D1508013

The Digital Scholar

The Digital Scholar

How Technology Is Transforming Scholarly Practice

Martin Weller

BLOOMSBURY ACADEMIC

First published in 2011 by

Bloomsbury Academic
an imprint of Bloomsbury Publishing Plc
36 Soho Square, London W1D 3QY, UK
and
175 Fifth Avenue, New York, NY 10010, USA

CIP records for this book are available from the British Library and the Library of Congress

ISBN 978-1-84966-497-4 (hardback)
ISBN 978-1-84966-617-6 (paperback)
ISBN 978-1-84966-625-1 (ebook)

This book is produced using paper that is made from wood grown in managed,
sustainable forests. It is natural, renewable and recyclable. The logging and
manufacturing processes conform to the environmental regulations of
the country of origin.

Printed and bound in Great Britain by the MPG Books Group, Bodmin, Cornwall

Cover image: © PeterPhoto123/Shutterstock

www.bloomsburyacademic.com

To Ellen

Contents

Acknowledgements

This book has grown out of a number of converging projects and interests, some of these related to my institution, the Open University (OU), some from research and others from my online network.

In my workplace at the Institute of Educational Technology at the OU, there are a number of colleagues who I have worked with on various projects and talked through many of the issues in this book. These include Patrick McAndrew, Grainne Conole, Eileen Scanlon, Doug Clow, Nick Pearce, Josie Taylor, Will Woods, Sam Kinsley and Karen Cropper amongst many others. Elsewhere in the OU, Tony Hirst has acted as my archetype for a digital scholar, and John Naughton showed me the power of blogging before they were even called blogs. I'd also like to express my gratitude to all the colleagues who have patiently attended workshops where I have worked through these ideas and the various senior managers who have indulged half-baked project plans and supported the writing of this book.

My online network features far too many people to list, and I fear I will offend people by not including them, but it would be remiss of me not to highlight the influence of early bloggers and online contributors, including Alan Cann, George Siemens, Josie Fraser, Scott Leslie, Brian Lamb, Brian Kelly, Alan Levine and Jim Groom.

I am aware that evenings when I should have been giving my family my full attention were occupied with writing, or 'playing with stuff', so thank you to my wife and daughter for allowing me to get on with it.

But most of all, my thanks go to all those who constitute my network, who, on a daily basis, share resources, thoughts, links, insights and poor jokes and thus enrich my professional and personal life.

1 Digital, Networked and Open

'Dad, you know that book you're writing, what's it about?' my daughter asked, as I walked her to school.

The 'elevator pitch' is always difficult for academics, who prefer to take their time to explain things in depth and give all sides to an argument. An elevator pitch for a nine-year-old is almost impossible.

'Well,' I pondered, 'it's about how using technology like the Internet, dad's blog, and Wikipedia is changing the way people like daddy work.' Having recently completed a school project, she was well acquainted with Wikipedia.

She considered this and then concluded, 'da-aaaaad, *no one's* going to want to read that!'

I fear she may be right, but I realised I have been writing this book for the past four years, mainly through my blog, which I have been using to explore what the advent of technologies, which offer new ways of communicating, collaborating and creating knowledge, mean for higher education. I figured if it had kept me interested for this long, it might be useful to share some of that with others.

A tale of two books

So what are these new ways of working that I had hinted at to my daughter? I'll start with an example that is in your hands now – the process of writing this book. Six years ago I wrote my last book, and halfway through writing this, I thought I'd compare the two processes. Below is a list of some of the tools and resources I used to write this book:

- Books – they were accessed via the library but increasingly as e-books, and one audiobook.

- E-journals – my university library has access to a wide range of databases, but I also made frequent use of others through tools such as Google Scholar and Mendeley.

- Delicious/social bookmarking – as well as searching for key terms I would 'forage' in the bookmarks of people I know and trust, who make their collections available.

- Blogs – I subscribe to more than 100 blogs in Google Reader, which I try to read regularly, but in addition I have cited and used many posts from other blogs.

- YouTube, Wikipedia, Slideshare, Scribd, Cloudworks and other sites – text is not the only medium for sharing now, and for certain subjects these 'Web 2.0' services offer useful starting points, or overviews, as well as insightful comment.

- My own blog – I have kept a blog for around five years now, and it provided a useful resource for items I have commented on and drafts of sections of this book. I also keep a scrapbook-type blog using Tumblr where I post any interesting links or multimedia and revisited this for resources I had harvested over the past few years. The blog was also a means of posting draft content to gain comments and feedback, which could then be incorporated into further iterations of writing.

- Social network – my Twitter network is especially useful for gaining feedback, asking for suggestions and, on a daily basis, as a filter and collection mechanism for sharing resources.

- Work and personal network – undoubtedly working in an intellectually lively environment and having face-to-face discussions with colleagues have been invaluable.

- Google alerts – I have set up alerts for a few key phrases which would then provide me with daily email updates on new content containing these keywords. This allowed me to find new resources, track conversations and stay abreast of a field which was changing as I wrote the book.

- Seminars and conferences – my attendance at face-to-face conferences has declined due to other commitments, but I regularly attend or dip into conferences remotely (see Chapter 10 for a more detailed exploration of the changing nature of conferences).

If I compare this with the tools I used when I wrote my last book in 2004, then many of these services did not exist or were in their infancy. Of this list I probably used books, journals and face-to-face conferences, with maybe some initial exploration of blogs.

In many ways the changes are not dramatic – books and journal articles still constitute a large part of the information sources I draw upon, although inspection of the references section will reveal the significance of blogs in particular. And the output of all this is still that most traditional of information sources, a book. But the changes are also significant for three reasons, I would suggest. First, the quantity of this information that is available online has increased considerably. I could access nearly all of it from my desk at home; there was no need to visit a physical library or bookstore. The digitisation of relevant content was almost total for the information sources I required for this book, compared with about half of that in 2004. The second factor is the significance of my online network in the writing process. I have around 3,000 followers in Twitter and around 2,000 subscribers to my blog (often they are the same people), which represents a wide pool of experience to draw upon. Sometimes I would put out a direct call to this network, along the lines of 'Does anyone have a good example of … '. In other cases I would post drafts of the content to my blog and receive comments and links to relevant material. Even without these direct appeals this distributed, global peer network represents an invaluable information source, comprising links to resources, commentary on issues, extended debate, use of new methods and technology, and contributions in the form of blog posts, videos and audio. This last item leads me to the third significant difference from the previous book, which is the range and variety of content that I drew upon. Even six years ago the type of content was largely limited to journal articles and books. Now, this has diversified to include blog posts, videos, draft publications, conference presentations and also the discussion, comment and debate surrounding each of these. The change from 2004 is partly a result of the first factor, quantity. There is just more of this stuff around. But it is also a result of a shift in attitude (at least on my part), in the legitimacy of these other forms of output and their central, vital role in everyday scholarly activity.

The comparison of writing these two books is instructive, I feel, because it gets to the heart of what we might term 'digital scholarship': it is both a profound change and a continuation of traditional practice. This can be seen with the final output also: the previous book existed only in traditional, paper format, and the copyright to this was owned by the publishers. This book is available not only in the traditional format but also online, freely accessible under a Creative Commons licence. In addition there is a set of resources, such as videos, presentations and blog posts, which relate to the book, with comments and reaction to these. The boundary to what constitutes the book is blurred; it is both the physical object and its complementary material. And this is becoming more common: my colleague Grainne Conole is writing a book by blogging chapters and gaining feedback in a site called Cloudworks (http://cloudworks.ac.uk/cloudscape/view/2155). Conor Gearty, a Professor of Law at the London School of Economics, is writing a book by posting a weekly video which sets out his theme and encourages discussion (http://therightsfuture.com/). The boundary between Gearty's book and a course, and the comments of the participants is deliberately blurred.

This conflict between what, from one perspective, seems a substantial change in practice and, from another, what appears to be a conservative, minor adjustment to standard approaches characterises not just book production but any aspect of scholarly activity, including research, knowledge dissemination, public engagement and teaching. Both radically different and yet familiarly traditional seem to be the story of digital scholarship at the moment, and it is the tension between these two forces that this book sets out to explore.

What is digital scholarship?

In Chapter 4 the concept of scholarship, and digital scholarship, will be addressed in detail, but it is worth providing an example now to illustrate the scope of this book.

'Scholarship' is itself a rather old-fashioned term. Whenever I ask someone to think of scholarship they usually imagine a lone individual, surrounded by books (preferably dusty ones), frantically scribbling notes in a library. This is somewhat removed from the highly connected scholar, creating multimedia outputs and sharing these with a global network of peers. Scholarship is, though, a sufficiently broad term to encompass many different functions and so has the flexibility to accommodate new forms of practice. It is not only focused on teaching, or research, but also on a wide range of activities. In fact, a rather tautological definition of scholarship is that it is what scholars do. And a 'scholar' can be defined as a learned person or a specialist in a given branch of knowledge.

Traditionally we have tended to think of scholars as being academics, usually employed by universities. This is the main focus of this book; it is the changes to university and higher education practice that will form the main discussion and research. However, digital scholarship broadens this focus somewhat, since in a digital, networked, open world people become less defined by the institution to which they belong and more by the network and online identity they establish. Thus a well-respected digital scholar may well be someone who has no institutional affiliation. The democratisation of the online space opens up scholarship to a wider group, just as it opens up subjects that people can study beyond the curriculum defined by universities.

A simple definition of digital scholarship should probably be resisted, and below it is suggested that it is best interpreted as a shorthand term. As Wittgenstein argued with the definition of 'game' such tight definitions can end up excluding elements that should definitely be included or including ones that seem incongruous. A digital scholar need not be a recognised academic, and equally does not include anyone who posts something online. For now, a definition of someone who employs digital, networked and open approaches to demonstrate specialism in a field is probably sufficient to progress.

Perhaps more fruitful is to consider an example of a particular technology-based approach, to demonstrate the issues that digital scholarship raises. At the outset of this chapter it was mentioned that I had been writing this book, although I hadn't conceptualised it as a book, for several years through my blog. We can take blogging as a microstudy of all the issues in digital scholarship, although almost any of the new internet technologies would suffice. First, it has the digital, networked and open approach in its DNA – these are not attributes that have been grafted onto it as an afterthought. The significance of these three factors is outlined below. Bloggers link to each other and usually have open comments; blogs have been responsible for driving the success of many other tools such as YouTube and Flickr as bloggers embed content to make their posts multimedia; they are democratic and easy to set up.

Blogs are also the epitome of the type of technology that can lead to rapid innovation. They can be free to set up, are easy to use and because they are at the user's control, they represent a liberated form for expression. There is no word limit or publication schedule for a blog; the same blog may mix posts about politics, detailed subject analysis, sport and personal life. Blogs can remain unread or have thousands of subscribers.

This freedom of expression is both their appeal and problem for scholarship. The questions one might ask of blogs in relation to academic practice are true of all digital scholarship:

1 Do they represent 'proper scholarship' (however that might be defined)?

2 Are they central or peripheral to practice?

3 Are they applicable to all domains?

4 Are they more applicable for some scholarly functions than others, for example, teaching?

5 How do we recognise quality?

6 Do they complement or replace existing channels?

7 Should we reward them through official routes such as tenure?

8 Should bloggers use institutional systems or separate out their blogging and formal identities?

9 What is their impact on academic communities?

If any of these questions interest you, then I hope you will find the remainder of this book relevant as I seek to unpack some of these issues.

Digital, networked and open

I suggested that the three ways in which my book-writing process differed from that of a few years ago were in terms of the quantity of digital content, the role of the social network and the types of information sources. What the combination of these three factors creates is a shift in the practice of writing. These three factors are representative of three characteristics, which when they intersect provide fertile ground for the transformation of practice.

The concept of digital scholarship will further be explored in Chapter 4. It is a term which has gained some currency and one which has an immediate appeal. It is something of a shorthand term though, since 'digital' is only one aspect. It is necessary, but not sufficient, for any substantial change in scholarly practice. Almost all scholars are 'digital' now, as they will invariably use a word processor to produce their articles and Powerpoint (or a similar tool) for presentations. If they are publishing these articles in a traditional journal and teaching via Powerpoint in a standard lecture model, it would be difficult to argue that this is worthy of particular interest; instead this represents a 'business as usual' model.

The impact of the digitisation of content should not be underestimated, however. What it provides is a common format for all types of media: image, text, video or audio. They are all just digital files, which means that they can all be shared by the same method. Much of the scholarly process we have currently can be viewed as a product of the medium in which they are conducted. A journal article is a certain length, and the journal publication cycle is determined as much by the economics of printing as it is by any considerations of the best methods for sharing knowledge. The size, location, length and format of a conference are influenced by the considerations of bringing together a group of people to one location and making best use of their time, within certain financial restrictions. But once these become digital then many of the current restrictions are removed: a journal article can be as long or as short as it needs to be, a journal can be published whenever the articles are ready or a continual publication of articles, conferences can be online and discussion can be asynchronous and distributed over any time frame, the format can be based around multimedia instead of presentations and so on, for almost any example of scholarly practice you care to consider. I will explore later in this book that this does not mean all existing practices *should*, or will, be replaced but that the range of alternatives is now greatly increased. This is a direct product of the shift to digital.

The second key feature for transformative practice is for it to be networked, as digital content that sits isolated on an individual's machine may represent a change in her own practice but does not constitute one for the community. It is the easy distribution of digital content over a global network that has led to the dramatic changes we have seen in many content industries. The possible lessons that can be drawn from these are examined in Chapter 3. Just as much of scholarly practice was shaped by the format of analogue systems, so has the distribution of these been influential. Prior to the Internet, academic knowledge was restricted to academic libraries, conferences, seminars or courses. Some of these may have been open, or have systems for sharing such as inter-library loans, but they all had a relatively high inbuilt threshold to accessing that knowledge. Once that content is digitised and made available online, that threshold to access effectively disappears and becomes a mouse click or a search term away.

It is not just the Internet that is significant in terms of networks but, more recently, the advent of social networks that is having an influence on scholarly practice. Networks of peers are important in scholarship – they represent the people who scholars share ideas with, collaborate with on research projects, review papers for, discuss ideas with and get feedback from. Prior to the Internet, but particularly prior to social networks, this kind of network was limited to those with whom you interacted regularly. This could be via letters, but usually it meant people you worked with and met at conferences. Maintaining a large network of peers requires a lot of effort, which is why Dunbar's (1992) research on friends and group size suggests that it has a capacity of around 150. It necessitates keeping in touch with a lot of people, often reinforcing that contact with physical interaction. In academic terms this kind of networking was most often achieved by being on the 'conference circuit'. Online social networks allow interaction with a wide group of peers (I won't go into the question here of whether online connections or relationships are inferior to face-to-face ones), often through relatively light touch mechanisms, such as Twitter, Delicious, blogs, and Flickr. Without having to attend every conference in their field, it is possible for scholars to build up a network of peers who perform the same role in their scholarly activity as the networks founded on face-to-face contact. Whether these are different in nature or are complementary to existing networks is still unknown, but for those who have taken the step to establishing an online identity, these networks are undoubtedly of significant value in their everyday practice.

This brings us onto the last feature to influence practice, namely openness. This is both a technical feature and what might be called a 'state of mind'. Technically, it can mean a number of things, including open source software, which is developed by a community for anyone to use, open APIs (application programme interfaces), which allow other software programs to interact with it (such as the applications in Facebook), or open standards (which are not owned by any one company and any software can adhere to, such as the IMS standards for metadata). All of these have been significant in creating a more general culture of openness, which has been fostered by many of the Web 2.0–type tools. At the heart of this has been what Tim O'Reilly (2004) calls 'an architecture of participation', an infrastructure and set of tools that allow anyone to contribute. It is this democratisation and removal of previous filters that has characterised the tools which have formed the second wave of web popularity, such as YouTube, Wikipedia, Flickr, blogs, Facebook and Twitter.

Openness then refers not only to the technology but also to the practice of sharing content as a default. Content in the scholarly context can mean data, journal articles, teaching material, presentations, discussion, seminars and comment. The removal of limitations inherent in analogue systems and their distribution has meant that the type of things people share has changed – if the only means of disseminating knowledge is a costly print journal then the type of content it contains tends to be finely worked and refined material. If there are almost cost-free tools for instant sharing, then people can share ideas, opinions, proposals, suggestions and see where these lead. More significantly perhaps the audience for the well-considered research publication is greatly increased by it being made open to all.

Digital content, distributed via a global network, has laid the foundation for potential changes in academia, but it is when the third element of openness is added in that more fundamental challenges to existing practice are seen, as I hope to demonstrate throughout this book. Let us take an example to illustrate this combination of a digital, networked and open approach, that of the life of a journal article.

The authors, let's call them Frank and Sally, know each other through a combination of commenting on each other's blogs, being part of the same network on Twitter where they share many of the same contacts and some email exchanges. Following a blog post by Frank on pedagogy for networked learning, Sally posts a long piece in reply. They decide to collaborate on a paper together and work in Google Docs to produce it. Sally gives a presentation about the subject to her department and shares the presentation on Slideshare. She posts the link to this on Twitter, and it gets retweeted several times by people in her network, some of whom comment on the presentation. Frank posts a draft of their chapter on his blog and again receives a number of comments which they incorporate into the paper. They submit it to an open access journal, where it is reviewed and published within two months. They both tweet and blog about the paper, which gets widely cited and has more than 8,000 views. As a result of the paper, they give a joint presentation in an open, online course on networked learning.

This example is fairly modest; I have not suggested the use of any particularly uncommon tools or any radical departure from the journal article format. It is also increasingly common (I could substitute many real people for Frank and Sally, including myself). As with the example of book writing, this scenario is both conservative and radical. It demonstrates the value of an individual's network as a means of distribution. This removes the authority of processes which had a monopoly on distribution channels for analogue content, such as publishers, libraries and book retailers. The open access journal means that knowledge created by academics, who are usually publicly funded in some form, is now available to everyone. Others may take that content and use it in their own teaching, perhaps informally and outside of a university system. The collaboration between two academics arises outside of any formal structures and as part of a wider network. They share their outputs as they go along, with the result that the overall output is more than just the article itself.

For each of these factors one can say that this is simply an adjustment to existing practice and not in itself of particular relevance. When considered across the whole community, however, the potential impact of each factor on scholarship is revolutionary, as it could lead to changes to research definition, methodology, the publishing industry, teaching, the role of institutions and collaboration. This reflects the somewhat schizophrenic nature of digital scholarship at the current time.

Fast, cheap and out of control

Particular types of technology lend themselves to this digital, networked and open approach. Brian Lamb (2010) borrows the title from Errol Morris' 1997 documentary to describe the kind of technology he prefers and thinks is useful in education as being fast, cheap and out of control. As with digital, networked and open, it is the intersection of the three that is the area of real interest. These three characteristics are significant for education in the following manner:

Fast – technology that is easy to learn and quick to set up. The academic does not need to attend a training course to use it or submit a request to their central IT services to set it up. This means they can experiment quickly.

Cheap – tools that are usually free or at least have a freemium model so the individual can fund any extension themselves. This means that it is not necessary to gain authorisation to use them from a budget holder. It also means the user doesn't need to be concerned about the size of audience or return on investment, which is liberating.

Out of control – these technologies are outside of formal institutional control structures, so they have a more personal element and are more flexible. They are also democratised tools, so the control of them is as much in the hands of students as it is that of the educator.

Overall, this tends to encourage experimentation and innovation in terms of both what people produce for content services and the uses they put technology to in education. If someone has invested £300,000 in an eportfolio system, for example, then there exists an obligation to persist with it over many years. If, however, they've selected a free blog tool and told students to use it as a portfolio, then they can switch if they wish and also put it to different uses.

There are, of course, many times when this approach may not be suitable (student record systems need to be robust and operate at an enterprise level, for example), but that doesn't mean it is *never* appropriate. Writing in *Wired*, Robert Capps (2009) coined the term 'the good enough revolution'. This reflects a move away from expensive, sophisticated software and hardware to using tools which are easy to use, lightweight and which tie in with the digital, networked, open culture. Capps cites the success of the small, cheap Flip video camera as an example:

> The Flip's success stunned the industry, but it shouldn't have. It's just the latest triumph of what might be called Good Enough tech. Cheap, fast, simple tools are suddenly everywhere. We get our breaking news from blogs, we make spotty long-distance calls on Skype, we watch video on small computer screens rather than TVs, and more and more of us are carrying around dinky, low-power netbook computers that are just good enough to meet our surfing and emailing needs. (Capps 2009)

In terms of scholarship it is these cheap, fast and out-of-control technologies in particular that present both a challenge and opportunity for existing practice. They easily allow experimentation and are founded on a digital, networked, open approach. It is these tools, and more significantly, the ways of working they allow and facilitate, that this book will focus on.

Technology determinism

This talk of technology 'allowing', 'facilitating', 'affording' or 'suggesting' methods of working or approaches raises the issue of technological determinism. This subject arises in almost every discussion around technology and education, so it is worth addressing it early. Technology-related viewpoints tend to be dystopian or utopian in nature. Examples of such views are not only to be found in science fiction. Educational technology literature over the past twenty years shows the promises and fears that have been associated with a variety of technologies, including computers, CD-ROM, computer-assisted learning, artificial intelligence, virtual reality and videodisc. The Internet and social media are just the latest in this list.

What both the positive and negative viewpoints have in common is that they see the technology itself as shaping human behaviour, so-called technological determinism, a phrase first coined by American sociologist Thorstein Veblen. The technological deterministic viewpoint is that technology is an autonomous system that affects all other areas of society. Thus human behaviour is, to a greater or lesser extent, shaped by technology. This seems to remove human will, or ingenuity, from the social process, and is thus usually rejected as excessively mechanistic. However, there seems to be such an anxiety about being labelled a 'technological determinist' that many people in education seek to deny the significance of technology in any discussion. 'Technology isn't important', 'pedagogy comes first', 'we should be talking about learning, not the technology' are all common refrains in conferences and workshops. While there is undoubtedly some truth in these, the suggestion that technology isn't playing a significant role in how people are communicating, working, constructing knowledge and socialising is to ignore a major influencing factor in a complex equation.

As this book seeks to explore the ways in which approaches founded in new technologies can influence scholarly practice, the charge of technological determinism may well be raised. It is not my contention that the presence of the technology will automatically lead to certain changes. Indeed, many of the interesting examples of digital scholarship are entirely unpredicted, what is often termed 'emergent use', which arises from a community taking a system and using it for purposes the creators never envisaged. This is particularly a feature of the kind of fast, cheap and out-of-control technologies that constitute much of the social media/ Web 2.0 collective. For instance, it has been well recorded that Flickr developed from a company which was aiming to manufacture an online game, and the photo-sharing application was just a simple tool to aid the game. As founder Caterina Fake commented, 'Had we sat down and said, "Let's start a photo application," we would have failed. We would have done all this research and done all the wrong things' (Graham 2006). Similarly, the proliferation of applications that have been built to interact with Twitter and Facebook were not predicted by the founders of those companies, nor the way in which people have used them (for a more detailed analysis of the development of the Twitter community norms, see Chapter 6).

A deterministic perspective would underestimate the role of people and the context in which the technology is used. Kling, McKim and King (2003) propose a 'sociotechnical interaction network', which emphasises the interaction between people, institutions and technologies. They analysed 'e-scholarly communication forums' to reveal the relationship between participants, resource flows, business models and other individuals and groups who do not participate in the network directly. Their work builds on what has been termed 'social construction of technology' (or SCOT), which is seen as a direct response to technological determinism (Pinch and Bijker 1984). In this perspective technology development is seen as the result of competition and negotiation between different groups or actors, rather than a finished artefact that is released (or inflicted) upon a rather submissive society.

SCOT is not without its critics, for example, Clayton (2002), and the detailed debate around the interplay between actors and technology is beyond the scope of this book. What the work of Pinch and Bijker and Kling *et al.* highlights is that it is possible to examine technology, technological influence and practice without falling into the trap of technology determinism. In this book it is the complex co-construction of technology and associated practice that is intended, with an iterative dialogue between the technology and the practices that it can be used for. Inevitably though, for the sake of simplicity and to avoid repetition, this complexity may be somewhat glossed over, and I will refer to a technology or an approach as if there is a direct line between them. For this I ask the reader's indulgence and request that it should not be taken to be demonstrative of a technological deterministic mindset, while at the same time recognising the significance of technology in the overall process.

The structure of this book

If I had given my daughter the full answer to her question regarding the nature of this book, I would have said it was essentially about three things: how the adoption of new technology *is* changing scholarly practice, how it *could* change practice and what questions does this raise for all academics?

This book has four main sections that seek to address these issues. The first section, comprising of Chapters 1 to 3, details the broad social context in which digital scholarship is taking place. Having made reference to the potential impact of new technologies and approaches in this chapter, Chapter 2 will look at some of the evidence for, and rhetoric surrounding, an imminent revolution in higher education. Chapter 3 examines other industries where digital, networked and open approaches have had a significant impact on established practice, including the music and newspaper industries. Possible similarities with higher education are examined and, significantly, the key differences are highlighted.

The second section forms the main section of this book and is concerned with scholarship. Chapter 4 draws on Boyer's 1990 study which proposed four scholarly functions, namely discovery, integration, application and teaching. Each of the subsequent four chapters explores one of these functions and how the digital, networked, open approach can impact upon practice. Each chapter focuses on just one demonstrative impact. For example, Chapter 7 explores how public engagement can be viewed from a digital scholarship perspective, but public engagement is only one form of the application function. Similarly, Chapter 8, which is concerned with Boyer's function of teaching, addresses the significance of a shift to abundant content and not all possible uses of technology for teaching. The aim of this section is to demonstrate that such technology-influenced approaches can have an impact in all aspects of scholarship and are not restricted to one function, such as teaching, or a particular discipline. This section in particular addresses the question of how technology is changing practice.

The next section, consisting of Chapters 9 to 12, explores the scholarly context in more detail, focusing on key practices, and can be seen as addressing the question of how digital scholarship could change practice. Chapter 9 looks at the open education movement, the various definitions of openness currently in operation and some of the issues it raises. In Chapter 10, using the metaphor of 'network weather', I argue that even if an individual does not engage with new technology, its adoption by others is beginning to change the environment within which they operate, and the academic conference is an example of this. Chapter 11 is concerned with the process of reward and tenure, and the challenges digital scholarship raises for institutions. This theme is continued in Chapter 12, which is focused on the publishing industry and its process, and in particular how open access publishing and the use of free communication tools are changing this core academic practice. The intention of this section is to return to the context within which digital scholarship exists, which was addressed in a broad sense in the first section, but to focus more closely on the academic environment. There are a number of areas of tension for digital scholarship, for instance, between the use of new technologies and tenure processes which are based on traditional publications. We are also in a period during which new practices are being established, as the possibilities that a digital, networked and open approach offers are applied to existing practice, for example, in the creation of new publishing models or conference formats.

The last section is a concluding one and addresses the issue of questions digital scholarship raises for all academics. Chapter 13 examines some of the issues and concerns about the adoption of new technologies and approaches. Chapter 14 continues this by addressing some of the reasons for anxiety surrounding digital scholarship and proposes a perspective based on 'digital resilience'.

2 Is the Revolution Justified?

t is common for observers and bloggers (including myself) in educational technology to proclaim that the current educational practice is, in some way, 'broken'. It is seen as not delivering deep learning, or failing to meet the needs of students, and of potentially becoming irrelevant to a new generation of digital learners. Before exploring the potential impact and benefits of a digital, networked, open approach, it is worth taking time to place these claims within some context and to give a sober assessment of much of the rhetoric that surrounds technology and education.

These calls for revolution have a certain innate appeal and are often based on a genuine concern for the well-being of higher education. For example, here I am arguing that the online learning environment can be seen as a metaphor for the change needed by universities:

> ... that the online learning environment is not peripheral, or merely a technological issue for universities and educators to resolve, but rather that it represents the means by which higher education comes to understand the requirements and changes in society, and thus the route by which it maintains its relevance to society. (Weller 2009a)

And here is John Seely-Brown (2006) making a compelling claim for the need for change in education:

> As the pace of change in the 21st century continues to increase, the world is becoming more interconnected and complex, and the knowledge economy is craving more intellectual property.

And Marc Prensky's (2001) opening statement for his article on digital natives claims that students have changed radically:

> It is amazing to me how in all the hoopla and debate these days about the decline of education in the US we ignore the most fundamental of its causes. *Our students have changed radically. Today's students are no longer the people our educational system was designed to teach.* (Prensky 2001)

Carie Windham (2005) makes a claim about the irrelevance of higher education:

> In a world where technologies change daily and graduates armed with four-year degrees are entering the workforce in record numbers, there is an

increasing fear among the Net Generation that a four-year degree will be neither relevant nor sufficient preparation when it becomes time to enter the work force.

The aim of this chapter is to examine the empirical evidence for any such revolution in higher educational practice, based on the behaviour of online learners.

The net generation

This isn't a book about the net generation, but that literature represents a good starting point for examining some of the claims on the impact of technology, since many of the claims for educational reform are justified by reference to the net generation or digital natives. There is some appeal in this, and we feel that a generation which grows up with access to the kinds of information and tools the Internet offers will be likely to use these for learning, which will therefore differ substantially from the kind of educational experience most people over the age of 35 experienced. However, separating myths and hype from the evidence in this literature is often difficult. The following are potential areas where we could extrapolate a need to alter educational practice.

Context

There is a need to start with some solid foundations to move forward from. So, first, let's examine the evidence that students use computers and the Internet at all in learning.

It seems a truism to say that current university students and those who are younger to them have greater exposure to information and communications technologies (ICTs) than previous generations. Marc Prensky (2001) bases much of the digital natives argument on the fact that 'today's average college grads [in the United States] have spent less than 5,000 hours of their lives reading, but over 10,000 hours playing video games (not to mention 20,000 hours watching TV)'. We know that accessing computers and the Internet for learning is now so commonplace as to seem normal.

The UK Children Go Online report (Livingstone and Bober 2005) states that

90% of 9–19 year olds who go online daily or weekly use the internet to do work for school or college and 94% use it to get information for other things. And that 75% of 9–19 year olds have accessed the internet from a computer at home.

Further to this, we know that students value computers and the role they play in learning. For example, in a study on higher education students in South Africa,

Czerniewicz and Brown (2008) found that '72% of students were extremely positive about the role of computers in learning and have a high opinion of their own abilities/self efficacy'.

They also found that students used computers for learning even when they were not asked to do so, and they used computers informally. This was particularly evident in the case of communicative media where 55 per cent of staff asked students to use communicative media as part of their courses; yet 75 per cent of students reported using communicative media regularly for their learning.

This informal learning theme is continued by Oblinger and Oblinger (2005), who reference Grunwald (2003):

> When teenagers are asked what they want from the Internet, the most common response is to get 'new information.' Close behind, at about 75 percent, is to 'learn more or to learn better.' The use of the Internet to learn is not limited to school work. Students are often informal learners, seeking information on a variety of topics, such as personal health.

We therefore have a basis to go forward – that students do at least use technology, value it and go beyond what they are formally required to do. This in itself, of course, does not necessitate a revolution, so let us examine some further areas under the general 'net generation' research.

Lack of relevance

Having established that students seem to value ICTs, we could ask the same of educators. Here the picture is less clear, and Czerniewicz and Brown (2008) found that unlike students, staff

> didn't know whether or not their colleagues thought computers were important. When they did report knowing about their colleagues use and attitudes towards computers, they were divided about their opinions as to their colleagues' values and use, indicating limited support networks and communities of practice.

There are some differences in the use of technologies across generations; for example, Oblinger and Oblinger (2005) report that 74 per cent of teenagers use instant messaging (IM) as a major communication tool compared with 44 per cent of online adults. Livingstone and Bober (2005) have similar differences in ICT competence, 'only 16% of weekly and daily user parents consider themselves advanced compared with 32% of children'.

Hartman, Moskal and Dziuban (2005) looked at reactions to online courses across three 'generations' and found that '[t]he Net Gen respondents were disappointed; they perceived a lack of immediacy in their online courses and felt that faculty response times lagged behind their expectations'. The attitude towards online learning seems to change across the generations.

> Baby Boomers preferred some face-to-face encounters with their instructors; Generation X students reported substantial, pointless interaction in class, and the Net Gen students felt that the interaction mechanisms designed by their instructors were much less adequate than their personal technologies. (Hartman *et al.* 2005)

This would suggest that the net generation does have a comparison to make about interactivity that may be relatively new.

Roberts (2005) reports the findings of a survey which suggests that 'customization is central to the definition of technology for Net Geners. Technology is something that adapts to their needs, not something that requires them to change'.

There may be proxies that we need to examine for the alleged irrelevance of education; for instance, truancy rates are now at their highest levels in England (Lipsett 2008), and there is also an increase in the number of students suspended from schools (Curtis 2008).

These figures themselves are subject to much interpretation, and what they signify is even more ambiguous. Of course, none of these necessarily point to problems with education; it could be a result of social pressures, for instance, and even if it does relate to educational irrelevance, that does not entail that technology is necessarily the solution.

In conclusion, then, there is some moderate evidence that there are some differences in the expectations of net generation learners and possibly an increase in dissatisfaction with education. There is a question of whether these expectations are really unique to the net generation, which we will look at later.

Different attitudes

A Pew Internet report (Lenhart *et al.* 2008) on teens and writing points at some differences in attitude between generations. Parents believe that teenagers engage in more 'writing' than they did, but the teenagers don't perceive what they do as writing; they see it as communication or socialising. They distinguish between academic writing and informal communication using technology. They have found some use of technology to improve writing:

> Teens who communicate frequently with friends, and teens who own more technology tools such as computers or cell phones do not write more for school or for themselves than less communicative and less gadget-rich teens. Teen bloggers, however, are prolific writers online *and* offline.

- 47% of teen bloggers write outside of school for personal reasons several times a week or more compared to 33% of teens without blogs.

- 65% of teen bloggers believe that writing is essential to later success in life; 53% of non-bloggers say the same. (Lenhart *et al.* 2008)

Of course, this does not mean blogging *causes* them to write more, so making the non-bloggers to keep blogs would not necessarily improve writing – those who like writing and have an aptitude for it are likely to keep blogs.

Another area where there may be a difference in attitude relates to 'cut and paste' or plagiarism, with younger people seeing less of a 'crime' in relation to copying. Livingstone and Bober (2005) report that '[a]mong 12–19 year olds who go online daily or weekly, 21% admit to having copied something from the internet for a school project and handed it in as their own'. Comparative figures for previous generations who may have copied from text books are not available, however.

Again the evidence is weak to absent to show that there is a major generational shift here, but there does seem to be some hints at subtle differences regarding standard educational practice and the way technology affects this.

Overestimating skills

A common theme from a number of recent reports seems to be that far from being the tech-savvy, digitally immersed cyborgs portrayed in much of the literature, there are some relatively poor information skills amongst the net generation and a good deal of variance.

For example, Brown (2009) reports,

Recently, the Nielsen Norman Group study of teenagers using the web noted: 'We measured a success rate of only 55 percent for the teenage users in this study, which is substantially lower than the 66 percent success rate we found for adult users'. The report added: 'Teens' poor performance is caused by three factors: insufficient reading skills, less sophisticated research strategies, and a dramatically lower patience level'.

The Google Generation report produced by the British Library (Rowlands *et al.* 2008) also explored some of the myths and its findings are listed below:

1 Young people have a poor understanding of their information needs and thus find it difficult to develop effective search strategies.

2 As a result, they exhibit a strong preference for expressing themselves in natural language rather than analysing which keywords might be more effective.

3 Faced with a long list of search hits, young people find it difficult to assess the relevance of the materials presented and often print off pages with no more than a perfunctory glance at them.

And as Livingstone and Bober (2005) state,

Many children and young people are not yet taking up the full potential of the internet, for example, visiting a narrow range of sites or not interacting with sites ... 38% of pupils aged 9–19 trust most of the information on the internet, and only 33% of 9–19 year olds daily and weekly users have been taught how to judge the reliability of online information.

Bennett, Maton and Kervin (2008) provide an excellent analysis of many of the claims around the net generation and have found a similar pattern of overestimating the information skills of the young: 'These studies also found that emerging technologies were not commonly used, with only 21 per cent of respondents maintaining a blog, 24 per cent using social networking technologies, and 21.5 per cent downloading podcasts.'

This leads onto the next point about the net generation literature, which is that it makes claims of generational difference with little basis.

Seeing difference where there is none

Some of the net generation literature seems to make claims of supposed generational difference when none exists. For example, multitasking is often set forward as a new 'skill', but Bennett *et al.* (2008) respond that 'there is no evidence that multi-tasking is a new phenomenon exclusive to digital natives. The oft used example of a young person doing homework while engaged in other activities was also applied to earlier generations doing homework in front of the television'.

And Oblinger and Oblinger (2005) claim as one of the defining characteristics of the net generation that 'they want parameters, rules, priorities, and procedures ... they think of the world as scheduled and someone must have the agenda. As a result, they like to know what it will take to achieve a goal. Their preference is for structure rather than ambiguity'. This rather begs the question, 'was there evidence that previous generations had a stated preference *for* ambiguity and chaos in their learning?'

Mark Bullen (Hanson 2008) makes a similar point about claims to the increased irrelevance of education to net geners: 'The relevance of education has been source of debate for as long as I have been in education. I remember, as a student, participating in a "walkout" from my high school in 1970 over the perceived irrelevance of our education.'

And while we may point to factors such as an increase in truancy to support the claim that school is seen as irrelevant, similar angst was to be found about truancy rates in1908 in New York (*The New York Times* 1908).

One issue is that people are often making claims when we have no comparison to judge them against. We don't know if students today are less satisfied with education than, say, 40 years ago, and even if we did, assigning causality would be difficult – it could be the result of massive expansion in higher education, for example.

One of the conclusions we may reach is that differences *within* generations seem as great as those between them. For example, compare responses of the young to the general population in the OCLC (2007) survey in which college students and members of the general public were asked the following question: 'How likely would you be to participate in each of the following activities on a social networking or community site if built by your library?'

The numbers are those who say they are *extremely likely* or *very likely* to do so (general public responses in brackets):

- self-publish creative work: 7 per cent (6 per cent)

- share ideas with/about library services: 10 per cent (7 per cent)

- share your photos/videos: 7 per cent (6 per cent)

- participate in online discussion groups: 6 per cent (6 per cent)

- meet others with similar interests: 6 per cent (7 per cent)

- describe your own personal collections: 9 per cent (6 per cent)

- view others' personal collections: 12 per cent (6 per cent)

Of course, the students could be objecting to the 'built by your library' element of the question, not the tasks themselves, which they might happily perform in Facebook, but the differences between the usually younger students and the general population are not significant.

There are, however, changes which we might attribute to the digital age that seem to be cross-generational; for instance, there seems to be a general decline in the amount of literature reading (NEA 2007). This may have a greater impact on the younger generation, who may never develop reading skills, but it does not necessarily separate them out from other generations.

Overall, as Bennett *et al.* (2008) suggest, there is little strong evidence for the main claims of the net generation literature, which they summarise as follows:

1 Young people of the digital native generation possess sophisticated knowledge of and skills with information technologies.

2 As a result of their upbringing and experiences with technology, digital natives have particular learning preferences or styles that differ from earlier generations of students.

However, for education it may not matter if this is a generational or a societal shift. If *everybody* is changing their behaviour, then education still needs to respond. 'Mature' students now exceed those in the traditional age range of 18–22 in the United States (Morrison 2003). So in this respect the net gen discussion is something of a red herring. What we need to be concerned about are the changes in the digital *society*.

People are learning in different ways

If the focus is less on the net generation, but with changes in society as a whole, then there is a need to look beyond students in formal education. First, some broad statistics of internet usage, which may relate to learning, starting with the behemoth of the Internet: Google. Statistics vary, with one report stating that in December 2009, Google was accounting for 87 billion search queries out of a global total of 131 billion (Comscore 2010).

Obviously, these searches are not all related to learning, and when they are, it may be learning at a very cursory level. In 2007, 55.6 million of these searches were referrals to Wikipedia (Schutz 2007), which hint at a greater depth of learning, at least that level of interest we see when people consult an encyclopaedia. If we take Wikipedia as the exemplar for online information resource, then at the time of writing it had 3,541,655 articles in the English version (http://en.wikipedia.org/wiki/Wikipedia:Statistics).

If Facebook is taken as the representative for social activity online, then, reportedly, there are more than 500 million active users; the average user has 130 friends; 50 per cent of users update their statuses at least once each day, and there are more than 900 million objects people interact with (web links, news stories, blog posts, notes, photos etc.) (http://www.facebook.com/press/info.php?statistics).

And lastly, YouTube as an example of new content creation. In June 2008, 91 million viewers watched 5 billion user-posted videos on YouTube, and 1–10 per cent YouTube users are creators (http://www.comscore.com/press/release.asp?press=2444).

This indicates a scale of activity online that has at least some passing relevance to education. Of course, none of this tells us much about how, what, or if people are learning. It is difficult when dealing with such global statistics to appreciate what they mean and how far we should be guided by them. But it is possible to at least conclude that there is significant activity online across a range of society, and the intersection of these activities (socialising, sharing, content creation, information seeking) has a direct relevance to education.

Interpreting these statistics in terms of educational change is difficult – do they point to the need for total revolution or merely that an adjustment such as a social network for students might be a useful addition to a virtual learning environment (VLE)? There is a need to explore beyond the headline statistics, to look at some more specific examples.

Meeting unmet needs of learners

One claim often made is that higher education has a necessarily limited curriculum and that in a digital society we will see a liberation of the topics people want to learn about. For instance, here I am (Weller and Dalziel 2009) making reference to the long tail:

> [A] distributed model of learning design production is the best way to attack the long tail (Anderson 2006) of possible learner interests. If a user wants to find small courses to formally accredit their understanding of highland knitting patterns, history of Sydney in the 1960s or anthropology amongst football fans, then most current formal providers will not meet their requirements, but a sufficiently distributed pool of user generated designs might.

Getting any general statistics to support this, beyond those in the previous section, is difficult. But we can look at some examples and make extrapolations; for example, Griffiths (2008) details how YouTube is being used by graffiti artists to share techniques and also create social norms. This is not likely to be a subject or skill taught in any conventional sense, and yet the peer assessment, commenting and reflection shown by participants map onto the types of behaviour we foster in formal education.

And similar examples can be found for almost any topic one could think of, ranging from knitting (e.g. http://www.ravelry.com, http://www.knittingdaily.com) to running (http://www.runnersworld.com, http://www.fetcheveryone.com). Closer to formal education, there are sites such as PhysicsForums, which is an informal space to talk about science, maths and physics and has more than 100,000 members.

Perhaps the most highly developed and relevant area of interest is that of Free/Libre Open Source Software (FLOSS) communities. From surveys of open source participants (Ghosh et al. 2002), it is known that the desire to learn is a key motivational factor for participating in FLOSS projects. The manner in which FLOSS communities operate demonstrates many of the educational characteristics educators hope to realise, including mentorship, communities of practice, learning by doing and self-directed learning.

Participation in FLOSS activities is also an example of bridging the gap between formal education and informal learning. Ghosh *et al.* (2002) also report that four-fifths of FLOSS community members are convinced that proven FLOSS experience can compensate for a lack of formal degrees, and three-fifths consider the skills they learn within the FLOSS community as core skills for their professional career.

Perhaps, because they have been around for some time and have a robust reputation, we can also see from FLOSS some of the potential threat to formal education. In another survey, Ghosh and Glott (2005) found that except for other forms of self-study, which are performed by 58 per cent of the community members, the most common ways to learn are those that provide the opportunity to either read or work on the code and that depend on internet-based technologies. Participating in training courses is the learning approach with the lowest uptake.

Clearly there are a wide range of interests out there that are uncatered for in traditional education, and while this may have always been the case, we can see that the Internet is enabling communities to form, which would have been previously limited by geographical factors, and the removal of these barriers has seen an unprecedented growth in communities for whom learning is a key objective.

Open education

The area where these changes find greatest expression in education is that of the open education movement. This seeks to make educational content freely available to all, through the advent of open educational resources (OERs) such as MIT's Open CourseWare and the Open University's (OU) OpenLearn projects. We will explore these and the changing nature of openness in education more fully in Chapter 9, but for now they can be taken as a signal of a potential shift in educational practice, driven largely by technology. There is also a move to make academic journals 'open access' so they are freely available, which is covered in Chapter 12. All of this can be seen as part of a broader trend and philosophy of the Internet, which sees openness as a key to technical development and social acceptance. The use of open APIs in many so-called Web 2.0 sites has allowed others to develop a range of software that interact and build on their core functionality, as seen with the proliferation of Facebook and Twitter applications. The general philosophy of the blogosphere and those who spend significant time online is to be generally open in terms of disclosure and sharing content. Of the top 10 sites in the world (Nielsen 2010), 3 are based around the public, or semi-public, sharing of personal content and information (YouTube, Facebook and Wikipedia), the others being search or mail related, with social media accounting for 22 per cent of all time spent online. In this respect, the open education movement can be seen as a response to, or at least as part of, a broader social change made possible by digital technologies.

The OER movement was begun in earnest by MIT's OpenCourseWare (OCW) project, launched in 2002, with the aim of making the whole of MIT's curriculum freely available. The site has more than 1 million visitors a month, the majority (41 per cent) coming from North America, although there is global usage, and self-learners represent the biggest group of users (Carson 2005). These are respectable, if not spectacular, figures when compared against the global population involved in education (132 million tertiary students worldwide in 2004).

The OU's experience with the OpenLearn project was that in the two years from the start of the project it had more than 3 million unique visitors, was accessed by more people (69 per cent) from outside the United Kingdom than within, 35 per cent of visitors returned to the site and 50 per cent of repeat visitors were 'new to the OU'. The project did not seem to affect core business; indeed there is some evidence that it helped recruit new students to formal courses, with at least 7,000 people registering on OU courses in the same online session that they were on the OpenLearn site (McAndrew *et al.* 2009). They also reported some evidence that the concept of openness was difficult to get across, and many users didn't believe (or appreciate) that this was free content.

The OER movement has grown quite rapidly from MIT's first venture; in January 2007 the Organization for Economic Cooperation and Development (OECD) identified more than 3,000 open courseware courses available from more than 300 universities worldwide (OECD 2007), although, as the report recognises, the sustainability of these projects is still an issue.

While the movement from within education has met with some success, commercial sites for sharing have often been far more successful. For example, the site for sharing and embedding presentations, http://www.Slideshare.net, has considerably more traffic than the MIT OCW site (http://compete.com/, February 2009).

The open education movement is still in its relative infancy, and so if it hasn't seen the widespread disruption to higher education some had hoped for, we shouldn't be too surprised. Education, as we know it today, has had several hundred years to develop the lecture-based model, so to expect an open model to radically alter this in just a few years may be expecting too much. There are a number of habits that will take some time to alter; for instance, educators are beginning to use a range of third-party material in their lectures (Flickr pictures, YouTube videos, OERs etc.), and so the 'market' for reusable content is growing. But suggesting that change *may* come is different from arguing that there is an urgent demand which universities have to meet, or else they will find themselves irrelevant to society. In the OER movement, it is probably fair to say that they are leading the thinking and development of concepts about free education, not responding to a social demand.

Lessons from other sectors

Chapter 3 will look at similarities and differences between higher education and other industries, particularly newspapers and music, which have been profoundly changed by the arrival of new technology. The digitisation of content and its distribution via the Internet have seen a merging of previously distinct sectors; for instance, a computer company (Apple) has become the main music outlet (iTunes), broadcasters provide telecoms services (e.g. Sky) and vice versa (British Telecom), and newspapers host podcasts (Guardian Online). As higher education institutions seek to explore, and exploit, new technologies, some of this boundary confusion begins to be applicable in the education sector also. For instance, the OU produces a podcast that features in the iTunes top 10, Kansas State University professor Michael Wesch produces YouTube movies that are viewed by millions and many bloggers having subscription rates to rival those of satellite TV channels (e.g. Stephen Downes has more than 10,000 hits per day). All of these are outside of traditional academic outputs, that is, courses, books and journal articles. The reverse is also true with YouTube, Google, Sky and the BBC, all engaging in activity that has some bearing on education, and a number of smaller start-up companies (e.g. TeachThePeople, SchoolForEverything) offering services on informal learning.

The result is that boundaries between sectors are less clear cut and more permeable than they once were.

Conclusions from the evidence

In this chapter, several contributing factors to the claim that higher education needs to undergo a radical change have been examined. We can look at each of these and state the overall strength of each argument.

A new generation is behaving fundamentally differently – there seems little real evidence beyond the rhetoric that the net generation is in some way different from its predecessors as a result of having been exposed to digital technologies. There is some moderate evidence that they may have different attitudes.

There is a general change in society which has relevance for learning – certainly the overall context is an ICT-rich one, and people are using the Internet for a variety of learning-related activities.

People are learning in different ways – although firm evidence of informal learning is difficult to gather, there is much by the way of proxy activity that indicates this is the case.

There is growing dissatisfaction with current practice in higher education – there seems little strong evidence for this. Probably more significant to the culture of education has been the shift to perceiving the student as a customer. There is certainly little evidence that the dissatisfaction is greater than it used to be, but what may be significant is that there are now viable alternatives for learners. Universities have lost their monopoly on learning, which reinforces the next point.

Higher education will undergo similar change to that in other sectors – there are some similarities between higher education and other sectors, such as the newspaper and music industries, but the differences are probably more significant. However, the blurring of boundaries between sectors and the viability of self-directed, community-based learning means that the competition is now more complex.

It is possible, and at times tempting, to see these complementary factors as some kind of 'perfect storm' brewing for change in higher education. It is convenient for many who seek to implement change in higher education (for a variety of reasons) to portray it as an inevitable force that cannot be resisted or is resisted at the peril of higher education's continued existence. This may account for why the net generation literature has been so widely accepted – it creates a convenient backdrop against which to paint the need for radical change.

Having reviewed the evidence the claims for a perfect storm seem to be exaggerated, *but* there is a gathering of significant trends which higher education should seek to address. Undoubtedly the proclamations of the imminent demise of higher education are overblown; even if higher education did nothing, it would not see the rapid change in its practice that we have seen in other sectors. Rather we should see the response to these trends as having two main arguments:

1 Maintaining relevance – whilst the strong claims for the loss of relevance of higher education are not justified, there are some significant factors above, and just as higher education responds to any significant cultural change, so should it respond to these.

2 Opportunities – rather than portraying the digital culture as an impending threat to higher education, the only option being to adapt or die, it is more fruitful to perceive it as an unprecedented series of opportunities. The manner in which we have conducted scholarship has often been restricted by physical factors, and the removal of many of these should liberate both how and what we do as scholars.

An appropriate response

One possible conclusion from this might be that scholars should be cautious in their adoption of new technology and approaches, until we have the firm evidence that it is required or necessary. I think this is to misinterpret the role of scholars and to underestimate the potential significance of such approaches for our own practice.

There are several reasons why it is important to engage with a digital, networked, open approach, even if the urgent survival of higher education isn't one of them. The first is that there is lag between society's acceptance of a technology and then its adoption in higher education. Brown (2009) suggests that in society the stages of technology diffusion can be defined as *critical mass* (ownership by 20–30 per cent of the population), *ubiquity* (30–70 per cent) and finally *invisibility* (more than 70 per cent). If higher education were to wait for the invisibility stage to be reached *before* it engaged with a technology, then given the time it takes to implement policies and technology, it really will look outdated. For example, in 2007, those using social networks might have been in the minority; now they will be in the majority. This is the problem with waiting for data to determine decisions – if you made a decision based on 2007 data that social networks were largely unused, it would look out of date in 2010. What is significant is the *direction* of travel, not the absolute percentages at any given time.

Part of the role of education is to give students relevant skills, and by using a range of technologies for academic (rather than purely social) purposes, it could be argued that it is fulfilling this remit for the graduates who will then enter the workplace.

The second reason why scholars need to continue to engage with technology relates to pedagogy. Part of the role of educators is to assess which of these technologies will be significant, both in terms of students' lives (therefore, they represent a means of us reaching out) and also educationally, therefore, providing a means of utilising technology to improve education.

The wiki is a good example; scholars shouldn't be using wikis because they believe there is a Wikipedia generation and it will make them look relevant but rather because they allow them to achieve certain goals in teaching.

The next reason is that if technology isn't itself the cause for revolution, it is the enabler for maintaining relevance in a competitive market. The reasons students select universities are varied: when it comes to choosing a university, it seems that course suitability, academic reputation, job prospects and teaching quality are the main factors influencing prospective students (Soutar and Turner 2002). Non-academic factors also play an important part, including proximity to their homes, availability of scholarships and teaching and the range of non-academic student services (Drewes and Michael 2006). Students from low-income families will be influenced by financial factors, such as cost of living in the university locality and employment prospects (Callender and Jackson 2008).

It is notable that 'technology usage' is not listed amongst these. Students don't *choose* a university based on the particular VLE it deploys, but the use of new technologies will have a direct impact on many of these other factors. For instance, the range of courses and student satisfaction will be influenced by the deployment of innovative technology by educators.

The final reason is that of exploration and professional reinvention. The reason educational technology seems more prevalent, and indeed urgent, now is that we live in an age when the quantity of tools that can be put to a pedagogic use is at an unprecedented level and the rate of release of these is increasing. Just as significantly, as I argued in Chapter 1, many of these are free and easy to use. Thus, their adoption carries a much lower risk than with previous generations of technology. The opportunities for experimentation and finding new ways of teaching a subject, or engaging in research or disseminating knowledge, are therefore much richer and, given the ease of use, greatly democratised.

Conclusion

The evidence for radical and imminent revolution in higher education may not be as strong as I once liked to believe, but we shouldn't ignore the fact that there are also some very significant trends which are founded on data and research and not just on anecdote and rhetoric. These suggest very strongly that the engagement with new technologies is a core practice for higher education.

And more significantly, these trends indicate that we have a richer environment in which to explore changes in teaching and learning practice. We have a convergence of a base level of technological competence, an expectation of the use of ICTs in education, a range of easy to use tools and models from other sectors to investigate.

So while the absolute necessity for radical change is overstated, there are unprecedented *opportunities* for the use of technology in education. And as educators we shouldn't need to wait until the case has been proven for each one to try it because, as the saying goes, it doesn't take a whole day to recognise sunshine.

Chapter 3 will explore the impact new technologies have had on other sectors in more detail and look at what lessons might be drawn for higher education.

3 Lessons from Other Sectors

I n Chapter 2, some of the rhetoric for revolution in education was examined. While this seems to be rather overblown when examined in detail, observation of other sectors reveals something of a revolution having taken place over the past decade. The changes in other sectors have often occurred despite the incumbents in the industry embracing the potential of new technology, coming either from external agencies or bottom-up pressure from consumers. The two key elements driving these changes are the ones outlined in Chapter 1:

1 The digitisation of content – once content becomes digital it is easily and perfectly reproduced and distributed. Data are indiscriminate as to whether they represent an image, video or audio, so the analogue distinctions that existed between different industries to represent these media begin to blur.

2 A global, social network – the Internet allows for the easy distribution of content, but more crucially the social element has removed the function of the filter that many industries used to perform.

When these two elements combine they create a powerful mixture which undermines existing business models. We can see this with two pertinent examples, that of newspapers and music.

The newspaper industry

Newspapers have been affected by two complementary factors (outside of the impact of the recession generally): loss of advertising revenue and decreasing circulation. The advertising revenue has been lost to many online sites; for example, in the United Kingdom, *Trinity Mirror* reported a 20.1 per cent fall in underlying group advertising revenues since the end of June 2008 (Sweney 2008) and *The New York Times* reported a similar drop (MacMillan 2008).

Some of these can be attributed to the impact of the financial crisis, particularly on housing advertising, but it is part of a longer term trend. Papers have seen much of their advertising revenue move to specialised online sites; for example, craigslist in the United States has well over double the traffic of *The New York Times* (*NYT*) and considerably more than the *Guardian Online* (see http://siteanalytics. compete.com/craigslist.org+nytimes.com+guardian.co.uk/ for a comparison of web traffic).

What this illustrates is that newspapers are beginning to see an unbundling of their component elements. In addition, the advent of the Internet means that people now get their news from many different places, and much of it online. In the United States, the circulation of the top 25 newspapers has declined on average by 7.4 per cent over the 2005–8 period. Thus far, newspapers have failed to make paid-for subscription models work online; for example, the *NYT* closed its TimesSelect model in 2007 as readers can find the content free elsewhere, and have an expectation that it will be free, although the Murdoch group has recently implemented a paywall model for much of its content.

In an article entitled 'Newspapers and Thinking the Unthinkable', Clay Shirky (2009) explores the industry's reaction to two forces outlined above. He examines the economics of newspapers and argues that this is why they are threatened by digital media. The point he makes is that we confuse function with form: 'Society doesn't need newspapers. What we need is journalism. For a century, the imperatives to strengthen journalism and to strengthen newspapers have been so tightly wound as to be indistinguishable'.

Andrew Keen (2009) responds to Shirky's piece arguing that the 'let-it-happen' conclusion Shirky draws is not inevitable:

> [H]ow absolutely should we stand back and trust the free market to come up with a solution to the crisis of the news business? We certainly aren't trusting this unfettered market to solve Wall Street's financial crisis. … So if we can agree that the news business, like healthcare and the financial sector, is too important to fail, then shouldn't the government be taking a more active gardening/watering role in ensuring that at least one or two of today's digital flowers fully bloom in the future?

The difference here is that unlike some other industries that various governments intervened to save, such as the car industry in the United States or the financial sector globally, newspapers were seeing decline long before the financial crisis of 2008, and crucially, there is a replacement of newspapers by other means. The need to save the industry is not perceived as great, since it is in the process of evolving. This is not the case with the financial sector.

Drawing on Shirky's analysis, John Naughton concludes,

> So here are some principles for thinking intelligently about our emerging media environment:
>
> 1 Think ecologically.
>
> 2 Think long-term. What's happening might be as profound as what happened after the emergence of print – and look how long it took for those effects to work their way through society.

3 Don't confuse existing forms with the functions that they enable. It's the functions that matter. Forms may be transient, the product of historical or technological circumstances. (Naughton 2009)

These are lessons that might be applied to scholarship also. As we will see in a later chapter, the point about confusing form with function exists in many higher education practices also. They can be seen in the evidence we use for promotion, for example, where we have come to see journal articles (the form) as the measure for scholarly research (the function).

Why is there so much interest in the future of newspapers, you may wonder. Obviously, they represent significant social artefacts of our age, and so their rapid change is interesting in itself. But more significantly they can be seen as a case study, or a warning from the future, about the impact of the Internet on well-established, often highly regarded, businesses. Unlike the music industry, which largely ignored the Internet, newspapers have been exploring a range of models to deal with the change. As Shirky (2009) puts it,

> The problem newspapers face isn't that they didn't see the internet coming. They not only saw it miles off, they figured out early on that they needed a plan to deal with it, and during the early 90s they came up with not just one plan but several.

Most other industries haven't worked through the range of models that newspapers have already attempted and discarded. Watching what will happen next with newspapers as businesses and journalism as a practice will provide a rich source of models for others to adopt. More significantly, Shirky and Naughton's point about not confusing form with function should sound a warning for scholarship: maybe we are in danger of confusing higher education with the university system. The latter is a convenient financial and administrative method of achieving the former, but in a digital world there is now something that was missing previously: alternatives. That is the message, that is the real take away from the newspaper industry and one I will return to throughout this book – we are now in an age of alternatives, where previously there were none.

The music industry

The music industry has seen a dramatic impact from the move to digital, online content. Initially sales of CDs were affected by download purchases, but in 2008 even the inclusion of downloads saw music sales at their lowest since 1985 (IFPI 2009). Online digital sales now account for 20 per cent of the global market, up from 15 per cent in 2007. User behaviour is also changing, with single-track downloads far more popular than whole albums. The move to online downloading has seen many record and DVD stores close. Piracy is seen as the major threat to the music industry's traditional business model, with the IFPI (2009) estimating unauthorised file sharing at over 40 billion files in 2008 and accounting for about 95 per cent of downloaded music tracks.

In addition the industry has seen artists exploring business models which essentially disintermediate the record company; for example, Radiohead offered their album *In Rainbows* as a direct download from their website, and Madonna signed with a concert promoter rather than a record company.

However, although the underlying models may be changing, the overall relevance and desire for music has not changed (and may have increased with mobile devices). As *Rolling Stone* (Hiatt and Serpick 2007) reports, 'people are listening to at least as much music as ever. Consumers have bought more than 100 million iPods since their November 2001 introduction, and the touring business is thriving, earning a record $437 million last year'.

In *Everything Is Miscellaneous*, David Weinberger (2007) gives an analysis of how the digitisation of content has altered our perceptions of the basic unit of music:

> For decades we've been buying albums. We thought it was for artistic reasons, but it was really because the economics of the physical world required it: Bundling songs into long-playing albums lowered the production, marketing, and distribution costs … As soon as music went digital, we learned that the natural unit of music is the track.

Nick Carr (2007) disagrees with Weinberger, pointing to the overall artistic structure of the album, using *Exile on Main Street* as an example. Clay Shirky (2007) in turn refutes this saying that if the artistic integrity of Exile were as strong as he claims, then it would survive digitisation – and this is not the case when download patterns are examined on iTunes, where most people download the track 'Tumbling Dice'. While an artistic integrity around the album may have developed, as Carr suggests, the album didn't have an *intrinsic* artistic integrity, rather the economics as outlined by Weinberger came first, and then some artists began to explore the album as an integrated unit. If digitisation had come first then maybe they would have explored artistic avenues open to them through that means, but they would have been unlikely to come up with the album as the logical conclusion to musical output. It is the logistics of physical packaging and their economics that made the album the logical unit for music distribution.

As well as revealing the role the economics of physical artefacts plays in constructing an industry, what this demonstrates again is that once the two factors of digitisation and global network combine, many of the implicit assumptions of an industry are suddenly exposed.

As an aside, and perhaps closer to home for scholars, it may be interesting to consider if the same isn't true of books. They have a longer pedigree and greater cultural value than albums, but essentially they are containers for ideas. Their format, size and existence are largely a result of the economics of atoms. An individual could only be in one place at one time and speak to an audience of limited size. Therefore, to transmit an idea to a wider audience, a format that is transportable, easily interpreted and has a low threshold to participation was required, and the physical book meets these requirements.

In the academic world there is also the article, which because of the economics of the physical is bundled together with other articles into a journal, essentially a small book. So even though the article may be smaller in size, it still follows the economic route determined by the book. But with the digitisation of knowledge, it is free to follow its own path. We will explore this in more detail in Chapter 12 when the academic publishing industry is examined.

Ownership and identity

The music industry, like book publishing, generates a strong emotional attachment to the physical object. People loved their vinyl collections. The digitisation of content then causes a change in this, which is fundamental to the industry, and like some of the other changes, it causes people to question some assumptions they didn't even know they had. One of these is about the issue of identity.

For my generation you partly constructed your identity around what you owned – your bookshelf, record collection and DVD archive were important aspects of who you were (as anyone who has read Nick Hornby's *High Fidelity* will appreciate). But for the digital generation this strong link with ownership has been broken.

It took time and money to build up any of those collections. Therefore they demonstrated a commitment which was worth exhibiting. In a digital world this effort is greatly reduced, and as a result, so is the emotional attachment one feels towards them. How often would people say that their book collection or record collection would be the things they would want to save from a burning house? This simply doesn't apply anymore – you can just download again (iTunes keeps a record of what you've purchased or people can easily obtain entire back catalogues from pirate torrent sites).

But even more than this, the need to own anything is reduced. As we see a move to pervasive Wi-fi, then persistent connections become possible, which means music can always be streamed. The need to possess or own music disappears then, as people have access to an online library which far exceeds anything they could ever own.

For industries which were based on ownership, this shift to a streaming, cloud-based approach represents a fundamental challenge.

What we see then is less an emphasis on the artefact and more value placed on things that cannot be easily reproduced. In terms of the music industry this equates to the live concert. This can be seen as a return to the past – musicians originally made their money from live performance and then found that the record was a useful means to promote this. The record, the artefact, then became the prominent means of revenue. In a digital world the recording returns to being a means of promotion again.

The parallel with education may be that it is less the content (in the form of lectures or teaching material) that is significant, but the life experience.

Boundary wars

A final lesson from these two sectors, which may be relevant to education, is the blurring of boundaries between sectors. Here's a question you've probably never pondered: why didn't someone else invent iTunes? It's not as strange as it sounds, after all with their MSN network, Microsoft had a global media platform which they were seeking to exploit as a content delivery route. The incumbents in the entertainment industry, such as Time Warner, had the money, back catalogue and brand they could have used. Either of these had the financial and political clout; they could have wrapped up the music market in the way Apple has. If you had to place a bet back in 2001 on which company would have online music locked down, which one would you have bet on?

Unlike the newspaper industry which attempted many models, most music companies did not attempt to make use of the Internet in the way Apple did with iTunes. It would have been sensible for them to attempt such models, so why did Apple succeed so spectacularly? There are, of course, lots of reasons, but I would suggest it was a sense of passion and experimentation on the part of Apple.

Part of the reason Apple succeeded with iTunes and the iPod is because it had attracted staff who fundamentally cared about Apple products and loved well-designed artefacts. Microsoft's Sharepoint may be a good, functional product, but it's never going to evoke the kind of passion found in Apple employees, and so as an organisation the 'gene pool' of innovation available to draw upon is weaker.

The Apple and Microsoft wars are old news, so does this have any relevance now? The rise of Web 2.0 services with their open APIs and the ease with which content can be created and shared see a democratisation of this passion and its expression. Because you can build on top of existing services people now don't have to be an Apple engineer to be engaged with a tool they care about – Twitter and its myriad applications are an example. Because someone can create a YouTube video easily, she doesn't have to be a broadcaster to create a programme about something she is passionate about.

For now, the lessons we can draw from this for scholars are both positive and negative. On the negative side it demonstrates that boundaries between sectors count for little in a digital world, and so the place of universities as the providers of education is not assured. On the positive side it demonstrates that passion and interest can reap rewards and that there is now a global conduit for sharing these.

A component analysis

A useful, if slightly reductionist, way of considering the changes in each sector, and in turn higher education, is to view them as a set of component functions, which are bundled together.

The music and newspaper industries might thus be represented as the set of functions outlined in Table 3.1.

Table 3.1 The component elements of the music and newspaper industries

Function	Music	Newspaper
Content	Recorded music	Stories written by journalists
Filter	Artists are discovered for you	The editor(s) filter content for you
Sustainable business model	The cost of recording and distribution is offset against profits	Cost of journalists and productions is offset by sales of papers and adverts
Format	Music is packaged and distributed on vinyl and then CDs	Stories are bundled together in a portable format, paper
Quality	Only acts that are deemed to have an audience are signed	Qualified journalists and editors ensure a level of quality
Access	Recording companies have access to a network of talent in marketing, producing and so on	Journalists have privileged access to certain groups, for example, politicians

These functions are bundled together because of convenience. From a consumer's perspective it was easier to have them all in one place. This was essentially a result of the economics of physical atoms and the difficulty in sharing. Many of the functions in Table 3.1 can be interpreted as versions of filtering. This is where the second driver, that of the global social network, comes into play. David Weinberger (2007) makes the distinction between filtering on the way in and filtering on the way out. When a system has outputs which are expensive physical products, it is important to filter on the way in, since an excess of CDs sitting unused in a warehouse is costly. But in an online, digital environment these considerations disappear or at least diminish. Then the best approach is to publish first and allow the system to filter.

Table 3.2 demonstrates how each of the functions above has been altered and undermined by digitisation and the network.

Table 3.2 Functions of industries that have been affected by networked approaches

Function	Music	Newspaper
Content	MP3, freely available online	Blogs and online commentary
Filter	iTunes playlists, social services such as Blip.fm, LastFM, automatic recommendation such as iTunes Genius	Social networks, for example, recommendations through Twitter; metrics such as Technorati; lists such as Wikio
Sustainable business model	Lowering of costs, distribution straight to consumer, revenue from live performance	Low-costs, individual ads, for example, Google AdSense; indirect benefits to individual, for example, public speaking; consultancy
Format	Through services such as iTunes, Spotify and so on	Blogs, wikis, podcasts, accessed through subscription such as Really Simple Syndication (RSS)
Quality	Filtered on the way out, through recommendations and networks	Filtered on the way out through networks, lists and personalised feeds
Access	Broad base of users and networks	Citizen journalism

In both industries the functions can be realised to differing extents by the network-driven model. The end result is not exactly the same – a collection of blogs and podcasts is not the same as a newspaper, but it fulfils many of the same needs for individual consumers.

One way to think of the component functions in an industry is by analogy with the atoms in a molecule. These are held together by chemical bonds. In some molecules these bonds are relatively weak and the presence of an outside agent, such as heat or another chemical, can cause them to break (and maybe reassemble in a different format). For other molecules the bonds are relatively strong, and considerable energy is required to break them. For both the music and newspaper industries the bonds that held them together in their pre-digitisation phases have been shown to be relatively weak. Some of the functions have now reformed; for instance, in successful online newspapers such as the *Guardian*, we have seen the loss of the payment of content but a successful reinterpretation of filtering functions.

Turning to higher education, the component functions can first be delineated, and then possible alternatives can be examined for the networked version, to determine the strength of the 'chemical' bonds in our molecule. The functions are similar, but not identical to those above, I would suggest (see Table 3.3).

Each of these functions is prone to being undermined by the network, with alternatives offered online. The strength of resistance, if we wish to phrase it thus, varies though across the functions, and an examination of each function separately suggests which functions universities, and by extension scholars, should concentrate on strengthening and promoting. Table 3.4 lists suggestions for some alternatives to these functions as offered by the global network and an assessment of that function's resilience, ranging from weak (i.e. this function is likely to be replaced by the network alternative) to strong (i.e. universities still represent the best method of realising this function).

Table 3.3 Functions in higher education

Function	How it is realised in higher education
Content	Lectures, academic journals
Filter	Lectures, reading lists
Structure	Courses, research programmes
Social	Ready-made student cohort
Support	Tutorials
Recognition	Assessment and accreditation

Table 3.4 Network alternatives to educational functions

Function	Alternative	Resilience
Content	Open content, YouTube, Google	Weak
Filter	Search, social network, Delicious	Weak
Structure	Pathways, for example, Trailfire; recommendations, for example, Amazon	Medium
Social	Social network, communities, wikis	Weak
Support	Groups, peer to peer, expert sourcing, for example, Mahalo	Medium
Recognition	Reputation, prior learning recognition	Strong

The second element to consider is the strength of the bonds between these functions and not just their individual resilience. This comes down to a matter of convenience and cost – is it easier and more cost effective for an individual to get the functions bundled together in the current offering or to access them separately online? Social currency and recognition are the significant factors here, since, although it may be much easier to be an autodidact now and teach yourself about any subject, and possibly join a community containing peers and experts, having this learning recognised in society is more difficult. The undergraduate degree is the default recognition for a certain level of learning and skill acquisition. From an employer's perspective it fulfils a function that is difficult to realise in other ways, although, of course, it is far from perfect.

So while the recognition element maintains its strong social currency, this exerts a sufficient bond to tie the other elements together, even if individual elements are now as well, if not better, served by the network alternative. This should not be taken as an excuse for complacency, however. As we have seen with the newspaper and music sectors, seemingly unassailable market positions can be quickly undermined in a digital economy.

It would not be impossible to imagine a third-party provider, let's say Google, offering an accreditation service, which equate to a university degree. They could create a marketplace of approved 'accreditors' and freelance tutors, a kind of eBay for education. In this scenario, no matter what subject individual learners are interested in, be it Drupal site development, thirteenth-century European history, topiary or climate change, they can find a community of learners, approved mentors willing to offer tuition (for a price) and registered providers who will allocate credits based on the learning they can demonstrate (perhaps through a portfolio). With the backing of Google a critical mass of large corporations might sign up to the scheme to meet their staff development needs. Individual learners also find that it meets the long tail of interests that are currently not met by a restricted curriculum. Such a scenario may be difficult to realise, but not impossible, and if successful, the weakness of the other elements in the 'university bundle' could become apparent, and the overall attractiveness of the university system is seriously undermined.

Conclusion

So, is education, like newspapers or the music industry, minus five years or so? It's tempting to think so, and there are some parallels, but the differences are significant also. Higher education is not merely a content industry and has some relationship to a physical institution often. The focus in this chapter has largely been on the teaching element of universities since this is the most apparent one to society, but of course, universities, and scholars, perform other functions too, most notably research but also dissemination, outreach and curation. However, I would suggest that if the teaching and learning functions were seriously undermined, these functions would not be sufficient to maintain universities in their current state.

In Chapter 2 it was suggested that reference to a perfect storm of technological-driven change was overstated and not the way to engage with new technologies, but that there are some significant factors influencing scholarly practice. In this chapter the impact digitisation and the global social network have had on two industries have been examined. So what are the lessons for higher education?

The following are the six main lessons which I believe higher education can draw from newspapers and the music sectors:

1 Change, when it comes, can happen very quickly.

2 There are no assumptions that are unassailable, and there are many implicit assumptions that we are unaware of.

3 Do not confuse form with function.

4 The boundaries with other sectors become blurred.

5 Calls to protect a practice because it serves a social function are not sufficient to prevent it being radically altered.

6 The combination of digitisation of content and the global social network creates an unpredictable environment which requires flexibility and rapidity of response.

Lest this should seem like a call to radical change that undermines the measured approach in Chapter 2, it is worth tempering these lessons with some significant differences between higher education and the sectors we have examined:

- Higher education offers human elements in support and guidance which go beyond that of a content industry.

- The recognition function is strongly embedded in society and not easily replicated on scale.

- Although teaching and learning is the primary function, universities perform other functions which make their value to society more complex than single-content industries.

- Many universities have social and physical aspects, providing a life experience that is not easily replicated.

- Universities have a strong historical and social context which provides some resistance, although it should not be relied upon.

The tension between these two pressures, the irresistible force of the digital, networked and open approach and the unmoveable object of universities and the recognition of degrees, is another example of the schizophrenic nature characterising digital scholarship. As with the paradox, where the irresistible force stops and the unmoveable object moves, it is essential to consider both elements in this scenario, and too often the discussion is dominated by representation of only one side. I will return to the significance of maintaining a balanced perspective in the concluding section of this book.

In this chapter the role of universities as institutions has been the focus. In Chapter 4, this is continued by examining the practices of individual scholars and the nature of scholarship.

4 The Nature of Scholarship

aving examined broad changes in other sectors that have been shaped by the aspects of open, digital networks, in this chapter, the focus will be on the practices of scholarship.

Scholarship

There are different interpretations as to what constitutes 'scholarship' and different methods for representing it. For example, is scholarship best expressed as a set of actions that are common to all disciplines, or is it best viewed as the outputs it produces? Are all practices of equal significance? Are there commonalities across all disciplines? Research on the nature of scholarship has sought to answer these questions, and from this work we can then begin to consider how practices may be changing. The term digital scholarship has gained some currency recently, but the definitions of this are also varied.

Before we consider definitions of digital scholarship, we should look at concepts of scholarship which they build upon. Unsworth (2000) suggested seven 'scholarly primitives'. His work was focused around humanities, but he argues that

Primitives refer to some basic functions common to scholarly activity across disciplines, over time, and independent of theoretical orientation … These primitives are the irreducible currency of scholarship, so it should, in principal, be possible to exchange them across all manner of boundaries of type or token. (Unsworth 2000)

His list of primitives is as follows:

1 discovering – knowledge either through archives or research;

2 annotating – adding layers of interpretation;

3 comparing – for example, texts across languages, data sets;

4 referring – referencing and acknowledging;

5 sampling – selecting appropriate samples;

6 illustrating – clarifying, elucidating, explaining; and

7 representing – publishing or communicating.

Palmer, Teffeau and Pirmann (2009) build on this work to suggest an activity-centric categorisation of five key tasks: searching, collecting, reading, writing and collaborating, which they then subdivide. This further division reveals differences between the humanities and science disciplines; for example, searching is subdivided into browsing, which 'tends to be open ended with the searcher looking through a body of assembled or accessible information', and direct searching, which 'occurs when a scholar has a well-defined goal. For example, they may be looking for information on a particular chemical compound or trying to find a particular journal article'. They suggest that browsing is more prevalent in the humanities, while direct searching is more relevant to science.

Probably the most influential work on scholarship in recent years is that of Ernest Boyer. Using data gathered from more than 5,000 faculty members, Boyer (1990) classified the types of activities scholars regularly engaged in. This was partly a response to the research versus teaching conflict, with recruitment and promotion often being based on research activity, while it is teaching that is significant to most students and to more than 70 per cent of faculty. The report sought to place all scholarly activity on an equal footing: 'What we urgently need today is a more inclusive view of what it means to be a scholar – a recognition that knowledge is acquired through research, through synthesis, through practice, and through teaching' (Boyer 1990: 24).

In Boyer's definition of scholarship, there are four components, each of which, he suggests, should be considered as of equal value by universities and government policy.

Discovery – This is the creation of new knowledge in a specific area or discipline. This is often taken to be synonymous with research. This is probably closest to the public conception of scholarship, as universities are often the site of significant breakthroughs.

Integration – This is focused on interpretation and interdisciplinary work. It is moving away from the pure, 'genesis' research of discovery. Boyer states that it is 'making connections across the disciplines, placing the specialties in larger context, illuminating data in a revealing way, often educating non-specialists'.

Application – This is related to the concept of service, but Boyer makes a distinction between citizenship and scholarly types of service, and for the latter it needs to build on the scholar's area of expertise. It can be seen as engagement with the wider world outside academia, which might include public engagement activities as well as input into policy and general media discussions. This can also include the time spent peer-reviewing journal articles and grant applications and sitting on various committees.

Teaching – Much of the interpretation of Boyer can be seen as an attempt to raise the profile of teaching. He argues that 'the work of the professor becomes consequential only as it is understood by others. Yet, today, teaching is often viewed as a routine function, tacked on'.

Boyer's work was influential and many universities sought to implement reward and development schemes based on his four activities. It is not without criticism, however, in that it focuses on the individual scholar and is therefore biased towards the humanities, where there is a higher incidence of lone scholars and a culture of 'possessive individualism' (Rosenzweig 2007). It may be less applicable in the sciences, which are characterised by large-scale, capital intensive collaborations (Galison and Hevly 1992).

However, as a basis for examining changes in scholarly practice, it is well established and captures the range of scholarly activity sufficiently for the broad impact of new technologies to be seen. Subsequent chapters will look at each of Boyer's activities in more detail and outline how some practices are changing and what the possible implications are.

Digital scholarship revisited

The term 'digital scholarship' can be viewed as a convenient shorthand to contrast with traditional, 'analogue' forms of scholarship, although as set out in Chapter 1, 'digital' is only one aspect of a trilogy, the convergence of which makes for significant change. Digital scholarship itself has differing interpretations, in one flavour it refers to the curation and collection of digital resources, which places it in the information sciences, whereas others use it in a broader sense to cover a range of scholarly activities afforded by new technologies. It is this more wide-ranging interpretation that is the focus of this book.

As the American Council of Learned Societies Commission on Cyberinfrastructure for the Humanities & Social Sciences observes, there are multiple interpretations of digital scholarship.

In recent practice, 'digital scholarship' has meant several related things:

1 building a digital collection of information for further study and analysis,

2 creating appropriate tools for collection building,

3 creating appropriate tools for the analysis and study of collections,

4 using digital collections and analytical tools to generate new intellectual products, and

5 creating authoring tools for these new intellectual products, either in traditional form or in digital form (http://www.cnx.org/content/m14163/latest/).

Christine Borgman (2007) discusses digital scholarship with a focus on data and somewhat addresses the humanities bias in Boyer's work by emphasising the significance of teams: 'The internet lies at the core of an advanced scholarly information infrastructure to facilitate distributed, data and information-intensive collaborative research'.

Borgman argues that the sharing of data and data itself constitute knowledge capital, comparable with published articles. This tension between Borgman and Boyer may indicate that there is no one interpretation of digital scholarship that encompasses all disciplines, as the work of Palmer *et al.* suggests. Similarly Fry (2004) suggests that the adoption of technology will follow different patterns in disciplines: '[academic] fields that have a highly politicized and tightly controlled research culture will develop a coherent field-based strategy for the uptake and use of ICTs, whereas domains that are pluralistic and have a loosely organized research culture will appropriate ICTs in an ad-hoc localized manner'.

Borgman's focus is on developing an information infrastructure that will facilitate the exchange of data and scholarly activity. She suggests that '[p]reservation and management of digital content are probably the most difficult challenges to be addressed in building an advanced information infrastructure for scholarly applications'.

While preservation and management are undoubtedly important, the focus of this book is on changes in the practice of scholars, particularly in how they communicate, the types of outputs they produce and the networks they operate within. As proposed in Chapter 1, it is the 'fast, cheap and out of control' technologies that perhaps have the greatest impact on scholarly practice. These are often tools produced outside of education, and their ease of use encourages innovation and exploration. Much of the digital scholarship work is centred on the curation and preservation of digital artefacts or the digitisation of content. The sort of changes we are seeing around open access publishing, development of blog communities, use of Twitter at conferences and easy sharing of content are driven not just by their digital nature but by the convergence of the three characteristics of digital, networked and open.

Before exploring the impact of such approaches on each of Boyer's four functions in subsequent chapters, the remainder of this chapter will provide some brief indicative examples of changes in them.

Discovery

Boyer's first function of scholarship is the discovery of new knowledge in a specific discipline or area, what is often termed 'genesis research'. An open, digital, networked approach to discovery could relate to the sharing of data. Particularly in scientific research, access to powerful computing tools at relatively low cost allows researchers to both generate and analyse unprecedented amounts of data. The development and adoption of digital data has led to the establishment of new (sub)fields so that '[a] growing number of sciences, from atmospheric modelling to genomics, would not exist in their current form if it were not for computers' (Foster 2006).

While the creation and analysis of digital data (like the digitisation of content we saw in Chapter 3) has been with us for a while now, it is the combination of the global network that is really beginning to alter research practice. This means that data forms can be easily shared with colleagues and the wider academic community in a way that was not possible previously, so that data sets can become part of scholarly communication:

> Datasets are a significant part of the scholarly record and are being published more and more frequently, either formally or informally … In short, they need to be integrated into the scholarly information system so that authors, readers and librarians can use, find and manage them as easily as they do working papers, journal articles and books. (Green 2009: 13)

Scientists, institutions, data centres, users, funders and publishers all have a part to play in the management of data (Lyon 2007), and increasingly the open provision of data is a required outcome from funding bodies.

A recent international collaboration has been set up with the aim of facilitating easier sharing through enabling organisations to register research data sets and assign persistent identifiers to them, so that research data sets can be handled as independent, citable, unique scientific objects. Combining data sets also encourages meta-analysis, so, for example, sites such as http://www.realclimate.org collate data sets from climate change studies which are open for others to process and use.

As well as raising the profile of data itself as a project output, this also changes the timescale and management of a project. Instead of waiting until data have been verified and analysed to be released, many projects are pre-releasing data with the specific intention of letting others work with it. The Human Genome Project was one of the forerunners in this respect, and as this discussion in *Nature* demonstrates (Birney *et al.* 2009), it is a practice many wish to be adopted more widely:

> One of the lessons from the Human Genome Project (HGP) was the recognition that making data broadly available prior to publication can be

profoundly valuable to the scientific enterprise and lead to public benefits. This is particularly the case when there is a community of scientists that can productively use the data quickly – beyond what the data producers could do themselves in a similar time period, and sometimes for scientific purposes outside the original goals of the project.

This 'liberation' of data has a number of implications for research practice which are summarised below.

The application of grid computing or crowdsourcing analysis

In *Wikinomics*, Tapscott and Williams (2006) give numerous examples of how sharing data sets allows multiple users to analyse data and return their results. SETI (the search for extraterrestrial intelligence, http://www.seti.org) is one of the best-known examples, with users downloading and analysing data sets on their own computers, but the example of the gold mining company in Canada is perhaps more telling. They set a prize fund to locate gold on their site and shared all the data they had available. The result was unexpected methodology being brought to bear and a number of successful new sites they had no previous intention of exploring.

Unexpected applications

Releasing data sets means that they can be applied in contexts that the original users would not have envisaged. Just as Twitter did not predict the different applications that can be built on top of it, so the providers of data sets do not predict or control the different uses to which they will be put. For example, in the United States, the Centre for Disease Control was able to monitor the spread of influenza more effectively by analysing Google search queries (Ginsberg *et al.* 2009).

Data visualisation

Related to the previous point, open data allow people to visualise it in different formats, thus making a statement, telling a narrative or revealing a trend from the data that may be otherwise hidden to a larger audience. The blog Information Is Beautiful gathers many of these together, and data visualisation is set to be a skill researchers will increasingly develop expertise in and seek to deploy (http://www. informationisbeautiful.net/).

Combination

This also applies to Boyer's next aspect of scholarship, integration, since open data allow researchers to combine data from different fields to produce new insights. This is addressed in Chapter 6.

It is the combination of openness, in terms of sharing data sets, digital provision of the data and sharing via a network, that allows these benefits to be realised; any one of these approaches in isolation would not be sufficient. The open, digital, networked approach then complements the use and development of free, easy-to-use tools, such as ManyEyes, Google Analytics and Gapminder, which in turn encourage an open, digital, networked form of dissemination and communication as these results are shared via blogs and social networks.

A second way in which scholars are utilising new technologies to adapt research practice is through the formation of networks and communities. What the global, social network allows everybody (not just scholars) to do is connect with those with similar interests. By establishing oneself in a network and sharing, a scholar connects with others working in the same field. This can be through blogging (where linking and commenting on others' blogs as well as blogging regularly is seen as an important function in a community), social networks or more structured community sites with forums, where one establishes a reputation by answering questions and engaging in discussion. For some subject areas it is in these distributed online communities that much of the relevant discussion in a subject takes place and not via the traditional forums of journals and conferences.

In addition these 'virtual' networks are now sufficiently well established to have connections through into traditional practice, so they are spawning research projects, writing collaborations, conferences and influencing research agendas, which is explored in more detail in Chapter 10.

Integration

Boyer's second dimension of scholarship is integration, where the discoveries of others are put into context and applied to wider problems. Following on from the discussion about the impact of networks on discovery, we can see that the mechanisms through which scholars publish and communicate their findings and learn about the work of others are undergoing radical change. This section will focus primarily on the journal article, although the publishing model is addressed in more detail in Chapter 12. Journal articles can almost be seen as the battleground between new forms of scholarly activity and traditional systems.

There are a number of issues that are converging into what has been labelled a journals crisis (Edwards and Shulenburger 2003; Willinsky 2006; Cope and Kalantzis 2009). These include long lag times between submission and publication, increasing subscription costs, the practice of bundling large numbers of journals together and the growing resentment over the reliance of journals on the volunteered labour of the writers, reviewers and editors for the content, which is then sold back to their employers (Harley *et al.* 2010).

This is exacerbated by the tendency to replicate the limitations of paper publishing even in digital formats, such as word limits, restrictions on dynamic content and links to data sets. Experiments in the possibilities of the digital format are taking place, such as the Journal of Visualized Experiments (JOVE http://www.jove.com/) in biology, which is a peer reviewed, and PubMed-indexed journal consisting of videoed contributions, which might suggest a radically different future for multimedia journals, but as yet this is not common.

There is also a wider philosophical point about the dangers of restricting access to knowledge to those working within the universities and research institutes that can afford to pay the subscriptions, excluding those researchers in other institutions and in particular in lesser developed countries (Willinsky 2006). The proponents of open publishing argue that making knowledge freely available enhances scholarship to everybody's benefit.

Peer-review processes have also begun to be adapted from established traditions in light of changes in the technologies of publication and means of access to what is published. These changes arise from the ability of users to copy, append and comment on the content of an article through the medium of distribution – the online forms of publication. The shift from a series of discrete and disciplined steps in a publication process that ends in a finished product to an ongoing system of regular commentary and conversation raises interesting questions about the function of peer review. The process of peer review has functioned as a filter, a means of ensuring quality, but there is a sense in which the normative effect of peer review has come to signify the process as being an end in and of itself, rather than the means to an end.

There are a number of modifications to peer review, such as open peer review and publishing or acknowledging the contributions of reviewers to the final text (Cope and Kalantzis 2009; Harley et al. 2010). In 2006 the journal Nature ran a debate and experiment with open peer review (http://www.nature.com/nature/peerreview/debate/index.html); this involved making articles which were undergoing the traditional process of peer review available on a publicly accessible server for wider comment, with the reviewers and public comments taken into consideration when deciding on publication. This trial was not particularly successful, with a low take-up by authors and a lack of high-quality comments.

Despite the possibilities for open publication made possible through a move to digital formats, there is still an inherent conservatism fostered through the current system of recruitment and promotion of scholars which prioritises traditional outputs (Borgman 2007; Harley et al. 2010). This is explored in Chapter 11.

The area of publication and dissemination is one that I will revisit in this book as it occupies a central role in scholarship and demonstrates several of the issues in digital scholarship, including the range of alternatives now available, the tensions with existing practice and the possible impact of adopting new approaches.

Application

Academics have been enthusiastic users of many new communication technologies in order to participate in wider global debates relevant to their field. Academic bloggers, for example, can gain large audiences and through this reach, engage with new audiences. We are seeing the development of a 'personal brand' amongst academics as new technologies allow them to establish an audience that is complementary to their institutional one. For example, Open University philosophy lecturer Nigel Warburton has achieved more than 5 million downloads of his podcasts, and Kansas State University professor Michael Wesch (2007) has had more than 10 million views of his YouTube video 'The Machine Is Using Us'.

These new channels are also beginning to compete with traditional means of public engagement in terms of influence. For example, Clow (2009) compares the traffic generated to a site by a 'tweet' from British celebrity Stephen Fry, which led to more than 50,000 hits in one day, with a feature on the Radio 4 news which led to 2,400 hits on a different site. While not directly comparable this illustrates the power of new technologies in 'outreach'.

These kinds of figures exceed the sales of most scholarly books and journal article access, so we can see that new technologies are facilitating access to a new audience which is disintermediating many of the conventional channels. A key element to realising a strong online identity is an attitude of openness. This involves sharing aspects of personal life on social network sites, blogging ideas rather than completed articles and engaging in experiments with new media.

This role of public engagement is one that will be explored further in Chapter 7.

Teaching

It is arguably in Boyer's fourth function, that of teaching, where we see the biggest impact of digital technologies and open approaches. The digitisation of learning and teaching resources means that they are easily reproducible and shareable at a global scale, although doing this raises serious challenges for universities accustomed to being the gatekeeper to such knowledge.

The advent of MIT's Open CourseWare project in 2001 initiated the advent of Open Education Resources (OERs). This has led to a broad OER movement with many universities embarking on similar projects (such as the OU's OpenLearn). While there is debate as to the direction, sustainability and impact of the OER movement (e.g. Wiley 2009a), it has raised the profile of openness in education and questions whether, as publicly funded institutions, universities have an obligation to release content freely. We will look at openness in education in more detail in Chapter 10.

With the advent of a wide variety, and high quality, of freely available academic content online, the individual student is no longer limited by the physical resources they can locate, and the lecturer is therefore no longer regarded as the sole source of knowledge, as the learner can pick and choose elements from a variety of courses provided by any number of diverse institutions and individuals.

Whilst there are institutional benefits to making its educational resources freely available, the large-scale projects such as OpenLearn have been made possible through significant external funding, and in the current economic climate some universities, such as Ohio State University, have backtracked from the Open Education agenda (McAndrew, Scanlon and Clow 2010).

The open, digital, networked approach also facilitates the creation of open courses, for example, Stephen Downes and George Siemens open course on Connectivism and Connective Knowledge. This course is open for both formally enrolled students as well as free learners, with approximately 2,200 participants taking the course in 2008 as free learners and 25 studying for credit. The course is open in terms of access, but also in digital and networked in terms of content, with students encouraged to create their own course components, including SecondLife communities, 170 different blogs, concept maps and Google Groups (Meiszner 2010).

Conclusion

It is clear from the preceding discussion that new technologies hold out very real possibilities for change across all facets of scholarship. In each case these afford the possibility for new, more open ways of working. Academic work has always contained a significant element of collaboration *within* academia, but now it is increasingly easy to collaborate with more colleagues within, and also beyond the academy, and for the varied products of these collaborations to be available to the widest possible audience. This reflects the kind of permeable boundaries seen in other sectors, as a result of digital network technologies.

In Chapter 3 the impact of digital and network technologies on other sectors was examined, but it is the third element of openness that is perhaps more significant for scholarship. Digital scholarship is more than just using information and communication technologies to research, teach and collaborate; it also includes embracing the open values, ideology and potential of technologies born of peer-to-peer networking and wiki ways of working in order to benefit both the academy and society.

The term 'open scholar' has also been used by some and can be seen as almost synonymous with digital scholar. The open scholar 'is someone who makes their intellectual projects and processes digitally visible and who invites and encourages ongoing criticism of their work and secondary uses of any or all parts of it – at any stage of its development' (Burton 2009). This is a significant and challenging step for scholars, especially when faced with norms and values which oppose, hinder or fail to recognise these forms of scholarship.

Chapters 5 to 8 will address each of Boyer's scholarly functions in turn. For each one I have selected just one perspective to demonstrate the possible impact of digital, networked, open approaches, which is not to suggest that this is the only, or even the most significant, impact but rather as illustrative of the potential changes and the issues.

5 Researchers and New Technology

This chapter will consider the first of Boyer's scholarly functions, termed discovery, by examining the use of new technologies and practices by researchers.

The current state

There have been a number of recent studies examining researchers' use of new technologies, and the conclusion one can draw from these is of cautious experimentation. Perhaps, more than any other of the scholarly functions, the use of new technology in research is the most conservative, maybe because research is the practice still most highly valued. This chapter will look at some of the current evaluation research and then look at some of the potential uses.

If technology uptake is examined first of all, most studies indicate that researchers tend to use a variety of tools, some of which are provided by their institution and others they have selected themselves (Kroll and Forsman 2010). In terms of Web 2.0 technologies, there is tentative take-up; for example, Proctor, Williams and Stewart (2010) in the United Kingdom found that

> a majority of researchers are making at least occasional use of one or more web 2.0 tools or services for purposes related to their research: for communicating their work; for developing and sustaining networks and collaborations; or for finding out about what others are doing. But frequent or intensive use is rare, and some researchers regard blogs, wikis and other novel forms of communication as a waste of time or even dangerous.

As we saw in Chapter 2, there is little evidence to suggest that age is a factor in the use of new technologies, as Carpenter, Wetheridge and Smith (2010) claim:

> [T]here are no marked differences between Generation Y doctoral students and those in older age groups. Nor are there marked differences in these behaviours between doctoral students of any age in different years of their study. The most significant differences revealed in the data are between subject disciplines of study irrespective of age or year of study.

There is a general suspicion around using social networks to share findings, although many researchers use them for personal and professional networking (James *et al.* 2009; Carpenter *et al.* 2010). Carpenter *et al.* describe researchers as 'risk averse' and 'behind the curve in using digital technology'. Similarly Harley *et al.* (2010) state that 'we found no evidence to suggest that "tech-savvy" young graduate students, postdoctoral scholars, or assistant professors are bucking traditional publishing practices'.

The relationship with publishing is a tense one (which we will look at in more detail in Chapter 12). While many researchers effused support for open access, for instance, with James *et al.* (2009) reporting 77 per cent agreement with the principle of open access publishing, there were also reservations about quality or, more significantly, perceptions by others of quality. Similarly Proctor *et al.* (2010) found that print journals were rated as more important than online ones.

What this indicates is the strong relationship between academic journals and recognition. It is through publishing in well-renowned journals that researchers are likely to gain tenure or promotion and also to be recognised in their own institution. There is thus a disincentive inherent in scholarly practice to explore new forms of publication, even when the majority of researchers themselves may support them. This is also related to reputation and identity. If other forms of output are perceived as frivolous then early stage researchers in particular will be discouraged from engaging with them. The academic with tenure, however, is often more willing to experiment with new technologies and forms of dissemination, as their reputation is already established. For instance, in the US context at least, Kroll and Forsman (2010) claim that 'the issue of open access publishing elicited strong support with faculty who want to share their publications freely. However, faculty express a strong preference for their graduate students to publish in traditional high-impact journal'.

Harley *et al.* (2010) put it even more bluntly:

Established scholars seem to exercise significantly more freedom in the choice of publication outlet than their untenured colleagues, …

The advice given to pre-tenure scholars was consistent across all fields: focus on publishing in the right venues and avoid spending too much time on public engagement, committee work, writing op-ed pieces, developing websites, blogging, and other non-traditional forms of electronic dissemination.

Academic research is then in a strange position where new entrants are encouraged to be conservative while the reinterpretation of practice and exploration is left to established practitioners. This seems to be the inverse of most other industries, where 'new blood' is seen as a means of re-energising an organisation and introducing challenging ideas. This should be an area of concern for academia if its established practice is reducing the effectiveness of one of its most valuable inputs, namely the new researcher.

As touched upon in Chapter 4, one area that is seeing significant change is the open access approach to data. There is a driver in this area from research funders, who are implementing policies which place data sets as a public good, with frameworks and services for discovery, access and reuse. In the United Kingdom, five of the seven research councils now have such policies (Swan and Brown 2008). There is variation across the disciplines, where many have an already established practice of sharing data and others where this is not the norm.

The use of social networks to form research teams is still rather tentative, with well-established practices still prevalent. Kroll and Forsman (2010) stress the importance researchers place in personal contacts:

> Almost all researchers have created a strong network of friends and colleagues and they draw together the same team repeatedly for new projects …

> Everyone emphasizes the paramount importance of interpersonal contact as the vital basis for agreeing to enter into joint work. Personal introductions, conversations at meetings or hearing someone present a paper were cited as key in choosing collaborators.

This perhaps indicates something of a closed shop – successful researchers have established personal networks which have been built up from years of attending conferences and previous collaboration. As financial pressures begin to bite in research funding, competition for grants becomes more intense, with success rate decreasing from 31 per cent in 2000 to 20 per cent in 2009. The average age of first-time principal investigators has increased over the same period (Kroll and Forsman 2010). Both of these factors may suggest that having previously successful teams will become more significant, thus creating a research funding spiral, where a greater percentage of the smaller funds goes to a decreasing set of researchers.

The picture we have then of research is one where scholars are exploring the use of a number of different technologies to perform certain functions individually, but the overall uptake and attitudes vary enormously. This is partly because 'research' is such a catch-all term which encompasses differences in disciplines, widely varying research methodologies and, of course, many different personalities and attitudes. The engagement or uptake with new technologies is less than might be expected or found in other communities. As Wu and Neylon (2008) put it,

> The potential of online tools to revolutionize scientific communication and their ability to open up the details of the scientific enterprise so that a wider range of people can participate is clear. In practice, however, the reality has fallen far behind the potential.

Given the potential benefits of new technologies (which I'll address below), why might this be so? The environment within which research operates can be seen as contributing to a lack of engagement. For example, in the United Kingdom, there was a Research Assessment Exercise, now superseded by the Research Excellence Framework (REF) (http://www.hefce.ac.uk/research/ref/), which assesses the quality of research in UK universities and then allocates funds on this basis. Similar schemes have been implemented in Australia, the Netherlands and New Zealand. The current proposals for the REF have an aim to 'support and encourage innovative and curiosity-driven research, including new approaches, new fields and interdisciplinary work'. However, the types of outputs mentioned focus on journal articles, and the exploration of metrics is restricted to a few commercial publishers' databases. There is no explicit encouragement to engage with new forms of outputs or to forefront an open access approach. As with all such exercises they significantly shape behaviour, and do not simply measure it, so the message researchers may have gained from their institution that the exploration of new approaches is discouraged becomes reinforced at a national level.

Where researchers are using new tools they are doing so in conjunction with existing ones, finding appropriate uses for the tools to make their work more effective. Proctor *et al.* (2010) summarise it thus:

> [T]here is little evidence at present to suggest that web 2.0 will prompt in the short or medium term the kinds of radical changes in scholarly communications advocated by the open research community. Web 2.0 services are currently being used as supplements to established channels, rather than a replacement for them.

This may be an entirely reasonable approach, since research is at the core of what it means to be a scholar, and issues around quality and reliability are essential in maintaining the status and reputation of universities. A cautious approach is therefore not surprising as researchers seek to understand where the potential of these new tools can enhance their practice, while simultaneously maintaining the key characteristics of quality research. I would argue that it is this integrity of research which should frame discussions and experimentation with new technologies, and not the negative influence of promotion criteria and funding frameworks, since a concern about the nature of research is just as likely to accept new methods if they improve its efficacy as reject them if they threaten its reputation.

The research context, in particular funding and publication models, may work against the adoption of new approaches, but that may not be the only reason. There may be intrinsic conflicts with the ingrained practices of the discipline itself. For example, examining 'Science 2.0' in *Nature*, Waldrop (2008) found that while wikis were being used regularly as collaborative research tools, blogging was less popular. The reasons for this may not be simply a reluctance to embrace new technology but rather that the form of communication runs against the training and values scientists have developed over many years:

> 'It's so antithetical to the way scientists are trained,' Duke University geneticist Huntington F. Willard said at the April 2007 North Carolina Science Blogging Conference, one of the first national gatherings devoted to this topic. The whole point of blogging is spontaneity – getting your ideas out there quickly, even at the risk of being wrong or incomplete. 'But to a scientist, that's a tough jump to make,' says Willard, head of Duke's Institute for Genome Sciences & Policy. 'When we publish things, by and large, we've gone through a very long process of drafting a paper and getting it peer reviewed'.

There may be a dilemma with science in particular and the informal lightweight technologies: scientists are engaged in the business of predicting the future. Given certain variables then these outcomes will ensue with a certain probability (or these outcomes are a result of these input variables). But as we have seen already, the benefits of many 'Web 2.0' ways of working are wrapped up in unpredictability. Authors won't know which blog posts will be popular; they can share ideas on Twitter but can't predict who will take them up; they can release research data but won't know what the uses for it will be. It might be the case then that scientists in particular want predictable benefits and outcomes from engaging in this type of activity, and at least at this stage these benefits are less than predictable.

A networked research cycle

There are many proposed approaches to conducting research through a 'research cycle' (e.g. McKenzie 1996; Hevner and March 2003). This section will adopt a basic cycle of plan, collect data, analyse and reflect to demonstrate how an open, digital, networked approach to the process might be realised, using a variety of tools. This is intended to be indicative of how new approaches could be used in the research process and not a claim that all research can or should be performed in this manner:

1 Planning – researchers establish their research question through iterative exposure, using social networks and blogs. They seek feedback and ask for relevant experience. Using online information sources such as Delicious feeds and Google scholar they gather relevant information to inform their research proposal. They set up a series of Google alerts around a number of subjects to gather daily information. A plan is created that incorporates

    regular release and small-scale outputs. They hold an informal online meeting with some interested parties and establish a project blog or wiki.

2 Collect data – researchers continue to use online information sources for their literature review. They create an online database and seek user contributions, seeded by requested contributions from peers in their network. An online survey is created in SurveyMonkey.

3 Analyse – researchers use Google analytics to examine traffic data and SurveyMonkey analytics to analyse responses. They use data visualisation tools such as ManyEyes to draw out key themes in responses.

4 Reflect – reflection occurs throughout the process by means of a series of blog posts and video interviews.

This would constitute a valid approach to research which would be comparable with current approaches. New methods then could be, and frequently are, deployed within a conventional structure. It is the development of new approaches and interpretations of what constitutes research that I think is more interesting, and more challenging to our notions of scholarship, and it is these that will be explored in the next section.

Themes

Having set out the overall view of the landscape as it pertains to research and open, digital, networked approaches, I now want to look at a number of themes which I believe will have increasing relevance, whether it is because they become accepted practice or because the research community reacts against them.

Granularity

Changes in granularity are one of the unpredicted and profound consequences of digitisation. As we saw in Chapter 3 the music industry has seen a shift to the track becoming the standard unit, rather than the album. A similar process has happened with newspapers, where the impact of search and social networks has seen individual articles being circulated, linked to and discovered, whereas with the physical artefact it was usually at the level of the whole paper that sharing occurred. As suggested in Chapter 3 a similar breakdown in granularity for books has yet to materialise.

    The books and journals will undoubtedly continue to exist, but they will not hold the monopoly on being the conduit for ideas. Just like some albums, some books have an integrity that justifies the format, the whole product is worth the investment.

But just like many albums used to consist of a handful of good tracks padded out with what we might generously term 'album tracks', so many books seem to be a good idea stretched over 100,000 words. This isn't the author's fault necessarily, rather a result of the book as the dominant route for transmitting ideas in society.

But this need no longer be the case – an online essay, a blog, a podcast, a collection of video clips – all these are perfectly viable means for disseminating ideas. As well as the book losing its monopoly, so does text – audio and video can be used effectively. Text became the dominant form largely because it was transportable when ideas were tied in with physical objects. And if ideas become the equivalent of tracks, then perhaps users create the equivalent of a playlist by pulling these together around a subject of their choice.

As a blogger, this range in granularity has been one of the most appealing aspects. A post can vary from a link to an essay; it can be a commentary on someone else's work, a piece of parody, a research finding, a suggestion, an appeal for contributions and so on. Having alternative outlets creates a backward reaction, in that it then influences the type of research people perform, which is my next category.

Pushback from outlets

In *The Adventures of Augie March*, Saul Bellow (1953) famously observes that 'there is no fineness or accuracy of suppression; if you hold down one thing, you hold down the adjoining'. The reverse would seem to be true also, let's call it Bellow's law: *There is no targeting of liberation; if you release one thing, you also release the adjoining.* It is this knock-on effect that creates the era of uncertainty we are now in. We are seeing the liberation of a number of activities that are facilitated by the open, digital network. These include the removal of filters, freedom to publish and broadcast, the ability to share easily, establishing peer networks without the need for travel, creating communities of interest around diverse subjects and so on.

For each of these there are consequent effects. So if we take the change in granularity in outputs, combined with the removal of filters such as publishers, then we see an example of Bellow's law in action. What constitutes research itself begins to change, since what we regard as research has been partly determined by the process of communicating its outputs. The general approach is to conduct research and disseminate at the end of the project, with maybe a conference presentation on work in progress about halfway through. This can be seen as a necessary approach when conducting large-scale research and also of ensuring what is communicated is reliable and backed up by evidence. But it might also be influenced by the nature of outputs – if you are required to write a 5,000 word paper (or 10,000 word report), then it needs to be based on something substantial. There is an analogy with software production – the traditional model was to expend years in development and then release a finished product. The open source software approach, saw a reversal of this, with developers using the community to find bugs and help fix them, which Raymond (1999) has termed a 'release early, release often' approach. He compares the two approaches thus, talking about Linux developer Linus Torvalds:

> If the overriding objective was for users to see as few bugs as possible, why then you'd only release a version every six months (or less often), and work like a dog on debugging between releases.

> Linus's innovation wasn't so much in doing quick-turnaround releases incorporating lots of user feedback … , but in scaling it up to a level of intensity that matched the complexity of what he was developing. In those early times (around 1991) it wasn't unknown for him to release a new kernel more than once a *day!* Because he cultivated his base of co-developers and leveraged the Internet for collaboration harder than anyone else, this worked. Raymond (1999)

A similar approach may suit some elements of research (I would not suggest it suits all projects or disciplines). A researcher releases, or communicates, ideas, progress, mock-ups, prototypes, draft results and so on throughout their project, gathering feedback as they go.

Perhaps more interesting is that the granularity of what we consider to be research may then alter. The UK REF uses the following definition of research: 'a process of investigation leading to new insights effectively shared'.

The REF is a fairly traditional, conservative view of research concerned with promoting research which is universally recognised as excellent, so their definition is not one we can assume is directed at revolutionising research practice. But if one examines it, there is nothing in its definition that specifies the length of a project or the size of the outputs it produces.

Let us take the example of my OU colleague Tony Hirst, who blogs at OUseful. info. He typically explores new technologies and data visualisation in particular. A random sampling of recent posts include the following:

1 an analysis of Twitter connections between UK politicians,

2 a representation of online communities who use the same hashtag,

3 an interrogation of the Mendeley software to show users by institution,

4 sharing his own promotion case, and

5 a presentation on 'data-driven journalism'.

Each of these is intended to promote discussion and has suggestion for implications, for example, how higher education can make effective use of data. None of them arise from a specific research project, and each of them is fairly small in terms of time and resource. The existence of his blog, though, allows Hirst to engage in this ongoing experimentation, as it has an outlet, but it simultaneously encourages it also, since discussions will arise on the blog (or in other places such as Twitter). Taken as a whole then, the blog *itself* represents the research process, and in this context it is difficult to say that it is not demonstrating 'a process of investigation leading to new insights effectively shared'.

What this may indicate is a shift from specific outputs and a focus on ongoing activity, engagement and reputation, which would be more difficult to measure and reward. Most people know what a good publication record looks like, but could we recognise a good blog track record?

Crowdsourcing

Again building on the open source model, researchers are beginning to realise the potential of a distributed model gathering user input. This can be in the form of grid computing, which utilises the computing power of individual computers to crack complex tasks. An example of this was Oxford University's screensaver project which sought to find a cancer cure by using the distributed computational power of 3.5 million individual computers to screen molecules (http://www.chem.ox.ac.uk/curecancer.html). Other approaches include user contributions, such as the iSpot project, where users upload photographs of wildlife to be identified by experts. This can be used to develop an overall picture of the distribution of species, and in one case revealed a moth never seen before in the United Kingdom (http://www3.open.ac.uk/media/fullstory.aspx?id=17208).

Similarly the Reading Experience Database (http://www.open.ac.uk/Arts/reading/) seeks to gather examples 'of the reading experiences of British subjects and overseas visitors to Britain from 1450–1945, whoever they were, and pretty much whatever they were reading'. This type of extensive record can only be achieved by opening it up to a wider audience, who not only will have access to different experiences but who may also have a different perspective on what constitutes reading matter than if the database were solely populated by academics, who might have a literary bias.

Whereas many such projects seek to encourage input from everyone, others are adding in a layer of filter and publication. For example, the Stanford Encyclopedia of Philosophy has a Wikipedia-type approach, but with an additional layer of editing, so that 'all entries and substantive updates are refereed by the members of a distinguished Editorial Board before they are made public' (http://plato.stanford.

edu/about.html). In this way they hope to combine the power of user-generated content with the reliability of a scholarly reference work.

The demonstrable advantage of such open approaches to data gathering for specific projects is leading to this being an increasingly popular methodology. The problem for such projects is in gaining sufficient contributions, and knowing how to promote this and generate appropriate levels of interest will become a relevant research skill.

Light connections and nodes

As the reviews above highlighted, collaboration and teams are still formed through personal contacts which are established through conferences, previous research, other professionals and so on. This is one area where I suspect we will witness a gradual alteration. As academics establish networks of peers online through blogs, Twitter, Facebook, Friendfeed, LinkedIn and other tools, and these become a more established part of the working pattern, the peers who constitute them come to be seen as another source of contacts. This will arise through the development of an online reputation, which will lead to collaboration. For example, if researchers are constructing a research proposal and realise they need a partner with experience in a particular subject, they will approach someone in their online network who has blogged or tweeted knowledgeably about the subject. Or they may even put out a direct request, asking for partners with appropriate expertise.

In this respect online social networks can be seen as a complement to existing ones. What may be more interesting is whether networks allow different forms of collaboration, just as open databases allow different forms of user contributions. Maintaining personal networks is hard work, since they operate on a one-to-one basis. They are therefore relatively small by nature. Maintaining online networks is less arduous, since an individual is effectively broadcasting to all those in their network. A Facebook status will be read by (potentially) all of your friends. One can view online relationships much more like activity networks; at different times certain nodes or clusters will be 'activated' or more intense. It is therefore possible to maintain a diverse and large network of peers through a series of light connections, just as content can be shared in a frictionless manner (more on this in Chapter 7).

If the definition of research becomes altered (or expanded) to include the smaller granularity outputs mentioned above, then it follows that the type of collaboration needed to realise these may vary from the large-scale, management-intensive project teams we currently operate. Collaboration may be to ask a number of peers within a network to contribute, or to come together for an online event or to engage in a distributed debate across blogs. All of these would constitute research but would not require face-to-face meetings or large investment.

Rapid innovation

In a presentation for TED (Technology, Entertainment, Design), founder Chris Anderson (2010) explores the idea of rapid innovation being driven by the sharing of video on a global scale. He gives the example of dancers sharing moves via YouTube, which they then learn, innovate upon and then share back. Anderson suggests that they have seen a similar effect with TED talks, where each speaker was effectively being challenged by the quality of previous ones which they had viewed online. He refers to it as 'crowd accelerated innovation', which requires three elements to flourish: a crowd, where people will occupy a number of roles; light, which can be interpreted as the ability to be able to see what people, particularly the innovators, are doing; and desire, which is the motivation to spend the required time in attempting innovation and is driven often by competition and the potential to be seen by a large audience.

This rapid innovation can be seen in skills such as dance, guitar playing, skateboarding and so on, which both lend themselves to the visual medium and also appeal to a younger audience. But it is interesting to reflect whether a similar phenomenon will arise in research. Will the early sharing of research, with a global audience, drive innovation and reduce time lags between cycles of research? A small example I have witnessed is with the improvement of presentations. Once individuals start sharing presentations on tools such as Slideshare, they both encounter good presentations and also realise that their slides are available to a potentially much wider audience. One way to reach that audience is to move away from the 'death by bulleted list' approach and make slides more visually engaging and the message clearer. The same may well happen with research in general, if we see a move to sharing smaller granularity outputs earlier in the research cycle. If a research project takes two years to complete and there is an 18-month delay in the publication of a paper, then a four-year cycle between rounds of research can be expected. But this could be reduced dramatically by the adoption of digital, networked, open approaches.

Conclusion

In this chapter the current attitude of researchers to new technologies and communication forms was reviewed. There are islands of innovation, but in general the attitude of the research community is one of caution and even occasional hostility. This can be partly attributed to the context within which research occurs and is recognised and rewarded, which acts to discourage use of different approaches by focusing heavily on the traditional peer-reviewed journal. It is also a product of inherent values and attitudes within research and disciplines which are at odds with many of the affordances of lightweight, informal communication channels. Researchers, in this respect, are engaging with new technologies when they complement existing practice and offer a more efficient means of realising their goals.

Some emerging themes and their implications were then drawn out, including changes in granularity, changes in the nature of research as a result, the use of crowdsourcing techniques and the development of light connections and online networks. These emerging themes sit less comfortably alongside existing practices and can be seen as a more radical shift in research practice. A combination of the two is undoubtedly the best way to proceed, but the danger exists of a schism opening up between those who embrace new approaches and those who reject them, with a resultant entrenchment to extremes on both sides. This can be avoided in part by the acknowledgement and reward of new forms of scholarship, a subject we will return to in Chapter 11.

Boyer's function of integration is the focus of Chapter 6 and in particular interdisciplinary work.

6 Interdisciplinarity and Permeable Boundaries

The second of Boyer's scholarly functions was that of integration, which he described as 'making connections across the disciplines, placing the specialties in larger context, illuminating data in a revealing way, often educating non-specialists'. In this chapter we will look at one aspect of this, interdisciplinarity, and the possible impact of new technologies on the boundaries between disciplines.

Interdisciplinarity

The cross-fertilisation of knowledge from different disciplines has a long history. Indeed, much of history was dominated by the pursuit of unified knowledge, a broad definition and approach to science and the pursuit of knowledge, a *Wissenschaft*, and the differentiation of knowledge into separate disciplines was seen as problematic. However, in order to progress knowledge in ever-more complex fields, specialisation became inevitable and productive. Simultaneously there was an acknowledgement that the application of knowledge across domains was also fruitful and should be actively encouraged. This can lead to a rather schizophrenic attitude towards interdisciplinarity – it is seen as both essential and yet not as pure as disciplinary study. As Klein (1991) puts it, 'interdisciplinarity has been described as both nostalgia for lost wholeness and a new stage in the evolution of science'.

Moti (1995) provides a useful definition of 'bringing together in some fashion distinctive components of two or more disciplines' and suggests that there are four 'realms' of interdisciplinarity:

1   interdisciplinary knowledge – familiarity with distinctive knowledge of two or more disciplines;

2   interdisciplinary research – combining approaches from two or more disciplines while searching or creating new knowledge;

3   interdisciplinary education – merging knowledge from two or more disciplines in a single programme of instruction; and

4   interdisciplinary theory – takes interdisciplinary knowledge, research or education as its main objects of study.

Interdisciplinarity has seen something of a revival of interest recently partly in recognition that many of the substantial challenges facing society will not be solved by a single disciplinary approach, including climate change, dwindling resources, global health epidemics and the impact of global information networks. Indeed the globalisation of many issues, often driven by the Internet, can be seen as an impetus for interdisciplinarity. Kockelmans (1979) summarises that there is an 'inexorable logic that the real problems of society do not come in discipline-shaped blocks'.

However, even with an agreement that interdisciplinary approaches are necessary for the solution of some problems, it is not always easy to achieve. C.P. Snow (1960) famously decried the two cultures' division of arts and science; yet the cultural differences can be seen as even finer grained than this broad binary division. There are differences in disciplines and even sub-disciplines, in terms of how research is performed, what constitutes valuable knowledge, approaches to collaboration and what form dissemination should take. For instance, in many 'hard science' disciplines, work is performed by large teams, and the conference publication is seen as a primary means of dissemination, whereas in the humanities work is often performed by the lone scholar, researching in archives and publishing in journals. Overcoming many of these explicit and implicit differences is one of the challenges of interdisciplinarity. It is by no means an easy task as Bauer (1990) suggests:

> Interdisciplinary work is intractable because the search for knowledge in different fields entails different interests, and thereby different values too; and the different possibilities of knowledge about different subjects also lead to different epistemologies.

> Thus differences among practitioners of the various disciplines are pervasive and aptly described as cultural ones, and interdisciplinary work requires transcending unconscious habits of thought.

Some of the barriers to interdisciplinarity can be seen in Chapter 5; for example, journals tend to be disciplinary in nature, and publication in such journals is closely allied with promotion and tenure. The prestigious journals tend to be strongly disciplinary, and research communities have views regarding quality outputs and research which are either expressed indirectly or reinforced directly through exercises such as the REF (Conole et al. 2010). So while there are calls for interdisciplinary work to tackle some of the 'big problems', the culture created in higher education and research works against this.

What we are concerned with here is the role that technology, and in particular an open, digital, networked approach, can play in interdisciplinarity. Roco and Bainbridge (2003) argue very positively for the role of technology, suggesting there is a convergence occurring in science as a result of three developments: scientific knowledge now being applicable from the nano- to the macro-scale, technology and suitable methodology. Hendler *et al.* (2008), however, propose that the study of the technology itself should be an interdisciplinary field, what they term 'web science'.

Some of the barriers to interdisciplinarity may be attributable to the different cultures which have arisen in disciplines, but there is also an economic aspect – interdisciplinary work is often not profitable to engage in. If one considers interdisciplinary study as the intersection of two separate disciplines, then that intersection is likely to be less than either discipline in terms of interested audience. The interdisciplinary journals which do exist need to be very specific in the areas of intersection they address; in short, they need to have an identifiable market. However, much of the positive benefit of interdisciplinarity can arise from the unexpected collision of distinct areas of study. This unpredictability is an area that current economics of practice is not structured to capture or encourage, as it are often grounded in the limitations of physical constraints. Journals need to have an identified market to interest publishers, people need to be situated within a physical department in a university, books are placed on certain shelves in book shops. Digital classification of books allows them to occupy many 'shelves' simultaneously, but even more relevant the low, or zero, cost associated with other forms of digital outputs means they can be produced without the need for identifying a particular audience, and once produced, because they are easily shareable, they can be used in unpredicted contexts or combined with dissonant material. This is an aspect we will look at in more detail in Chapter 7.

The potential of technology

The potential of new technologies to encourage interdisciplinarity may be greater than their use in research, which was addressed in Chapter 5. Because interdisciplinary work is often not well represented by the existing funding and publishing environment, it is also not subject to the restrictions this places on practice and innovation. The lightweight and unrestricted forms of communication found in many Web 2.0 tools may serve the needs of interdisciplinarity to overcome existing disciplinary and geographical boundaries (Anderson 2007).

Taking blogs as an example Aemeur, Brassard and Paquet (2005) suggest they act as a form of personal knowledge publishing which fosters interdisciplinary knowledge sharing.

An interesting, but as yet probably unanswerable, question is, to what extent do the new technologies and associated practices create a common set of values, epistemological approaches and communication methods? That is, do the cultural norms associated with the use of the new technologies override those of the separate disciplines? Obviously there is nothing inherent in the technologies themselves that force users to behave in a specific manner; for example, one could use Twitter to simply repeat the same sentence every day. But *successful* use of the technologies often requires the adoption of certain approaches or cultural norms, whether it is deliberate or not.

Continuing with the example of blogging, regardless of the subject matter of a particular blog or the informal community to which that blog may belong to, there are some persistent cultural norms. Shaohui and Lihua (2008) suggest the following three characteristics of blog culture:

1 Thought share – if the first generation of websites were characterised by information sharing, then blogs mark a move to sharing thoughts.

2 Nonlinearity and concentricity – through linking, embedding, within blogs and then aggregation of blogs, there is a nonlinear construction of knowledge.

3 Criticalness and multivariate collision – specifically this arises from a personal, subjective standpoint that attracts varied comments and views.

The blogger and entrepreneur Loic Le Meur (2005) suggested a number of aspects of a blog community, including

- a willingness to share thoughts and experiences with others at an early stage;

- the importance of getting input from others on an idea or opinion;

- launching collaborative projects that would be very difficult or impossible to achieve alone;

- gathering information from a high number of sources every day;

- control over the sources and aggregation of their news;

- the existence of a 'common code': a vocabulary, a way to write posts and behaviour codes such as quoting other sources when you use them, linking into them, commenting on other posts and so on;

- a culture of speed and currency, with a preference to post or react instantaneously; and

- a need for recognition – bloggers want to express themselves and get credit for it.

By becoming a blogger then, one begins to adopt these practices, because they make for a successful blog, and they are represented in the blogs that constitute the cultural norms. Ehrlich and Levin (2005) state that 'norms and metanorms provide a cultural stickiness or viscosity that can help sustain adaptive behaviour and retard detrimental changes, but that equally can inhibit the introduction and spread of beneficial ones'. The cultural stickiness of the blogging community then is to share ideas, link and acknowledge others, gather and share information quickly, and operate in a timely manner. These could also be presented as attributes which can be seen to serve the needs of interdisciplinarity.

Precisely because it is relatively new, there has been a good deal of interdisciplinarity in the blogosphere. Although many bloggers will tend to read the blogs within their subject area, they will also come across those of overlapping or even distinct disciplines. But also *within* any given blog there is an element of interdisciplinarity or at least variety. Because blogs operate at the intersection of personal and professional life, unlike a journal, their content is not bounded by discipline. While a blogger may post predominantly on a particular subject (say 'Open Science') they may also have an interest in other areas, for example, Haikus and Japanese poetry, which they will bring into their posts, precisely because this personal mix is what renders blogs interesting. Open Science and Haikus would not be a combination one is likely to find in a conventional journal, but when the publishing filter is removed, and the community norms promote an element of personal interest, then this kind of mix arises. For example, one of my favourite blogs is Jim Groom's Bavatuesdays, which mixes thoughts on educational technology and advice on the blogging platform Wordpress with meditations on B-horror films. The mix seems perfectly logical and acceptable within the norms of the blogging community.

This may not constitute interdisciplinarity in an academic sense, but we can see interdisciplinary knowledge arising in at least four ways in blogs:

1 as the formal communication platform of a department, project or individual with a specific interdisciplinary remit;

2 through the historical context of the individual, who may have specialised in a different domain previously and can reference this in a personal blog;

3 informal interests which overlap with the more substantive content of the blog, such as the examples above; and

4 through comments and links from the blogs' wider readership.

Each of these routes for interdisciplinarity would be difficult to realise through the more formal mechanisms of journals or conferences.

What is potentially significant for interdisciplinarity then is not so much the technology itself but the practices that are associated with it. This is particularly relevant with regard to openness.

Twitter as interdisciplinary network

Blogs provide a good example of how interdisciplinary knowledge can be disseminated.

Another example is the social network, which potentially allows for connections between people and content across disciplines. I will take Twitter as the example for a social network here to explore this, although it could be applied to other tools equally well.

First, some history on Twitter as it is pertinent to how it can act as a tool for interdisciplinarity. Developed in 2006 when their initial podcasting company Odeo was floundering, Twitter focused around status-type updates delivered via mobile phone. This focus on being able to text was the reason for the 140 character limit, and the initial prompt was to answer the question 'What are you doing?' People could follow others, so it provided a means of broadcasting a message to all friends.

It was launched into the mainstream in 2007 and was a big success at the influential SXSW conference that year. One of the key elements in its success has been its open API, which allowed other developers to build applications using the Twitter data. This meant that people didn't need to even visit the Twitter website to use it; they could instead use one of the many different clients. This open API approach has seen unpredictable and wide-ranging uses of Twitter, including use as a public log for activities such as running and weight loss, picture sharing services, data analysis, news and market trend monitoring, management of Twitter network, link shortening, archiving tweets, polling and so on.

Although Twitter is not open source, this open approach in terms of how people access it and what they use it for has allowed the network to grow and make it a default network for many different groups of people.

Three key features of Twitter demonstrate how an open approach has allowed community norms to emerge. The first is the convention of putting an @ sign in front of a person's Twitter ID to send them a reply (e.g. @mweller). This was a user convention first of all, so it would designate that a particular tweet was for the attention of a particular user. As Twitter developed it became a standard convention, and then incorporated into the software, so now users can see all replies to them listed separately. The @ reply rule grew out of the email naming convention but has almost become synonymous with Twitter now.

The second convention was the use of hashtags to define a particular comment which could be grouped together. The use of the # was proposed by Chris Messina in a tweet: 'how do you feel about using # (pound) for groups. As in #barcamp [msg]?' Hashtags can be seen as metadata, describing the content of a tweet. They became relevant as the use of search on Twitter grew. People could search on a hashtag and thus gather all of the tweets on a particular topic. This was seized on by conferences, so all the delegates at a conference would agree to use a hashtag, and later conference organisers began specifying an official hashtag. Search was originally performed by a third-party service (using the open API), but in July 2008, Twitter bought Summize, the most popular Twitter search tool. Hashtags could now be incorporated into standard Twitter practice, and 'trending' became a relevant term as topics grew on Twitter, often denoted by a hashtag. Apparently the Twitter team initially rejected hashtags as 'too nerdy' (Gannes 2010), but their simple, and unregulated, creation has allowed them to flourish.

Hashtags can now be used as the means to define a community, particularly around an event, course or topic. The open data approach of Twitter means that these can in turn be analysed to reveal connections between members, subjects of discussion, locations and prominent members (e.g. Hirst 2010). As well as a useful means of categorising tweets, hashtags are now so ingrained in practice that they form a part of humour on Twitter, with people often creating 'mock' hashtags (although there are no official hashtags) as an ironic counterpoint.

The third norm to emerge is that of the retweet. This is the practice of passing on someone's tweet. Originally, this was achieved by copying and pasting the tweet and adding RT and the user's ID at the start. Boyd, Golder and Lotan (2010) identify the following motivations for retweeting:

- to amplify or spread tweets to new audiences;

- to entertain or inform a specific audience, or as an act of curation;

- to comment on someone's tweet by retweeting and adding new content, often to begin a conversation;

- to make one's presence as a listener visible;

- to publicly agree with someone;

- to validate others' thoughts;

- as an act of friendship, loyalty or homage by drawing attention, sometimes via a retweet request;

- to recognise or refer to less popular people or less visible content;

- for self-gain, either to gain followers or reciprocity from more visible participants; and

- to save tweets for future personal access.

As with the other community behaviours, the retweet became enshrined in code, when in late 2009 Twitter implemented a retweet function on its site. This allowed users to easily retweet a message by simply clicking a button, without the need for copy and paste, but some of the subtlety as to how it appears in timelines was lost (it is shown coming from the originator and not the retweeter).

What these three examples demonstrate is that the community has evolved over time, suggesting, experimenting and then adopting norms of behaviour – the 'stickiness' we saw with blog culture. Once it has become established, and proven to add value, Twitter has then moved to implement it in code to make it easier and also to further spread its use. It has not imposed the practice from the start, and sought to define how users will interact, which has often been the case with software development; instead it has allowed the community itself to develop its own norms.

If I analyse my own Twitter network (using the free service TwitterAnalyzer.com) it reveals that the geographic spread of my followers is mainly across the following countries: United Kingdom, United States, Australia, Germany, Canada, France and China.

By analysing the biography details people provide the top professions amongst my followers are consultant, technologist, PhD student, lecturer, manager, teacher, librarian and author.

Amongst these I can identify a number of communities and networks, some of which will intersect. These include the following:

- Bloggers – many of the people I follow are those I already had an online connection with via blogs, and Twitter was an extension of this.

- The Open University – I have acted as an advocate for Twitter in the Open University and see it as a means of knowledge sharing within an organisation.

- Cardiff – I live in Cardiff, Wales, and there is an active Twitter community, which often meets face to face.

- UK Higher Education – As well as bloggers and Open University people there is a large contingent of peers in other universities, funding bodies, libraries and so on.

- Journalists and media – a number of journalists and media consultants use Twitter regularly.

- Tottenham Hotspur – I support Spurs and a number of people I follow for this reason, but also there is a wider group for whom football is an interest (who are also members of the other networks).

There are a number of subgroups in this also; for example, Canadian bloggers form a coherent network of their own, and many individuals will occupy more than one category. One can view these many different groups and subgroups as networks that will become more or less active, and distinct, according to external events. For example, during the general election in the United Kingdom, this geographic grouping became more significant because there was a unifying theme. This is seen particularly with large, synchronous events such as the televised debates during the election.

Huberman, Romero and Wu (2009) have investigated interactions on Twitter and find that despite many followers the number of people a user interacts with (i.e. sends replies to) is relatively small. This reflects findings in Facebook and is interpreted as the existence of Dunbar's number (1992), as mentioned in Chapter 1, in social networks. While this may well be true for the more stable relationships, the use of functions such as hashtags and retweets allows for a finer grading of online acquaintance. I can read, or retweet, someone else's posts without ever interacting with them, and they may reciprocate, without engaging in direct conversation; yet these people form part of a valuable network.

As an interdisciplinary tool the Twitter network has a number of advantages and associated issues.

Geographical diversity – while my network is inevitably centred on the United Kingdom and North America, it is a global community which brings together different perspectives. It is limited by language though, and the immediacy does not allow for translation, so there is a danger of English language views dominating.

Professional diversity – within the different networks a range of professions and experience can be found, which will inevitably bring a degree of interdisciplinarity. One of the benefits of Twitter has been to improve interdepartmental communication within an institution. However, while the list above shows a reasonable range of occupations, it is still largely centred on higher education. There are, for example, very few (or no) priests, builders, make-up artists or senior retail managers in my network (which is not to say they are not present on Twitter). For interdisciplinarity this may not be an issue.

Size – at the time of writing I follow about 1,100 people and have approximately 3,400 followers. That represents a considerable network and pool of expertise which will share a wide range of knowledge and will also respond to requests for advice on topics outside of my own domain.

Immediacy – one of the changes Twitter required in my behaviour was a shift from exhaustive reading to regular sampling. As a blog reader I tried to keep up with most posts from those I subscribed to, with subsequent guilt when the unread count on my blog reader mounted. As my Twitter network expanded this behaviour was not possible and so a shift was required, which means I 'dip into' Twitter, sometimes more intensively and other times I am completely absent. This is the concept of the stream; it is not meant to be consumed in its entirety but sampled on occasion. Twitterers are responding in real time, and thus it is ideal for capturing diverse reactions and interpretations before they are filtered into disciplines. There is a consequent danger though that this relentless churning of information means useful research will be missed via this route.

Interdisciplinary bridges – the ease of sharing provides a means to bridge disciplines, in particular the retweet can be viewed as a tool for bridging audiences and disciplines as a twitterer in one domain can rebroadcast to their network, which will have the types of subgroupings shown above.

An inherent set of cultural norms – the three features we saw above, as well as other practices, indicate that, as with blogs, Twitter has its own set of cultural norms, which provide the required 'stickiness' for communities to develop. These may be sufficient to overcome the differences in cultural norms across disciplines and provide a common framework.

Professional and personal mix – Twitter occupies an intersection between professional and personal, formal and informal, and resource and conversation. In many previous tools we have sought to separate out these elements; for instance, when we create forums for students in VLEs it is a common practice to have a separate 'Chat' or social forum so that this doesn't interfere with the academic discussion. However, this blend in one place in Twitter both provides motivation to partake (we don't separate out our thoughts or lives so neatly) and also provides hooks into other areas of interdisciplinarity.

One of the reservations regarding Twitter, and other forms of online community tools, is the possibility of an echo chamber, which is the antithesis of what is desired for interdisciplinarity. As the amount of information available increases, there is an argument that it becomes more difficult to hear distinct and different voices. This occurs for two reasons: first, there is so much information arising from your immediate area of interest that it becomes difficult to keep up with this; second, it is now possible to find a group of like-minded people whatever your interests or tastes, so it is more emotionally 'comfortable' to spend time with these rather than with different voices. In a physical setting bounded by geographical constraints, one is more likely to be with a diverse group of people, but online the pool of people is larger so the grouping is more likely to be around interests and tastes than convenience or location. This is beneficial for many things; working with like-minded people often leads to quick development, but for interdisciplinarity it may create new types of boundaries. One can create a distorted view of what is a general consensus because dissenting voices are not heard. Of course, this is equally true (if not more so) with controlled media who will reflect certain positions.

The solution to the potential for the echo chamber to arise is to cultivate networks with a reasonable level of diversity and follow people who share diverse resources. It is not necessary to go to extremes in this for interdisciplinarity to be fostered but simply to ensure that there are some people who are in other disciplines and those who are in roles that cross boundaries.

The list above shows a number of benefits in developing a networked approach to interdisciplinarity, which may address the issues which have plagued it for many years. Indeed if researchers had intentionally set out to create a tool for promoting interdisciplinary discourse, then the resultant service may have not looked dissimilar to Twitter.

Conclusion

One way of approaching Boyer's category of integration is to consider the combination of different academic disciplines. While interdisciplinarity is seen as a necessary approach to solve many of the complex real-world problems, some of the cultural practices in research create obstacles to its realisation. In this chapter the possible role of two technologies to address this was explored, namely blogs and Twitter (as an example of a social network). In both cases there exist strong cultural norms of their own, which may address some of the cultural barriers within disciplines by providing a common set of values, so it may be that bloggers in different disciplines are more alike than non-bloggers and bloggers within the same discipline. Similarly, the history and approach of Twitter have been one of allowing community norms to develop and then reinforcing these through software implementation. The result is a tool with features and associated practice which can positively encourage interdisciplinarity. In both cases it is the cultural norms that have developed around the tools rather than being determined by the technology.

If we return to Moti's (1995) four realms of interdisciplinarity, we can consider how such approaches can be used to address them:

1 Interdisciplinary knowledge – the easy and varied publication in blogs creates less rigid boundaries between disciplines and allows for unpredictable interactions.

2 Interdisciplinary research – using social networks, loosely coupled teams across different disciplines can provide input to research.

3 Interdisciplinary education – the proliferation of free, open content means that courses can be created by collecting resources from a range of disciplines, and these resources are easily discoverable through search and network recommendations.

4 Interdisciplinary theory – the development of the previous three approaches can lead to a richer and broader study of interdisciplinarity, and using different dissemination methods, this work can be applied to diverse areas.

What underlies much of the potential for new tools to enhance interdisciplinarity is the easy, cheap and unfiltered production of content which can be shared effectively, which is also a factor in realising public engagement, which is the subject of Chapter 7.

7 Public Engagement as Collateral Damage

This chapter will focus on the third of Boyer's scholarly practices, which he terms 'application'. This comprises a number of different practices, including sitting on committees, inputting to policy, advising charities and so on. The major practice I will address in this chapter though is that of public engagement.

Public engagement

This is defined by the Higher Education Funding Council for England (HEFCE) in the following way (HEFCE 2007):

> 'Public engagement' involves specialists in higher education listening to, developing their understanding of, and interacting with non-specialists. The 'public' includes individuals and groups who do not currently have a formal relationship with an HEI through teaching, research or knowledge transfer.

Hart, Northmore and Gerhardt (2009) summarise seven dimensions of engagement:

1 public access to facilities

2 public access to knowledge

3 student engagement

4 faculty engagement

5 widening participation

6 encouraging economic regeneration and enterprise in social engagement

7 institutional relationship and partnership building

It can therefore be realised in a number of ways, from student volunteering to opening university libraries to the public, to authoring a general interest book. Perhaps the most visible and commonly cited example though is that of broadcasting, where an academic is used to present a television or radio programme or used as an expert in discussion programmes. The Hart *et al.*'s report lists some excellent case studies, but these are often bespoke and expensive projects within universities as they seek to promote their reputation and establish links with communities. In this section I want to look at how open, digital, networked approaches to scholarly practice can provide a different perspective on public engagement.

The first step in this is to consider the production of digital outputs. In terms of traffic to sites, the user-generated content sites have impressive statistics: more than 100 million monthly for YouTube, 4.3 million for Scribd and 1.75 million for Slideshare (figures from http://www.compete.com for July 2010). These dwarf the statistics for most higher education projects; for instance the most well-established OER site, MIT's OpenCourseWare site (http://ocw.mit.edu), has 200,000 visitors monthly, the OU's OpenLearn 21,000 and the learning object repository MERLOT 17,000. Perhaps the best site for education-related material is the TED talks (available at http://www.ted.com) with 1.5 million monthly visitors, and through third-party platforms such as iTunes U, where the Open University iTunes project registers around 1.6 million downloads a month (http://projects.kmi.open.ac.uk/itunesu/impact/).

What these figures indicate is that there is potentially a significant impact to be realised in the use of Web 2.0-type output. Commercial, third-party providers have the most traffic, but here educational content is mixed in with a wide range of materials, which increases the likelihood of serendipitous encounters with university content but dilutes the overall institutional presence.

We know then that the potential audience is significant through such avenues; the next issue is the comparison with the effort required to reach that audience. Traditional broadcast requires a large team effort usually, whereas digital, networked and open approaches require relatively little effort and associated cost.

I'll use an example of my own experience to illustrate the point. In March 2010 two of my network contacts (George Siemens and Dave Cormier) announced that they were running a short, free, online course about the future of the course and asked for contributions. One evening, I created a Slidecast with accompanying music for them to use (http://www.slideshare.net/mweller/future-of-education-3475415). The production of this short presentation required approximately two hours worth of input, using images from Flickr with a Creative Commons licence. It didn't 'cost' anything apart from the time investment, and the technical expertise required was minimal. Perhaps more significant was a familiarity with creating these types of presentations and feeling comfortable with sharing content.

The Slidecast generated about 4,500 views over the coming months. These figures do not compare with the type of audience that might be reached through a television or radio programme, but the cost and effort required was also considerably less. And I was not the only person to contribute a free object to their course (see http://edfutures.com/contributions). The reason that a global network of experts could contribute artefacts to a course for free is because of the low threshold to content production. The reasons *why* people did it are more complex, but include the following:

- A social connection with the course organisers – whether they have met face to face or not, the contributors had a connection with the organisers, so felt well disposed towards their request.

- Interest in the subject – creating the object gave each of the contributors an opportunity to explore ideas that were of interest to them also.

- Creativity and fun – unconstrained by the conventional requirements of scholarly outputs it allowed the contributors to play with format and ideas.

- To engage with the community – sharing content is seen as a default action for many of the contributors.

- Ego – we should not underestimate the selfish, more egotistical reasons for generating content, including positive feedback and reinforcement of status.

A long-tail content production system

The overall reach of any one such artefact may not compare with that of traditional broadcast outputs, but collectively we may see similar levels of impact. This is a good example of Anderson's long tail (2006). Traditional broadcasting can be seen as embodying the classic Pareto principle, which suggests that 20 per cent of your products account for 80 per cent of sales or views. These are the blockbusters. But as Brynjolfsson, Hu and Simester (2007) demonstrate when products move online the concentration of sales becomes more distributed. They compared a shopping catalogue with the online version of the same products and found that 'the Internet channel exhibits a significantly less concentrated sales distribution when compared with the catalog channel, even though these two channels offer the same products at the same set of prices'. Being online encourages a more 'long tail' oriented set of behaviours. They further argue that as 'search costs' reduce, sales concentration becomes more skewed towards niche products. Search costs in this sense refer to the effort required by the individual, so the more experienced they become at searching, the more these costs decrease. This suggests that long-tail-type behaviour will continue to increase as people become more experienced at searching, evaluating and locating content that appeals to them.

If we consider the types of outputs generated in higher education, then it is possible to re-conceptualise universities as 'long-tail content production environments'. In Table 7.1 the range of content that universities can produce is listed, matched with

Table 7.1 University content matched to open, distributed channels

Output	Type of outlet	Example
Data	Data repositories	RealClimate, Gene Expression Omnibus
Research paper	Open access journals, repositories, individual websites	Mendeley, Google Scholar, Open Research Online (ORO)
Software code	Open source repositories	Sourceforge
Lectures/teaching content	OER projects, learning repositories, commercial sites	iTunes U, YouTube edu, MIT OpenCourseWare, Slideshare
Ideas, proposals	Individual sites	Blogs, Twitter, YouTube
Conferences, seminars	Conference sites	TED talks, YouTube, Twitter hashtag, Cloudworks
Debate, discussion	Public engagement sites, subject community forums	Blogs, Twitter, discussion boards

some of the examples of the open, digital network outlets that might be used to disseminate them.

Table 7.1 includes some examples which may not, at first glance, seem like outputs, such as ideas and discussion. However, when an individual shares, or conducts, these via digital networked means, they become a shareable artefact. In open source communities, the discussion forums are viewed as a valuable learning resource (Glott, Meiszner and Sowe 2007). Ideas and proposals, or suggestions, can be seen as a further example of the change in granularity in output. For example, my colleague Tony Hirst recounts how he suggested on Twitter that someone should take the Digital Britain report (a UK government proposal to develop the digital economy), break it into chunks and make it commentable. A response from Joss Winn led to them forming the company WriteToReply which does exactly this with consultation documents (Hirst 2009).

Potentially then higher education produces, as part of its everyday function, a large amount of long-tail content. All of the outputs listed above are unlikely to attract large audiences, but all of them are capable of gathering niche audiences, which collectively would fulfil a large element of a university's public engagement function.

This can be realised through specific projects, such as the OER projects many universities are initiating. However, long-tail models only work when there is sufficient content to occupy the tail. In order to achieve this scale of content in a sustainable manner, the outputs listed above need to become a frictionless by-product of the standard practice, rather than the outcomes of isolated projects.

To return to the three key characteristics of this book, what is required then to realise this frictionless generation of content is to embed the practices of generating digital, networked, open outputs. While many of the outputs in Table 7.1 are already in a digital format (e.g. code and data), there is still a cultural and institutional change required in order to make these outputs open and networked. The open aspect can be addressed in one of two ways: the first is to have an institutional policy on open access, and the second is to encourage staff to adopt the kinds of sharing practice outlined in Chapter 1.

Some universities have developed policies around open access of teaching and research content. Wiley (2009a) states that 'as of July 2009, forty one organizations in the United States have open access mandates: seventeen at the institutional level, ten at the departmental level, four at the college level, and six at the funder level'. These policies are categorised as dealing with four main issues relating to open access:

> access (i.e., access to scholarly works by faculty, students, and administrators), cost (i.e., the price of continuing to subscribe to increasingly expensive journals), copyright (i.e., the common practice where faculty members relinquish their rights to the written work), and tenure (i.e., the manner in which current tenure review procedures consider open access publications). (Wiley 2009a)

The biggest shift though is likely to occur when we consider the outputs which are not necessarily digital in nature and make the shift to realising these in digital, shareable formats. This is only achievable through such practices becoming second nature for academics.

Two common objections to producing these types of output are money and time. In both cases I would argue that we underestimate the time and money we spend in many current wasteful activities, which we do not question because they are standard practice in the workplace. For example, meetings can be notoriously expensive, and often unproductive, if one takes into account all of the salaries involved, yet are perceived as a necessary evil in the modern university. As with lectures, though they are often disparaged, meetings *can* be useful and the best way to achieve certain goals, but as with lectures, they are also often uninspiring and ineffective. Holding virtual meetings is one approach (these can at least be recorded and shared if useful), but other means of achieving the same ends might be to share blog posts, brainstorm ideas in shared documents and so on.

Similarly keeping blogs is often seen as an additional activity, but it can be seen as a by-product of academic activity, such as keeping notes, working up ideas and so on. Clay Shirky (2008a) talking of cognitive surplus, recounts how a TV producer responded when he told her about Wikipedia:

> She heard this story and she shook her head and said, 'Where do people find the time?' That was her question. And I just kind of snapped. And I said, 'No one who works in TV gets to ask that question. You know where the time comes from. It comes from the cognitive surplus you've been masking for 50 years'.

The same might be true of generating outputs. The analogue methods of working may well be hiding the sort of cognitive surplus Shirky refers to. They don't necessarily take extra time, but we have spent much of that time creating non-shareable resources. A small but indicative example is that when I used to attend conferences I was required to write a report on the conference which would go to the funding committee in my department but which would not be read by anyone else. Now I write a blog post, or create a Slidecast or make a YouTube video which is accessible to everyone. The shift is to producing an output which is shareable.

Frictionless broadcasting

The advantages of a move towards a frictionless long-tail model are largely related to costs and resources. Because its cost is free or relatively low, it means that, unlike large-scale projects or traditional broadcasting, there is no need to consider audience demographics, to establish specific projects (with the associated management costs) or to set objectives and goals. The result of this means that, taken as a whole, the university can embrace the kind of unpredictability that is at the heart of the Internet, what Jonathan Zittrain (2008) refers to as 'generativity'. Unpredictability is an undesirable goal for any specific project to have as an aim because budget allocation entails project objectives, measures of success, intended audiences and lines of responsibility. This is one of the areas of tension for universities (and other large organisations) with the Internet culture – the project-focused method of working ingrained in many organisations is at odds with the bottom-up, unpredictable nature of internet innovation. There are two ways to address this; the first is to invest considerable amounts of money creating content which might take off and the second is to generate content at low cost as a by-product of normal operations.

A small, non-educational, example of this is that of the Downfall meme. These videos take the same segment of the (excellent) 2004 German film *Downfall*, when Hitler in his bunker rants against his imminent defeat. By overlaying different subtitles the first parody depicted his rage against being banned from Xbox Live. The ease with which it could be altered and the inherent comedy in seeing a despot savagely bemoan the unfairness of obscure topics led to it going viral. It generated thousands of reinterpretations and millions of hits, until the production company ordered a takedown notice of all parodies in 2010. In this it exemplifies the unpredictability that can occur online and the creativity which can be unleashed.

Memes such as Downfall (and others such as 'David After the Dentist') are a rarity, however. It is not that large numbers of views or remixes are possible that is significant, but that unpredicted use and adoption can occur. Very small viewing figures are the norm in the long tail.

If we consider public engagement from the perspective of the individual academic, then we can think of a continuum of possibilities. At one end would be relatively small-scale events such as a public lecture. This has a small, limited audience, but the filter is relatively open, in that many academics can at some point have an opportunity to deliver such a lecture. It is relatively low cost, with the venue often being provided free (as part of the university) and some refreshments. In the middle of our continuum we might place a general interest book. This will reach a larger audience, cost more to produce and have a stricter filter in place, in that publishers will determine who writes such a book. And at the opposite end of the continuum we can place broadcast activity, which is high cost, reaches a large audience and has a very fine filter with only a very small number of academics becoming broadcasters. The level of compromise or generalisation can also be seen to increase across this continuum, where with a public lecture the academic may speak in detailed terms about their subject, but with a general interest programme they are often required to 'dumb down' to an extent.

If we now consider the sort of digital outputs listed above, they have some similarity with these but also some areas of difference. They can be classified as follows:

- Low cost to free – if we assume they are by-products of activity which is already costed.

- Small but unpredictable audience – the long tail typically has small audiences but unexpected hits can occur.

- Open filter – anyone can publish.

- No compromise – with no associated cost the academic can be as general or detailed as they like.

- High reuse potential – the reuse potential of most other forms is low, either because they are in a format that is not reusable or copyright prohibits it, whereas small online artefacts can be easily aggregated into different contexts.

- Different distribution – such outputs are often distributed through search and social networks, so having a pre-established network is an important factor in seeding their uptake.

In order to encourage this frictionless type of output, universities can engage in several parallel functions. The first is staff development, although it is essential to promote a sense of independence, since most of the tools are very easy to use. Nevertheless what is often useful is a space, or allowance, that legitimises exploration with these tools, overcomes some initial concerns and establishes a peer support network. In the podstars project I ran at the Open University (Weller 2010), which encouraged academics to start generating video outputs, these were the most common positive elements of the project. For example, this participant commented, 'It gave me confidence to get on and try it. I am already using it in my research and indirectly I am using it for teaching, via communications to large cohorts of students on the science website'.

The emphasis on any staff development then should be on empowerment and liberation, rather than on training in specific software packages. The type of staff development required is probably located somewhere in between Google's 20 per cent time, which developers can use to work on interesting projects, and the standard IT training courses, in that it needs some direction and technical support but is best served by allowing a diverse range of projects and encouraging creativity.

A second function for universities to perform is to remove obstacles, or perceived obstacles, to the production of such outputs. This will be most apparent in promotion criteria, which almost exclusively focus on traditional outputs such as journal articles. We will look at rewards and recognition later in Chapter 11.

Related to the formal recognition of such outputs in promotion cases is the informal acceptance within an institution. The benefits of an open, digital, networked approach to research, public engagement and teaching need to be recognised by both senior management and colleagues and not dismissed as merely 'playing'.

Lastly, although third-party sites such as YouTube are often the best tools at delivering such content, the provision of educational and institutional context is important, as it provides both recognition and increases the profile of the individual and institution. This might be in the form of a YouTube channel, an iPhone app, a university portal, a departmental blog, a newsletter and so on.

It is through these approaches that the cultivating environment which will encourage the bottom-up production of varied content will emerge. Given the potential benefits in profile, engagement and costs, these are relatively small changes to introduce.

Conclusion

In this chapter I have argued that we can view higher education as a long-tail content production environment. Much of what we currently aim to achieve through specific public engagement projects can be realised by producing digital artefacts as a by-product of typical scholarly activity. My intention is not to suggest that this is the *only* means of performing public engagement; for example, engaging with local schools works well by providing face-to-face contact with inspiring figures. As with other scholarly functions, some will remain, but the digital alternative not only allows for new ways of realising the same goals but also opens up new possibilities.

I used the example of Dave Cormier and George Siemens' course in this chapter, and the advent of easy to produce content, which is shareable via a global network, means that this type of course is now possible to organise and construct (relatively) easily and offer freely. We are only at the start of exploring the possibilities this affords us, and in Chapter 8 we will look at this teaching function in more detail.

8 A Pedagogy of Abundance

When we consider the changes in scholarly practice, it is perhaps in teaching that we see the greatest potential for a radically different approach to emerge. The three key elements of digital, networked and open converge most significantly around the production, pedagogy and delivery of education. In this chapter I will examine some of the implications, focusing on the shift to abundant content as one pertinent issue. As with the preceding chapters, this is intended as one perspective that illustrates the impact of the digital, networked, open approach and not as the only issue of relevance.

Economics of abundance and scarcity

One perspective of relevance to teaching and learning is the effect that sudden, and great, abundance of learning content and resources has on how educators approach learning. There is an obvious relation to economics here. Traditional economics can be viewed as a study of the impact of scarcity. In his 1932 essay Robbins defined economics as 'the science which studies human behaviour as a relationship between ends and scarce means which have alternative uses'.

But when goods become digital and available online then scarcity disappears. They are non-rivalrous so that if a copy is taken, it is still available for others. They are distributed free on a global scale (if we ignore infrastructure costs which apply to all content). When analysing the lessons from other industries in Chapter 3 the problems industries have faced can be viewed as essentially making a transition from an economics of scarcity to an economics of abundance. If the music industry is considered from this perspective then the traditional model can be said to have been based around the following assumptions:

- talent is scarce

- locating it is difficult

- content is physical

- content is manufactured according to demand

- access to it is scarce

What follows from this set of assumptions is the structure of the entire industry. Talent is discovered by Artists and Reportoire (A & R) agents, who spend their time attending concerts, building networks and talking with bands to find new talent. Once discovered artists are signed exclusively to a label, who then record their content and produce this in a physical format. This is then distributed via a logistics network to a chain of shops. With limited opening hours, the consumer could then go to the shop to purchase the item, if it was in stock, or order it if not, because storage space would be limited. After a period, depending on popularity, the item would cease to be produced and become available only via second-hand record shops.

This model seems antiquated already, and yet it is one of recent history. The first 'attack' it suffered was that of online ordering, through the likes of Amazon. The small storage space of the local record shop was no longer a limiting factor, and entire back catalogues were available at the click of a mouse. The necessity of travelling to the shop was removed, and although there was no restriction on when you ordered, there was still a delay in receiving the physical goods.

The changes brought by the advent of online shopping were significant, but essentially it was the same model for the music industry but with an improved shop front. The structural change to the industry arose when the format of music changed to the digital file, which could be freely distributed online. In this model talent is still scarce, but the act of locating it has changed. The artists can promote themselves; listeners locate music through the routes we saw in Chapter 3 (such as LastFM and playlists) without the intervention of a record label. For the consumer the availability of music is instant, the granularity alters, and if the individual uses bit-torrent-type downloads then entire back catalogues are as easily downloaded as one track. This changes the consumers' relationship to content; their own time and attention become the key scarce resources now.

Responses to the digital era can be classified as 'abundance' and 'scarcity' responses. The former takes the assumption of new abundance and tries to work it to their advantage. The Freemium model is one such example, as realised by Flickr, for example. Here users get a good level of service free, to attract sufficient numbers. The additional value that requires payment only attracts a small percentage of users (estimates vary between 5 and 10 per cent of Flickr users who convert to 'Pro' customers), but with a large base it becomes significant. As Chris Anderson (2008) puts it,

> Freemium as the opposite of the traditional free sample: instead of giving away 1% of your product to sell 99%, you give away 99% of your product to sell 1%. The reason this makes sense is that for digital products, where the

marginal cost is close to zero, the 99% cost you little and allow you to reach a huge market. So the 1% you convert, is 1% of a big number.

Chris Anderson also coined the term 'long tail', which was examined in Chapter 7, and this too can be viewed as an 'abundance response'. The long tail argues that with an abundant stock range, businesses make money not by selling large quantities of a few items (the blockbusters) but by selling small quantities of a large number of items.

Other models include giving away the digital object free, and where one exists, charging for the physical object. This is a model being explored by publishers such as Bloomsbury Academic. Where no physical object exists, then it is associated services which attract a cost; for example, while many users download and install open software solutions freely, a small number are willing to pay for consultancy services around these. The most widely deployed abundance response is to use advertising revenue to allow free access to content. It still remains to be seen how successful many of these approaches will be; these are after all, transitory times.

Scarcity responses, however, seek to re-establish, or retain, the existing economic model by introducing scarcity into the digital content. An obvious example is that of digital rights management (DRM), which attempts to encode legislation and usage within the content itself. For example, iTunes limits the number of computers that you can have accounts on and restricts the devices you can associate with an iTunes account. DRM is often backed up with strong legal enforcement, where we have seen recent examples of the founders of torrent sharing site Pirate Bay being fined 30 million Swedish kronor and receiving a jail sentence for encouraging illegal file sharing. In the United Kingdom, the Digital Economy Act was passed in 2010, which will identify copyright infringements and then require the user's internet service provider to issue a notice. In many of the arguments put forward for such approaches analogies are made to rivalrous, scarce goods or services; for example, Paul McCartney, commenting on the Pirate Bay case, said 'if you get on a bus, you've got to pay. And I think it's fair, you should pay for your ticket'. Paywalls and subscription models can also be seen as an attempt to re-establish the scarcity of content.

Education and abundance

If we use this perspective to examine education we can consider how education may shift as a result of abundance. Traditionally in education expertise is analogous to talent in the music industry – it is the core element of scarcity in the model. In any one subject there are relatively few experts (compared with the level of knowledge in the general population). Learners represent the 'demand' in this model, so when access to the experts is via physical interaction, for example, by means of a lecture, then the model of supply and demand necessitates that the learners come to the place where the experts are located. It also makes sense to group these experts together, around other costly resources such as books and laboratories. The modern university is in this sense a solution to the economics of scarcity.

The production of books and journals can be seen as an initial weakening of this model, as it separated some level of expertise from the individual. However, access was still limited to physical artefacts, and the prohibitive costs of many of these meant that the only way to access them was through libraries, reinforcing the centralised physical campus model.

As a result, a 'pedagogy of scarcity' developed, which is based around a one-to- many model to make the best use of the scarce resource (the expert). This is embodied in the lecture, which despite its detractors is still a very efficient means of conveying certain types of learning content. An instructivist pedagogy then can be seen as a direct consequence of the demands of scarcity.

While expertise is still rare, the access to content associated with it is now on a different scale. We have (often free) access to journal articles, videos, podcasts, slidecasts and blog posts. And it is not only content we can access but also discussion through forums, comments and blogs. In addition there is access to your own or other's social networks. The experts themselves may be more approachable, or there may be discussion around their content in dedicated forums. People may have shared annotated versions of their work or associated reading lists through social bookmarking. This scale and range of learning-related content at least raises the question of whether we have developed the appropriate teaching and learning approaches to make best use of it. In short, what would a pedagogy of abundance look like?

The advent of elearning has seen an exploration of new pedagogies or at least a shift in emphasis onto different ones. Siemens (2008) argues that '[l]earning theories, such as constructivism, social constructivism, and more recently, connectivism, form the theoretical shift from instructor or institution controlled teaching to one of greater control by the learner'. In examining the current physical space of a lecture hall, Wesch (2008) asked students what it 'said' about learning, in essence what were the affordances of the physical learning environment. His students listed the following:

1   to learn is to acquire information;

2   information is scarce and hard to find;

3 trust authority for good information;

4 authorised information is beyond discussion;

5 obey the authority; and

6 follow along.

These are obviously at odds with what most educators regard as key components in learning, such as dialogue, reflection, critical analysis and so on. They are also at distinct odds with the type of experience students have in the online world they inhabit regularly, particularly the social network, read/write web. These environments are characterised by

- user-generated content

- power of the crowd

- data access

- architecture of participation

- network effects

- openness

It may be that we do not require new pedagogies to accommodate these assumptions as Conole (2008) points out:

> Recent thinking in learning theory has shifted to emphasise the benefit of social and situated learning as opposed to behaviourist, outcomes-based, individual learning. What is striking is that a mapping to the technologies shows that recent trends in the use of technologies, the shift from Web 1.0 to Web 2.0 echoes this; Web 2.0 tools very much emphasise the collective and the network.

But she goes on to say that

> Arguably then there has never been a better alignment of current thinking in terms of good pedagogy – i.e. emphasising the social and situated nature of learning, rather than a focus on knowledge recall with current practices in the use of technologies – i.e. user-generated content, user-added value and aggregated network effects. Despite this, the impact of Web 2.0 on education has been less dramatic than its impact on other spheres of society – use for social purposes, supporting niche communities, collective political action, amateur journalism and social commentary. (Conole 2008)

In examining the changes that education needs to accommodate to be relevant to the digital society, Seely-Brown and Adler (2008) emphasise the shift to participation, arguing that in order to meet the growing demand for education, and the requirements of a rapidly changing workplace, the traditional model of supply-push needs to be replaced with one of demand-pull. Learners need to be able to learn throughout their lives and to be able to learn about very niche subjects (Anderson's long tail again). The only way to accommodate these needs they argue is to move to a more participatory, socially constructed view of knowledge. They stress the significance of new technologies in realising this:

> Tools such as blogs, wikis, social networks, tagging systems, mashups, and content-sharing sites are examples of a new user-centric information infrastructure that emphasizes participation (e.g., creating, re-mixing) over presentation, that encourages focused conversation and short briefs (often written in a less technical, public vernacular) rather than traditional publication, and that facilitates innovative explorations, experimentations, and purposeful tinkerings that often form the basis of a situated understanding emerging from action, not passivity.

Any pedagogy of abundance would then, I suggest, be based on the following assumptions:

- Content is free – not all content is free, but increasingly a free version can be located and so an assumption that this will be the default is more likely than one based on paywalls or micropayments.

- Content is abundant – as covered above, the quantity of content is now abundant as a result of easy publishing formats and digitisation projects.

- Content is varied – content is no longer predominantly text based.

- Sharing is easy – as I have suggested in Chapter 7, there are now easy ways to share, so the 'cost' of sharing has largely disappeared.

- Social based – this may not necessarily entail intensive interaction; filtering and sharing as a by-product of individual actions constitutes a social approach to learning.

- Connections are 'light' – as with sharing, it is easy to make and preserve connections within a network since they do not necessitate one-to-one maintenance.

- Organisation is cheap – Clay Shirky (2008b) argues that the 'cost' of organising people has collapsed, which makes informal groupings more likely to occur and often more successful: 'By making it easier for groups to self-assemble and for individuals to contribute to group effort without requiring formal management, these tools have radically altered the old limits on the size, sophistication, and scope of unsupervised effort'.

- Based on a generative system – Zittrain (2008) argues that unpredictability and freedom are essential characteristics of the Internet and the reason why it has generated so many innovative developments. Any pedagogy would seek to harness some element of this generative capability.

- User-generated content – related to the above, the ease of content generation will see not only a greater variety of formats for content but courses being updated and constructed from learner's own content.

Possible pedagogies

As Conole suggested, there are a number of pedagogies which meet some of these assumptions. In this section some of the contenders for a pedagogy of abundance are examined.

Resource-based learning (RBL)

This places resources in the foreground of learning, and the learner's interaction and selection of these (which may include human resources) is the driving principle. Ryan (2000) uses the following definition for RBL, taken from the Australian National Council on Open and Distance Education. RBL is 'an integrated set of strategies to promote student centred learning in a mass education context, through a combination of specially designed learning resources and interactive media and technologies'. If one views the abundance of resources as the primary factor in a pedagogy of abundance then RBL looks like an appropriate strategy. I would suggest that it is often still grounded in a scarcity approach, however; for example, Ryan goes on to argue that 'these integrated strategies for RBL should be based on the application of a range of instructional design principles to the development of learning materials'. In a world of abundance the emphasis is less on the development of specific learning materials than on the selection, aggregation and interpretation of existing materials.

Problem-based learning (PBL)

Barrows and Tamblyn (1980) summarise PBL as 'the learning that results from the process of working toward the understanding or resolution of a problem. The problem is encountered *first* in the learning process'. In PBL students are given an ill-structured or open-ended problem. They work often in small collaborative groups towards a solution, but often there is no definite answer. The role of the teacher is one of facilitator, helping groups if they get stuck, providing useful resources and advice. In medical education in particular, PBL has been well researched and there has been some modest evidence that it is more effective than traditional methods (Vernon and Blake 1993; Smits, Verbeek and de Buisonjé 2002), so it has a solid grounding. With its emphasis on learner direction, use of diverse resources and open-endedness it meets many of the requirements set out above. As with RBL it may need recasting to fully utilise the new found abundance of content, where there is greater stress on finding and evaluating wide range of resources, and the utilisation of social networks as a resource.

Constructivism

This theory of learning gained much popularity in the 1990s, particularly with the advent of elearning. It is a view of learning that places the focus on individual learners who constructs their own knowledge through activity. Jonassen (1991) describes it thus:

> Constructivism … claims that reality is constructed by the knower based upon mental activity. Humans are perceivers and interpreters who construct their own reality through engaging in those mental activities … What the mind produces are mental models that explain to the knower what he or she has perceived … We all conceive of the external reality somewhat differently, based on our unique set of experiences with the world.

In practice this has been realised as courses which often have a strong group, discursive and reflective component, with the emphasis on individuals to develop their own interpretations, with the educator in less of a teacher role and acting more as a facilitator. Given that it has a loose definition, it is hard to pin down a constructivist approach exactly. Mayer (2004) suggests that such discovery-based approaches are less effective than guided ones, arguing that the 'debate about discovery has been replayed many times in education but each time, the evidence has favoured a guided approach to learning'. It could be argued that with everyone able to publish content in a Web 2.0 world, the 'dangers' inherent in constructivism become more pronounced, as the proliferation of conspiracy theories might attest. However, given that this is the environment everyone has to operate within, the ability to construct appropriate and rigorous knowledge from a range of sources is even more relevant. When Kirschner, Sweller and Clark (2006) claim, with some justification, that 'the epistemology of a discipline should not be confused with a pedagogy for teaching/learning it' that only highlights that the epistemology of a discipline is now being constructed by all, so learning how to participate in this is as significant as learning the subject matter of the discipline itself.

Communities of practice

Lave and Wenger's (1991) book on situated learning and Wenger's (1998) influential book on communities of practice highlighted the social role in learning and the importance of apprenticeship. They proposed the concept of 'legitimate peripheral participation', whereby participants move from the periphery in a community to its core by engaging in legitimate tasks. A very practical example of this is seen in open source communities, where participants move from reading and occasionally commenting in forums to suggesting code fixes and taking on a range of functions such as moderation and code commenting. Crowston and Howison (2005) propose a hierarchical structure for FLOSS communities, consisting of the following layers:

1 At the centre are core developers, who contribute the majority of the code and oversee the overall project.

2 In the next layer are the co-developers who submit patches, which are reviewed and checked in by core developers.

3 Further out are the active users who do not contribute code but provide use-cases and bug-reports as well as testing new releases.

4 Further out still are the many passive users of the software who do not contribute directly to the main forums.

Bacon and Dillon (2006) suggest that some of the practices seen in open source communities can be adopted by higher education, in particular, the process of peer-production and the situated method of teaching and learning. With its practical approach, self-direction, user-generated content and social aspect, the communities of practice approach as realised in open source provides an interesting model, since it devolves much of the work to a community, from which all benefit. However, the number of successful open source communities is relatively small compared with the number of unsuccessful ones, and thus the rather tenuous success factors for generating and sustaining an effective community may prove to be a barrier across all subject areas. Where they thrive, however, it offers a significant model which higher education can learn much from in terms of motivation and retention (Meiszner 2010).

Connectivism

This is a learning theory proposed by George Siemens (2005). Of the theories listed here it is the only post-network theory, which has as its starting assumption the

Internet and the mass of connections we establish. As Siemens states, 'Learners as little as forty years ago would complete the required schooling and enter a career that would often last a lifetime. Information development was slow. The life of knowledge was measured in decades. Today, these foundational principles have been altered. Knowledge is growing exponentially'. Connectivism then stresses that learning takes place within a network. The following are the principles of connectivism:

- Learning and knowledge rests in diversity of opinions.

- Learning is a process of connecting specialised nodes or information sources.

- Learning may reside in non-human appliances.

- Capacity to know more is more critical than what is currently known.

- Nurturing and maintaining connections is needed to facilitate continual learning.

- Ability to see connections between fields, ideas and concepts is a core skill.

- Currency (accurate, up-to-date knowledge) is the intent of all connectivist learning activities.

- Decision-making is itself a learning process. Choosing what to learn and the meaning of incoming information is seen through the lens of a shifting reality. While there is a right answer now, it may be wrong tomorrow due to alterations in the information climate affecting the decision.

Connectivism can be seen as an approach to learning that foregrounds the significance of the network and connections. Using its principles Downes and Siemens have run large-scale open online courses. Given its starting assumption it is probably closest to a pedagogy of abundance, but it is still relatively new and, while it sets out some clear principles and draws on other theories, it is not yet fully formed as a pedagogic theory.

Conclusion

The intention here was not to set out a how-to guide for teaching or even to evaluate the effectiveness of these theories. We are witnessing a fundamental change in the production of knowledge and our relationship to content. This is producing an abundance of content which is unprecedented. Google CEO Eric Schmidt claims that society produces more information in two days than was created from the beginning of human history until 2003, stating 'the real issue is user-generated content' (Siegler 2010). Many of our approaches to teaching and learning were developed in a different age, and this basic shift from moderate scarcity to excessive abundance constitutes a challenge to higher education and to individual information processing abilities. It may well be that the existing theories are sufficient; they just need recasting or reimagining for a world of abundance. Bill Kerr (2007), for example, argues that 'the new territory which George Siemens connectivism and Stephen Downes connective knowledge seeks to claim has either already been claimed by others or has been better done by others'.

Abundance does not apply to all aspects of learning; indeed the opposite may be true, for example, an individual's attention is not abundant and is time limited. The abundance of content puts increasing pressure on this scarce resource, and so finding effective ways of dealing with this may be the key element in any pedagogy. However, I would contend that the abundance of content and connections is as fundamental shift in education as any we are likely to encounter, and there has, to date, been little attempt to really place this at the centre of a model of teaching.

9 Openness in Education

aving looked at scholarship and Boyer's four scholarly functions in Chapters 4–8, this section of the book, Chapters 9–12, examines the context in higher education, academia and universities within which digital scholarship is establishing itself.

Of the three characteristics of digital, networked and open, it is the latter that perhaps has most resonance in the scholarly context, and so in this chapter I want to explore the changing nature of 'openness' in education and the different interpretations and issues it raises.

The changing nature of openness

When the Open University (OU) in the United Kingdom was founded in 1969, its mission statement was to be 'Open to people, places, methods and ideas'. The emphasis in open education then was on open access – thus a model was developed which had no prerequisites to study and was based around a flexible distance learning model. In this manner many of those who were excluded from higher education could participate. As more universities have developed distance education models, part-time study, blended and online offerings, the question of access to higher education in the developed world is less of an issue than it was at the inception of the OU. In the United Kingdom, the percentage of young people (18- to 22-year-olds) attending university in 2008–9 was 45 per cent, compared with about 5 per cent in the 1960s (with 51 per cent of young women attending university) (Coughlan 2010). In terms of access, the lifelong learning agenda and provision of flexible study has seen mature students (usually defined as over 25) now outnumbering traditional students in many countries (e.g. MacFadgen 2008). The current financial crisis has seen a drop in admissions for the first time in over a decade, so open access may become an increasingly significant factor again. In many developing countries, which are seeing a rapid expansion in higher education, open access is a highly relevant issue.

Returning to the OU mission statement, it has survived remarkably well, but the examples we might call to mind for realising openness with regards to people, places, methods and ideas would now be different from those envisaged in 1969. Although open access is still a relevant issue for education, we have also seen a plethora of other interpretations and nuances on the term 'openness' and how it relates to education over the past two decades in particular. This speaks to the evolving nature of the term and also the efficacy of openness as an approach, be it in developing software or conducting research. The following are amongst the terms that are relevant to education:

1 Open source – much of the open source software movement had its foundations in higher education, and universities both develop and deploy open source solutions.

2 Open educational resources – the term OER was coined in 2002 to describe the application of open source principles to the release of educational content, initiated by MIT's OCW project. We will look at OERs in more detail below.

3 Open courses – as well as releasing content as OERs a number of educators have begun exploring the concept of open courses, which are delivered online, with various models for payment (or entirely free).

4 Open research – researchers are using a number of approaches to perform research practices in the open, including crowdsourcing, open online conferences, open proposals and so on.

5 Open data – as well as sharing data openly (e.g. http://www.realclimate.org), there has also been a move to develop standards such as Linked Data, to connect and expose the vast quantities of data that are now available.

6 Open APIs – the recent Web 2.0 approach saw an increase in the use of open APIs. These allow other software developers to build tools and code that interrogate the data in one application. For example, both Facebook and Twitter have open APIs that facilitate the development of services which build on top of these existing tools.

7 Open access publishing – the ability to publish cheaply and quickly online has led to a movement around open access publishing, which is freely available and may use open peer review models. We will look at publishing in more detail in Chapter 12.

Openness has almost become a cliché in education now; after all, few people will argue in favour of a 'closed' education. It is a term which is loosely applied, and having gained currency, much like the 'Web 2.0', the term is now one that is being appropriated in many different sectors. What I will attempt to do in this section is not to create a tight definition of openness in education, but rather describe some of the features that characterise it.

Digital and networked

Open education can be realised in many ways – holding a public lecture, devising a mobile schools program and so on could all be deemed to be open education. While such approaches are important, and in many contexts appropriate, what we are concerned with in the current debates about open education are the changes in practice that are afforded and influenced by two technological aspects outlined in Chapter 1:

1   It is based on digital content, where content can include debates, video, text, audio, forums and so on.

2   Resources are shared via a global network, both technical and social.

The combination of digital content and a global, socially oriented distribution network has created the conditions in which new interpretations of open education can develop. Indeed, as mentioned in Chapter 4, some commentators have begun to talk of the 'open scholar', which is almost synonymous with the 'digital scholar'; so closely aligned are the new technologies and open approaches. For example, Gideon Burton (2009) makes the explicit link between openness and digital technologies:

> The traditional scholar, like the scholarship he or she produces, isn't open – open-minded, hopefully, but not 'open' in a public way. No, a typical scholar is very exclusive, available only to students in specific academic programs or through toll-access scholarly publications that are essentially unavailable to all but the most privileged. In the digital age, the traditional barriers to accessing scholars or scholarship are unnecessary, but persist for institutional reasons.

There are two questions this link between new technologies and open education raises. The first is, what are the mechanisms by which new technologies have facilitated openness? The second is, why is openness seen as a desirable and effective mode of operation in the digital networked environment?

I will address both of these questions, but first it is worth delineating some of the characteristics of openness in education. Anderson (2009) suggests a number of activities that characterise the open scholars, including that they

- create,

- use and contribute open educational resources,

- self-archive,

- apply their research,

- do open research,

- filter and share with others,

- support emerging open learning alternatives,

- publish in open access journals,

- comment openly on the works of others, and

- build networks.

We might argue about some of these and whether all are required to meet the definition of an open scholar, but Anderson's list matches many of the subjects in this book and represents a good overview of a digital, networked and open approach to practice. From my own experience I would propose the following set of characteristics and suggest that open scholars are likely to adopt these.

- Have a distributed online identity – using a variety of services an identity is distributed depending on the means by which the individual is encountered.

- Have a central place for their identity – although their identity is distributed, there is usually one central hub, such as a blog, wiki or aggregation service page (e.g. http://flavors.me/).

- Have cultivated an online network of peers – the open scholar usually engages in social networks through a preferred service (e.g. Twitter, Facebook, Friendfeed) and regularly contributes to that network.

- Have developed a personal learning environment from a range of tools – the open scholar develops a suite of preferred tools not through a deliberate policy of constructing a PLE but through personal trial and error.

- Engage with open publishing – when formal publications are produced open scholars will seek an open publishing route for their dissemination.

- Create a range of informal output – as well as producing traditional outputs, the open scholar produces and explores different forms of output such as video, podcast, slidecast and so on.

- Try new technologies – there is an acceptance that technology is not fixed and that new technologies are explored on an individual, *ad hoc* basis to ascertain where they fit into the individual's overall portfolio of tools.

- Mix personal and professional outputs – the social network space is characterised by the personal elements its participants reveal, which can be seen as the hooks through which connections are established. The open scholar deliberately mixes personal and professional observations in order to be an effective communicator within these networks and does not seek to keep them distinct.

- Use new technologies to support teaching and research – when assessing or adopting new technologies they will be appraised not only for their use on a personal basis but also how they can be used to support professional practice, such as using social bookmarking for a research group or creating student portfolios in Friendfeed.

- Automatically create and share outputs – the default position of an open scholar is to share outputs, be they presentations, ideas, suggestions or publications, using whatever route is appropriate.

While not every open scholar will adopt every one of these practices, they provide an archetypal set of characteristics which allow comparison with traditional scholarly practice and also move away from some of the limitations of a straightforward classification of 'digital'.

Having suggested a range of characteristics for open scholars, the two questions set out above can now be addressed, which seek to explore the connection between digital technologies and the evolution of open education.

The facilitation of openness

The first issue relates to the mechanism(s) by which new technologies have facilitated openness. In the characteristics set out above, it is the last characteristic that is arguably the most significant, the default assumption, desire and ability, to share. This can be seen as the one action that has been fundamentally altered by the digital network.

This has occurred because successive technologies have built on existing networks, and the Web 2.0 explosion in recent years in particular has seen a proliferation of free tools whose basic proposition is to distribute content across the network. While media sharing sites such as YouTube, Flickr and Slideshare are destination sites in their own right, much of their success has been built upon existing networks, particularly that of blogs and social media sites such as Facebook. The ease of sharing has been greatly increased by some data standards, including RSS and embed codes which allow users to take content from one site and easily import it into another.

Leslie (2008) comments on the ease of this everyday sharing, compared with the complexity inherent in many institutional approaches:

I have been asked to participate in many projects over the years that start once a bunch of departments, institutions or organizations notice that they have a lot in common with others and decide that it would be a good idea to collaborate, to share 'best practices' or 'data' or whatever …

But inevitably, with a very few exceptions, these projects spend an enormous amount of time defining what is to be shared, figuring out how to share it, setting up the mechanisms to share it, and then … not really sharing much …

Now I contrast that with the learning networks which I inhabit, and in which every single day I share my learning and have knowledge and learning shared back with me. I know it works.

An illustrative example here can be taken from the music industry. To share music with friends used to be costly, in terms of time and resource. So, to share music, an individual might be required to purchase a tape, record all the songs (which would take at least the length of the tape and probably longer) and then would give the tape away and so would no longer own the resultant mix. Compare this with digital network versions of sharing and the use of services such as LastFM, which allow people to share music they have been listening to and, through data mining, recommend similar music. Through tools such as Spotify and iTunes it is easy to share a playlist by simply making it public. Other tools such as Blip.fm allow easy sharing through social networks such as Twitter. In all of these cases the effort required to share is greatly reduced and is often a frictionless by-product of actions performed by the individual. In terms of both finance and time the cost of sharing has effectively disappeared.

This same ease of sharing applies in scholarly terms also. Three levels of this new, lightweight sharing can be categorised, showing increasing effort on the part of the sharer:

1 Frictionless – sharing that occurs without any additional effort required, for example, if a scholar is gathering resources for her own research, then using a social bookmarking tool is an effective tool for her as well as making the list public.

2 Quick sharing – this requires a small level of effort, so does not occur simply as a by-product, but the effort required is minimal, such as sharing a link via Facebook or uploading a Powerpoint presentation to Slideshare.

3 Content creation – this requires some effort to produce a digital artefact, for instance, creating a blog post, a YouTube movie, or adding and synchronising audio to a presentation to create a 'slidecast'. The effort and expertise required are still relatively low compared to many traditional forms of output.

In addition, there will be traditional artefacts, such as journal articles, which can take a long time to produce but can be easily shared online. There is an initial investment required in acquiring some expertise in using the tools necessary for effective sharing, but the technical ability threshold is low; it is rather a question of changes in practice. As Leslie's quote illustrates, some of the default attitudes towards sharing, from both institutions and scholars, are grounded in a model where the process of sharing is a logistical and categorisation issue.

The ease with which sharing can occur has inevitably led many scholars to adopt this practice as a means of dissemination, debate, teaching and research. However, being able to share easily is not the same as it being effective and worthwhile to do so. It is this aspect we will look at next.

The effectiveness of openness

This section will look at the second question about openness, that is, why has this mode of working been adopted, in varying degrees, across all aspects of education? Is it an inevitable consequence of the digital network or that previously difficult, but desirable, models of working are now realisable?

One way of approaching this is to look at the citation levels of articles that are published online versus those that are in closed access journals. Hajjem, Harnad and Gingras (2005) compared 1,307,038 articles across a range of disciplines and found that open access articles have a higher citation impact of between 36 and 172 per cent.

So publishing in an online, open manner aids in the traditional measures of citation. In addition, there are a number of other benefits. As outlined in Chapter 4, the crowdsourcing approach to research allows researchers to gather input from a wide range of users. In 'Amazing Stories of Openness', Levine (2009) crowdsourced contributions, and provided examples that include translations of resources, technical developments on an initial diagram, offers to give keynote talks, job offers, ideas for teaching, feedback on dissertations and so on.

The term 'lazyweb' refers to the practice of asking questions of one's network, rather than researching it yourself. This lighthearted term underplays a significant function of your social network, which is access to experts, peer and a wealth of experience which you can draw upon easily. However, you are only likely to get a response from your network if you have in turn been open. Reciprocity is key.

This notion of reciprocity is essential in maintaining an effective network of peers. Using blogs and Twitter as examples, the relationship between a blogger and a reader is maintained if the blogger provides interesting and regular updates. This notion of reciprocal, but not identical, activity can be used for more subtle interactions, what might be termed 'shifted reciprocity'. For instance, a lazyweb request on Twitter is likely to be successful if the requester has either responded previously to such requests (standard reciprocity) or has given enough of herself to the network such that people feel well disposed towards her (shifted reciprocity).

In this sense then we can begin to think of an economy of reciprocity. In this economy, the more you give online *that is of value* to those in your network then the more 'credit' you establish. This allows us to see that spamming is negative behaviour – it is not establishing a reciprocal relationship. But also if we look at, for instance, Sarah Horrigan's (2009) list of Twitter etiquette, she suggests the following for users:

- Fill in your profile.

- Picture please – it doesn't have to be anything much, but I do like to see that I'm talking to someone or something.

- Don't protect your updates – Twitter is social … it's not a private club.

- Participate, don't just aggregate – I'm sure no one minds the odd bit of blog promotion … but actively participating with a few thoughts of your own sure makes for a more interesting Twitter.

- Update, don't stagnate.

- Learn the importance of @ and 'd'.

- Retweet selectively.

Most of these suggestions can be interpreted as advice on establishing reciprocity. If someone doesn't have a profile, or doesn't update regularly, then her reciprocal currency is diminished. It also helps us frame our behaviour in any new tool; for instance, setting up auto-follows and direct messages in Twitter is devaluing the reciprocal nature of following – I know you'll follow me back if I follow you, but that means that decision isn't based on any assessment of my value to your network. Therefore the reciprocal value to each party is likely to be less. Within a reciprocity economy we build up a sense of identity capital, and reciprocity is the 'currency' through which exchange is realised. As in any economy establishing any status requires effort, time or innovation.

This is not as altruistic or unrealistic as it might seem. Nowak and Roch (2007) analysed 'upstream reciprocity' behaviour; that is, when the recipients of an act of kindness are more likely to help others in turn, even if the person who benefits from their generosity is somebody else. They conclude that although there is a cost associated with upstream reciprocity, it tends to evolve as a result of the positive feeling of gratitude and when direct reciprocity is also present, with a resultant increase in reciprocity and altruism in society as a whole.

Sharing, and thus openness, is the base, the *sine qua non* of an online social network, since if no one shares then you cannot even begin to establish a network. And once it has started, the evidence is that it tends to multiply, so reciprocity becomes a consequence of the network. Therefore, in order to realise many of the benefits of a social network, openness is a prerequisite, which means that it becomes an effective strategy for working.

Open education as a 'movement'

The open education approach can be viewed as more than simply an effective working method, however. There is a view which has it as a 'movement', which whilst not deliberately setting out to do so, has a broad set of agreed principles and a number of leaders or prominent figures, such as David Wiley, Michael Wesch and Larry Lessig. In general, the movement can be characterised as being

- technologically competent,

- interested in new technologies,

- active online,

- against proprietary copyright,

- in favour of new rights, such as Creative Commons,

- have a preference for loosely coupled technology systems compared with centralised LMSs, and

- have a preference for new forms of outputs.

Nearly all members of any movement will resist categorisation, but there is an increasingly political dimension to much of the open education movement, which is seen particularly when legislation seeks to curtail the rights of online activity; for example, the digital economy bill in the United Kingdom was widely protested against by those who could be classified as being part of the open education movement, and net neutrality is also seen as a key issue amongst this group.

Perhaps the most visible, and well funded, part of the open education movement is the generation of free, openly accessible content in the form of OERs, so it is worth looking at these in detail as they highlight many of the issues raised by open education.

Open educational resources

This section will look at the most concrete realisation of the open education movement, namely that of open education resources. In particular I want to revisit the notion of granularity and how changes in this, afforded by new technologies, are changing scholarly behaviour.

Open educational resources started in earnest with the MIT OCW initiative (http://ocw.mit.edu/index.html). This was started in 2001 through a grant from the Hewlett Foundation, with the aim of making all course materials available online. OCW constituted a very important statement. At a time when many universities and content providers were seeking to find ever-more stringent methods of protecting their materials, OCW acted as an antidote to this and made people think about an alternative, open source–based approach.

OERs can be seen as a development on the previous work of learning objects (Wiley 2001), which sought to develop reusable, shareable pieces of learning material. A number of projects were set up to generate learning objects and to create repositories to house them, for example, MERLOT.

Much of the focus on OERs has been around large-scale, externally funded OER projects such as MIT's OCW and the OU's OpenLearn projects. These have been successful in raising the profile of open education, creating a semi-politicised open movement and in generating impressive download figures of resources (e.g. Carson 2005).

If one broadens the definition of OERs to encompass resources produced by individuals and shared on sites outside the formal education portals, for example, YouTube, Slideshare and Flickr, then a continuum of resources can be considered. These vary in granularity, quality and explicit learning intentions. This wider definition of OERs to include any open resource used in learning can broadly be characterised into two types of OERs, namely 'big' and 'little' OERs (from Hoyle 2009). As with classification of science into big and little (Price 1963) the distinction is not perfect, but it addresses two fundamentally different approaches, which can be seen as complementary. For OERs the differences can be summarised as follows:

- Big OERs are institutionally generated ones that arise from projects such as Open Courseware and OpenLearn. These are usually of high quality, contain explicit teaching aims, are presented in a uniform style and form part of a time-limited, focused project with portal and associated research and data.

- Little OERs are individually produced, low cost resources. They are produced by anyone, not just educators, may not have explicit educational aims, have low production quality and are shared through a range of third party sites and services.

Using this simple granularity classification, we can explore some of the issues around OERs and open education in general.

Status

I was involved in a project promoting the use of OERs in some ACP (Asia–Caribbean–Pacific) countries. When we evaluated the uptake of the project, all of the partners reported reluctance by academics to reuse content from others. Much of this resistance was allied with notions of identity and status (Rennie and Weller 2010). To reuse someone else's content in teaching was interpreted as a sign of weakness or a threat to their (often hard-won) status as expert. This objection was somewhat alleviated when the provider of the content was a recognised university with an international reputation. In this case, the big OERs have an advantage, because there is both a sense of mistrust about the type of material produced for little OERs and also an anxiety that their use would be perceived as unprofessional. The large-scale OER projects tend to have a pre-publication filter policy, so only high-quality material is released. It also has the associated university brand linked to it, so there is a quality 'badge' and recognised reputation, which can be seen as enhancing the individual lecturer's quality and teaching.

Big OERs could be viewed as a 'colonising species', whereby their presence changes the environment to make it more favourable for subsequent acts of reuse, such as little OERs.

Aggregation and adaptation

Many of the big OERs have explicit learning aims associated with them or at least an intended level and audience. Little OERs, however, are created for a variety of purposes and rarely have explicit learning metadata associated with them. This means that big OERs are a useful starting point and can often be used 'wholesale', that is, without adaptation. Indeed, the experience of the OpenLearn project has been that very few units are changed or adapted for use. The OpenLearn research report states,

> In relation to repurposing, initially it was thought:
>
> 1 that it was not anyone's current role to remix and reuse;
>
> 2 the content provided on the site was of high quality and so discouraged alteration;
>
> 3 there were few examples showing the method and value of remixing;
>
> 4 the use of unfamiliar formats (such as XML) meant that users were uncertain how to proceed. (McAndrew *et al.* 2009)

There were a number of collaborative projects established between the OpenLearn team and other institutions whereby content was adapted for use, for example, translation into Spanish of all published resources.

With little OERs, their use is often unpredictable, precisely because they are a smaller granularity and do not have the same level of intentionality associated with them. An example might be an image shared on Flickr, which depicts, say, a collection of toys, and is used in a presentation as a representation of diversity within a community. The resource may not be adapted, but it is used in an unintended and unpredicted context. This is another example of what Zittrain (2008) terms 'generativity', which he defines as 'a system's capacity to produce unanticipated change through unfiltered contributions from broad and varied audiences'. Little OERs are high in generativity because they can easily be used in different contexts, whereas the context is embedded within big OERs, which in turn means they are better at meeting a specific learning aim.

This may indicate that different patterns of use will operate for big and little OERs. With the former the emphasis is on adaptation, taking large chunks of content and expending resource in adapting it to local use. An example of this is the essay writing course developed at the University of the South Pacific (http://www.usp.ac.fj/studyskills/CFDL/module1.html), which was adapted from a course developed by three New Zealand tertiary institutions. Little OER use tends to be focused less on adaptation and more on aggregation, that is, taking a number of different resources and creating a cohesive educational narrative that brings these together.

Models of sustainability

The sustainability of big OER projects has been an issue of concern since their inception. As Wiley (2007) puts it,

> [T]he William and Flora Hewlett Foundation has put millions of dollars into university-based open educational resource projects around the world. Given the current budget climate for education, a concern naturally arises about the future of the university-based open educational resource projects. What will happen when the targeted external dollars dry up? Will the initiatives themselves also dry up? How are these initiatives to sustain themselves over time?

Big OER projects have a variety of models of funding, and Wiley highlights three of these demonstrating a range of centralisation: a centralised team funded by donors and grants (such as MIT), linking it into teaching responsibilities (as practised at Utah State University) and a decentralised collaborative authoring approach (e.g. Rice Connexions, http://cnx.org).

The costs vary for these approaches, with MIT estimating it to be approximately US$10,000 per course, and the Rice model being close to free as courses are created by interested parties, as with open source software. The returns for institutions may vary also; for example, the OpenLearn project was responsible for generating about 7,000 course registrations in one year, improving the OU's global presence, generating publicity, operating as a basis for research funding and a means for establishing partnerships (McAndrew *et al.* 2009). This was partly a function of the OERs being direct OU content, unlike the Rice model.

The sustainability of little OERs is less of an issue and is probably closest to the second of Wiley's models. As outlined above little OERs arise from relatively low-cost forms of sharing. For example, if a presentation is given, then uploading it to Slideshare is a zero-cost activity, and adding a synchronised audio file to create a slidecast takes only a modest amount of time. The result is a shareable OER that can be aggregated and used elsewhere, as suggested in Chapter 7.

Affordances of OERs

Both Wiley and McAndrew *et al.* (2009) state that individual users don't tend to adapt OERs (which in this case refers to big OERs). The reasons for this are varied, including technical complexity and motivation. One other reason which the OpenLearn team suggest is that the 'content provided on the site was of high quality and so discouraged alteration'. This is an interesting observation as it seems to indicate that high-quality content encourages a somewhat passive acceptance. In this sense big OERs may be seen to be akin to broadcast content. The OpenLearn team also reported that social interaction was not a high priority for most users: 'a large choice of content is considered the most important feature of OpenLearn and that interacting with other learners is low on this list' (although there was an active subset of users who were identified as social learners and made extensive use of forums).

In contrast the low production quality of little OERs has the effect of encouraging further participation. The implicit message in these OERs is that the consumer can become a producer – they are an invitation to participate precisely because of their low quality. Whether this is in writing a blog post that links to it or in creating a video reaction, the low threshold to content creation is a feature of little OERs. Not all users of a site will become creators; YouTube claims that '52 percent of 18-34 year-olds share videos often with friends and colleagues', whereas the majority of Wikipedia edits are performed by a small group of users (Ortega 2009).

In educational terms it may be that both have a role to play within a learning context or course. Learners may want to feel the reassurance of the quality brand material for core content, but they may also want a mixture of the more social, participatory media that encourages them to contribute.

Portals and sites

The traffic to many of the big OER sites is reasonably impressive. Most big OER projects have a specific site associated with them, although their content may be used to populate other portals and repositories also.

Little OERs tend to be found on third-party, 'Web 2.0' type services, such as Slideshare, YouTube, Scribd and so on. There are advantages and disadvantages to both approaches, which are summarised in Table 9.1.

So, for example, Slideshare is a site for sharing Powerpoint presentations, to which you can add audio too, favourite, comment upon and embed elsewhere. It attracts significantly more web traffic than MIT's OCW site but, of course, features presentations about all manner of subject. This raises a number of questions:

- Are people more likely to share content through a service such as Slideshare? If so, why? Is it because it is easier or because they may gain a greater number of views?

- Is the basic unit of sharing (the presentation) at Slideshare a granularity, people understand more than courses and units at OER sites?

- Is the comparison fair? Can we consider Slideshare an OER repository of sorts?

Table 9.1 Advantages and disadvantages of OER portals and third-party sites

	Specific project site	Third-party site
Advantages	Greater brand link	Greater traffic
	Link through to courses	Cheaper
	Control	Greater serendipity
	Ability to conduct research	Expertise in social software development
Disadvantages	Requires specialist team	Can lose service
	Requires updating	No control, for example, over downtimes
	Lower traffic	Loss of ownership of data
	More expensive	Other non-educational content also present

- Are commercial operations better at developing sites and adding in the necessary functionality than educational ones?

- Are people learning from Slideshare? If so, how does it compare with learning from OERs?

- What are the dangers that your resources will be lost on Slideshare, and what use is your data being put to?

At the moment we are too early in the development of OERs and these third-party services to answer many of these questions, but the different hosting options of big and little OERs raise these issues for educators.

The role of context

The following anecdote is well known and, while true, was also concocted by *The Washington Post* (Weingarten 2007):

A man sat at a metro station in Washington DC and started to play the violin; it was a cold January morning. He played six Bach pieces for about 45 minutes. During that time, since it was rush hour, it was calculated that thousands of people went through the station, most of them on their way to work.

In the 45 minutes the musician played, only 6 people stopped and stayed for a while. About 20 gave him money but continued to walk their normal pace. He collected $32. When he finished playing and silence took over, no one noticed it. No one applauded, nor was there any recognition.

No one knew this but the violinist was Joshua Bell, one of the top musicians in the world. He played one of the most intricate pieces ever written, with a violin worth 3.5 million dollars.

Two days before his playing in the subway, Joshua Bell sold out at a theatre in Boston and the seats average $100.

The moral of the story is usually taken to be that people don't stop and appreciate what is around them, and in their busy lives they can pass by things of beauty and value. But it has some lessons for the discussion of OERs also.

The first may be that people don't value free things or are suspicious of free. We have become accustomed to roughly equating monetary price with value or quality. Free is therefore obviously of low quality or suspicious at least. There is a general expectation that online resources will be free, although the success of iTunes apps is beginning to challenge this. But in education there is still an expectation that high-quality education costs. OERs are, of course, only part of the educational offering – they are the content, and just as important are the associated elements outlined in Chapter 3, such as accreditation. But big OERs have a relationship to price when they are the learning materials used by universities. The message then is that some people have valued them highly enough to pay for them (and the associated services). Little OER, by its very nature, has not been paid for and so one variable people use to judge value is absent, namely whether someone would pay for it.

But perhaps what is more significant about the Joshua Bell story is what it says about context. The reason many people passed him by was because of context – they are in an underground station, which is an unpleasant place to be, and want to get out of it as fast as possible because they are probably on their way somewhere and want to be punctual or because they're not expecting to encounter classical music there and so have a different mindset in place and so on.

Big OER is often found in a specific repository and people have come to that site with the intention of learning. It is placed within an educational context. Little OER is often placed on third-party services which will contain a range of content and people may not have learning as their goal when encountering these resources. This may mean that a different audience is reached, but it may also result in any educational intention in the content being misconstrued or missed.

The importance of educational context was one outcome in a project I ran recently. In the podstars project I mentioned in Chapter 7 (Weller 2010) academics used Flip cameras and other tools to start producing multimedia content. They uploaded their content to YouTube and to a wiki. As one of the contributors commented,

> No amount of creativity in the making of an artefact will compensate for the absence of a framework within which to disseminate it. My Facebook postings (of links to my 2 videos) received brief comments from 3 of my 67 'friends'. Nothing on Twitter or Youtube. This demotivated me to continue investing the time. If I'd had, say, a teaching forum with students working on intercultural semiotics, I'd have had more of an impact.

As was suggested above, little OER encourages aggregation and through this, the creation of context. While this offers greater flexibility, it also requires greater effort, whereas the educational context of big OERs is inherent in both their location and their content.

Open courses

As well as open educational content, a number of educators have begun to explore the possibility of running courses entirely in the open. These are sometimes labelled MOOCs (Massively Open Online Courses). David Wiley, Alec Couros and Jim

Groom have all experimented with versions of open courses, but it is probably Stephen Downes and George Siemens' 'Connectivism and Connected Knowledge' courses, which have run annually since 2008, that are most representative. McAuley *et al.* (2010) suggest that a MOOC

> integrates the connectivity of social networking, the facilitation of an acknowledged expert in a field of study, and a collection of freely accessible online resources. Perhaps most importantly, however, a MOOC builds on the active engagement of several hundred to several thousand 'students' who self-organize their participation according to learning goals, prior knowledge and skills, and common interests. Although it may share in some of the conventions of an ordinary course, such as a predefined timeline and weekly topics for consideration, a MOOC generally carries no fees, no prerequisites other than Internet access and interest, no predefined expectations for participation, and no formal accreditation.

Models of open courses vary; some are created solely as open courses, with no associated accreditation; others combine fee-paying students, often on campus who are studying for credit, with those taking the course online purely for interest.

Completion rates are an issue for MOOCs, where the motivation and commitment to continue is not as great for those taking the course out of interest and who will not be assessed. However, as McAuley *et al.* (2010) argue, 'completion of all course assignments is neither necessary nor the goal of every student', so this may not be significant. As with OERs, sustainability and the impact upon a university's core business are also topics of interest, as it is not yet fully understood whether such courses act as recruitment vehicles for fee-paying students or result in a drop in student enrolment. There are, of course, many other reasons why courses may be delivered in the open, but their sustainability within a conventional university structure is likely to be the deciding factor for broader adoption.

Conclusion

In this chapter the nature of openness in education has been explored, particularly as it relates to content and courses. The categorisation of educational resources, as big and little, provides a lens on some of the issues and uses of the open education movement. One key difference is that of intentionality, where big OERs are created for the specific purpose of learning, whereas little OERs may be created from a variety of motivations but can have an educational intention ascribed to them by someone else.

There are significant differences between the way in which these types of OERs are used and interpreted by audiences, which relate to quality, reputation and ease of production. It may well be that a 'mixed economy' of both types of OERs is the best route to realising open education. Big OER is a useful means of raising the profile of open education and an initial way of approaching reuse that overcomes many of the objections based on quality and reliability. Little OER represents a more dynamic model that encourages participation and may be more sustainable. For learners, a mixture of both may also create a varied, engaging experience.

Open courses represent the type of experimentation and model that has been seen in other industries, as discussed in Chapter 3. Both OERs and open courses are a direct response to the challenges and opportunities of a digital, networked, open approach in education. They may not be the solutions in themselves, and maybe several years from now they will be superseded, but they can be interpreted as generating feedback and experimenting with possibilities and alternatives that were previously unavailable. It is the generation of alternatives that will be explored in more detail in Chapter 10 and particularly how this relates to another significant scholarly practice, the academic conference.

10 Network Weather

Previous chapters have looked at the potential for change in scholarly practice but deliberately avoided an argument based on compulsion or inevitability. This chapter takes a slightly different tack and suggests that the use of digital, networked open tools and approaches will have an impact on some areas of scholarly practice, which in turn will affect all scholars, regardless of whether they themselves use the technologies or not.

Network weather

The metaphor that will be adopted here is one suggested by Adam Greenfield (2010), which he termed 'network weather'. Greenfield is interested in the way technologies affect our physical environment, in particular life in cities. His argument is that, even if you are unaware of these technologies, they are beginning to have an impact on how we experience our daily lives in urban settings. He gives the following scenario to demonstrate his point:

> The irritating guy with the popped collar standing next to you at the bar? He paid less for his G&T than you did, because he's the Mayor of this place on Foursquare, and the management has cannily decreed Mayors get a 5% discount. Ten minutes from now, the place is going to fill up with his equally annoying buddies, absolutely ruining your hope of a quiet drink. And they're going to show up not because he did so much as call them to tell them where he'd be, but because he's got things set so his Foursquare account automatically posts to his Facebook page. Buddies of his that don't even use Foursquare will come, to slouch at the bar, stab at their phones and try and figure out where the party's going next.

> You'll settle up and leave, miffed, and ease on down the road a spell to a place you know where you can get a decent bowl of penne – nothing special, but good and hearty and cheap, and you'll chase it with the big bouncy house red, and all will be well and right with the world. Except the Italian place is gone, gone because it racked up too many nasty reviews on Yelp, or somebody Googlebombed its listing, or its hundred healthcode violations made it positively radioactive on Everyblock.

> ... if you don't know what they are and how they work, you'll never have the foggiest clue why things shook out the way they did. Your evening will have

a completely different shape and texture than what it would have prior to the advent of ubiquitous mobile Internet. You'll have been tossed this way and that by the gusts and squalls of network weather. (Greenfield 2010)

We can consider similar scenarios for scholarly practice and the way they are affected by network weather. A good example that is already happening is the nature of the academic conference – a practice and event that sits at the heart of scholarship. It achieves many vital functions in academic practice, including the following:

- Knowledge sharing – attendees get to present and listen to other talks.

- Validation – by sharing research and ideas within a subject community attendees gain validation of their own research.

- Networking – it is often through meetings at conferences that scholars develop their network of peers.

- Recognition – publishing conference papers is often a first step for researchers to publishing papers and are recognised outputs.

- Socialising – slightly different from networking, there is a social element to conferences which make them enjoyable.

Each of these functions is affected by network weather. I will address the changes in detail, but they can be summarised as follows:

- Remote participation – streaming events allows people to attend remotely and often put questions to the speakers.

- The backchannel – Twitter, in particular, has become a potent force for creating a backchannel of conversation, with positive and negative results.

- Amplified events – many conferences now seek to draw in a wider audience using remote participation, beyond the normal constituents.

- Socialisation – people will organise events before and during the conference using social networks.

- Alternative session formats – in response to the impact of such technologies, conference organisers are beginning to use the face-to-face element of conferences to do more than just content delivery.

Here, then, is my attempt at Greenfield's network weather scenario for an academic at a conference.

When you arrive you are disappointed to find out that someone who has attended for the previous three years, and who you always have a meal with, has stayed at home because they can attend remotely. In the opening session the keynote speaker makes a claim that someone checks and passes around via Twitter, and it seems they have misrepresented the research findings. There is a noticeable change in atmosphere and the questions the speaker receives are more challenging than you usually encounter. In another session the speaker takes questions from the remote audience, which includes students and this generates a very good discussion about the learner perspective.

That evening the conference bar seems rather empty, and seeing an old colleague he informs you that there is an alternative conference Facebook page, and they have arranged a meeting in a local bar, with a discussion theme.

The next day the afternoon doesn't have any presentations; instead it has an informal format where the participants seek to create a set of learning resources and a link up with four remote hubs in different cities.

This may not sound like an improvement to the conference, or in fact a substantial change, but each of these uses and impacts are all ones that have been implemented in the past year or so. They represent real changes to an activity at the core of scholarly practice and are therefore a good example of the type of network weather which we may experience across all areas of scholarly function.

Remote participation

Over the past few years remote participation of conferences has become more commonplace, as tools for streaming video have become cheaper and social tools have become widely adopted. Entirely online conferences will be covered later; this section is concerned with the often vicarious, casual participation at a distance of a physical event. This type of participation is often unofficial and uses low-key, free technology, although increasingly it is an official element of the conference. It is often a hybrid of the following examples:

- Twitter hashtags

- live video streaming (whether official or via an individual)

- blogging

- live blogging (i.e. reports during a session)

- video/audio updates and interviews
- Flickr photo streams
- Slideshare presentations
- Cloudworks/Friendfeed aggregations

There are at least three interesting issues this raises. First, how does it change the nature of the conference to have this broader participation? Second, how can conference organisers and presenters best take advantage of it and incorporate it into the conference? Third, what is the experience like for the remote participant compared with the 'real thing'?

It is changing the nature of the conference for the attendees because it means the boundaries of the conference become blurred. As well as engaging in dialogue with those who are present, there is a wider group who can engage in conversations on blogs or Twitter (or the conference may use an official remote presentation environment such as Elluminate for streaming). It also blurs the time over which these discussions take place with some pre-event discussion in anticipation and a good deal of post-event discussion as people blog and reflect on the conference.

The second question of taking advantage of remote participation is one where we are seeing a range of experimentation. This can include seeking questions from remote participants, asking them to send in online contributions (such as videos), organising virtual streams which run parallel to the main conference, and using their participation both as promotion for the conference (because it creates more online discussion) and analysing their involvement as part of the overall conference review.

There is a delicate balance for conference organisers to strike here, for if the remote participation becomes too effective then people may stop attending the conference, and it is difficult to get people to pay for remote participation.

For the last question relating to experience, I conducted a short online survey to gain an overview of how remote participation compares with real attendance. The first three questions asked how remote participation compared with face-to-face attendance on some of the main functions of conferences, namely networking, content and socialising.

For networking most people ranked it as between 25 and 50 per cent as good as attending face to face, while for accessing the content, most people ranked it as around 75 per cent as effective. Unsurprisingly, socialising didn't fare as well, with most people ranking it between 25 per cent as good and no good at all.

Lastly, I asked about how much time remote participation took compared with face-to-face attendance. An estimate of 25 per cent was the most popular response.

This gives an interesting starting point for considering remote participation at conferences. When considering attending a conference, an individual can ask oneself a question such as 'if I can achieve 50% networking, get 75% of the content for 25% of the time and it's 75% greener, then what are the real benefits of attending?'

This is not to argue that remote attendance is superior, or should completely replace face-to-face conference attendance, but it will need to be clearer what benefits are accrued from physically attending, and maybe individuals will trade-off some face-to-face attendance for remote participation.

Backchannel

The combination of a common (but not formally promoted) communication channel (such as Twitter, FriendFeed and Facebook) and pervasive Wi-fi access has led to the rise of the backchannel at conferences. Combined with the use of the hashtag, the audience of a talk don't need to agree to 'meet' in a common forum, or to even know each other to engage in discussion. This could be seen as another example of the technology and community norms of social media spaces such as Twitter overriding the boundaries between people that we saw in Chapter 6. In Chapter 6 we were concerned with interdisciplinary boundaries, for the conference the boundaries are more physical – how do you communicate with strangers who you share a room with but can't speak to?

The backchannel allows people to comment on the presentation, both with others at the presentation and also to their wider network. This can be a benefit, with positive feedback, following up links, real-time discussion before the ideas dissipate, the creation of an instant archive around an event and a means of connecting with others at the conference that can be followed up.

But the experience is not always a positive one, as Danah Boyd (2009) relates. She gave a presentation at a conference where the Twitter backchannel was displayed behind her, but she couldn't see it. She relates how the public commentary disrupted her talk:

> [W]ithin the first two minutes, I started hearing rumblings. And then laughter. The sounds were completely irrelevant to what I was saying and I was devastated. I immediately knew that I had lost the audience. Rather than getting into flow and becoming an entertainer, I retreated into myself … I fed on the response I got from the audience in the worst possible way. Rather than the audience pushing me to become a better speaker, it was pushing me to get worse. I hated the audience. I hated myself. I hated the situation. (Boyd 2009)

In an example of network weather she points out how the conference organiser's decision to foreground the backchannel changed the nature of the talk:

> The problem with a public-facing Twitter stream in events like this is that it FORCES the audience to pay attention to the backchannel. So even audience members who want to focus on the content get distracted. ... the Twitter stream fundamentally adds another layer of content that the audience can't ignore, that I can't control. And that I cannot even see. (Boyd 2009)

The vast majority of backchannel conversations are, in my experience, positive, encouraging and complementary (and complimentary) to the talk. When the backchannel has been negative it has often been because the speaker is being deliberately provocative, so this reaction is no doubt what they intend. But we should appreciate that the backchannel is a powerful element, and as with many emerging practices finding the balance of behaviour may take time; for example, turning the backchannel into a 'frontchannel' is probably something that should only be done if the speaker wants it and is planning to use it in some way.

Academics are accustomed to, and usually welcome, thoughtful criticism, but care must be taken to avoid the pack mentality the backchannel sometimes exhibits. Dave Ferguson (2009) relates his experience of witnessing a 'harshtag' incident, when the keynote speaker was deemed to be condescending. He argues that although the behaviour may be reprehensible, it should also make organisers think about the role of the keynote and how speakers use their time and the concept of an audience: 'I'm not going to talk about *audience* any more. An audience is what you have at a performance, like a concert or a play or a taping of *Wheel of Fortune*. When it comes to a professional presentation, what you have are participants – people who want to take part, who *plan* to take part, in what's going on'.

Amplified events

Remote participation can occur without the conference organiser's explicit backing or promotion, and the provision of easy broadcasting tools will only increase the extent to which this happens and the channels it occurs across. The amplified event (Dempsey 2007) is one where the conference organisers seek to reach out to audiences beyond the physical conference, to include input from remote participants using 'a variety of network tools and collateral communications' and also to provide attendees with an 'amplified' experience.

In its simplest form this might include live-streaming the talks and having an agreed hashtag. A more sophisticated approach would utilise environments to encourage remote participants, whether these are synchronous videoconferencing tools such as Elluminate or Big Blue Button, asynchronous discussion in VLEs such as Moodle or conference-specific social network spaces such as Crowdvine. The use of appointed bloggers and social media coverage may also contribute to the 'amplification' of the conference.

Another aspect of amplification is not only across physical distance but also across time. The archive of a conference will include a distributed record of formal and informal content, including the recordings of talks, the papers, participants' presentations on sites such as Slideshare, blog posts, Twitter archives, individual audio and video accounts, messages in discussion forums, official and unofficial photos on Flickr and so on. If there is a commonly used hashtag, then all of this material can be discovered and represents a much more complete picture of the conference and the issues than simply the record of the published papers. Compare the archive of a conference held in 1990 to one held in 2010 – the archive of the former is likely to consist of little more than the printed proceedings and maybe some photos in an album somewhere. The archive of the latter will be multimedia, distributed and feature a range of tone, from the formal academic one to informal, social chat. There are undoubtedly issues around the preservation and curation of such a record, but it represents a more complete representation of the conference. In this respect at least the open, networked, digital conference is already radically different from its historical predecessor.

Brian Kelly (2008) suggests the following eight forms of 'amplification':

1 Amplification of the audiences' voice: Prior to the availability of real-time chat technologies at events it was only feasible to discuss talks with immediate neighbours, and even then this may be considered rude.

2 Amplification of the speaker's talk: The availability of video- and audio-conferencing technologies makes it possible for a speaker to be heard by an audience which isn't physically present at the conference.

3 Amplification across time: Video and audio technologies can also be used to allow a speaker's talk to be made available after the event, with the use of podcasting or videocasting technologies allowing the talks to be easily syndicated to mobile devices as well as accessed on desktop computers.

4 Amplification of the speaker's slides: Sites such as Slideshare enable the slides used by a speaker to be more easily found, embedded on other websites and commented upon, in ways that were not possible when the slides, if made available at all, were only available on a conference website.

5 Amplification of feedback to the speaker: The backchannel acts not only as a discussion channel for conference participants but also as a way of providing real-time feedback to a speaker during a talk. There are also dedicated microblogging technologies, such as Coveritlive and Scribblelive, which aim to provide more sophisticated 'backchannels' for use at conferences.

6 Amplification of a conference's collective memory: The pervasive nature of digital cameras and mobile phones generates a collective representation of a conference, which are then shared via sites such as Flickr. The ability of such photographic resources to be 'mashed up' with, say, accompanying music can similarly help to enrich such collective experiences.

7 Amplification of the learning: The ability to be able to follow links to resources and discuss the points made by a speaker during a talk can enrich the learning which takes place at an event.

8 Long-term amplification of conference outputs: The availability in a digital format of conference resources, including both official and unofficial resources, may help to provide a more authentic record of an event, which could potentially provide a valuable historical record.

Socialisation

It is accepted that one of the functions of the academic conference is to 'network' and meet peers. Rather like study at a university, the exchange of academic knowledge is only one function – it is the most publicised one, but of equal importance is the human or social element. As we saw in Chapter 5, many academics have a network of colleagues with whom they form research teams, often using the same teams, and these connections are usually formed through face-to-face interactions.

New technologies allow this socialisation to occur before, during and after a conference, with a subsequent impact on the face-to-face socialising that occurs at the conference. A network of contacts may have been previously limited by physical networks, but now an academic with an online presence can have a range of contacts, and the conference is a means of reinforcing these or furthering discussion which has taken place online. The sense of meeting up with old friends is, as with above, amplified, since there will be a group of people who have not met face to face and yet feel as though they know each other, not just because they have engaged in discussion around their discipline but also because they will know an element of each other's personal lives. As I argued in Chapter 6, one of the key factors in Twitter's success is that people deliberately mix personal and professional messages.

They are, after all, called 'social networks' for a reason because they encourage social interaction. This needn't always culminate in actually meeting the person; meaningful interactions can occur between people who may never meet, and it undervalues online relationships to view them as 'face-to-face friendships in waiting'. The conference, though, can reinforce these relationships, with the result that ongoing virtual interaction is strengthened as a result of meeting physically.

Changing formats

These elements are combining to lead many conference organisers to explore different formats. An example is a hybrid approach where some people attend face to face and others sign up for a structured virtual event, or there are 'hubs' hosting a version of the conference in different locations. For example, the MacLearning 2010 conference took place simultaneously at MIT and Northwestern University with six other campuses joining in via a live videoconference. It was also open to online participation via the web.

Within conferences the range of sessions is also beginning to change. Recognising that it is the face-to-face social element that is the real virtue of physical conferences, organisers are seeking to capitalise on this. The BarCamp model has been adopted within some conferences. The BarCamp was initiated in 2005 as a developer workshop which deliberately eschewed much of the practice of conventional conferences. Participants are encouraged to share their work via social media, and the structure is much more fluid, with participants proposing and scheduling sessions each day as they progress and see what is of interest. This 'unconference' type approach has been adopted for non-developer events also. For example, the TeachMeet (http://www.teachmeet.org.uk/) events are organised as informal, unconference-type events where teachers can share good practice, practical innovations and personal insights in teaching with technology, and they often run in conjunction with conventional events. They have explored different formats, including

- micro-presentations – lasting 7 minutes;
- nano-presentations – lasting 2 minutes;
- random selection of speakers – from a pool of willing participants; and
- use of the backchannel – to let non-participants participate.

As with the Barcamp model, TeachMeet encourages others to organise their own version, rather than restricting the conference to one location.

In this section we have been looking at how the conventional face-to-face conference is experiencing change as a consequence of the top-down or bottom-up adoption of technologies. What this illustrates once again is that new technologies provide a range of alternatives where previously it was a distinctly binary choice: you either attended or not (although you could read the proceedings afterwards). Now there are a range of alternatives; individuals who may have attended some conferences previously may now choose to do so remotely, they may still attend some and other conferences which they would never have attended they may now dip into vicariously.

In the next section I will look at the wholly online conference, as an example of an alternative to hosting a conference.

Case study – the Open University conference

The Open University holds an annual learning and technology internal conference, and in 2010 I took over the responsibility for organising it. The format of the conferences had become rather staid, and the use of technology was conservative, so there was a remit to try new approaches. There was also a requirement to lower costs, with financial cutbacks, so there were a number of factors which suggested attempting a different format.

The structure we decided upon was to make the conference wholly online, free and open to all, with a theme of 'Openness in Education'. We used two main technologies: Cloudworks for asynchronous discussion and sharing resources, and Elluminate for the synchronous sessions of the conference itself. The conference was held over two days, with four synchronous sessions.

The Cloudworks site acted as the main hub for the conference, allowing participants to register and get information about the conference. Cloudworks allows content to be embedded from other sites such as Flickr, YouTube, Slideshare and so on. We added in the presentations that people gave us, contributions and interviews, but there was no need to host these; instead we relied on cloud services. Each Elluminate session was recorded and could be played back, so it could be accessed after the event had finished, the links being provided in the main Cloudworks site. Each section was also chunked into the separate smaller talks and delivered as podcasts so people could view or listen to them on mobile devices.

We made use of a range of other free online services around the conference also, including Twitter (we used the hashtag #OUConf10 to track conversations), twapperkeeper which archives tweets (for the hashtag), SurveyMonkey for the post-conference questionnaire, blogs for promotion, YouTube, Slideshare, Animoto and Xtranormal (all for creating content).

As well as the two-day conference, there was specific pre- and post-conference activity in Cloudworks. A number of interviews were filmed with the vice chancellor and others on the themes of the conference (see http://cloudworks.ac.uk/cloud/view/3959) and shared via YouTube. Instead of paper contributions we requested 'multimedia posters' where individuals or teams could create videos about their research or projects using a range of tools. After the conference we held an asynchronous discussion session focused around these contributions (see http://cloudworks.ac.uk/cloudscape/view/2012).

Organising the conference completely online offered a number of advantages. First, it meant we could get a wide range of speakers, usually willing to present for free. We had four external keynote speakers, including Wikipedia founder Jimmy Wales, all of whom presented remotely without any requirement to travel to the university. Most, but not all, of the OU presenters were on campus. Had we required presenters to travel to the OU we would certainly not have been able to get the same range of speakers.

Overall the conference attendance compared favourably to previous years, with 287 people attending the synchronous Elluminate sessions over the two days and 3,500 viewing conference content in Cloudworks. Approximately, 250 had attended the previous year's face-to-face conference.

A survey of those who attended the conference gave very positive responses, with 'excellent' or 'good' ratings of 83 per cent (for content), 79 per cent (use of technology) and 83 per cent (organisation). In addition 73 per cent said they would definitely attend another online conference and 25 per cent indicated they probably would, suggesting this is a medium the university can explore for other events.

Attendees came in from 14 different countries and 48 per cent indicated that they would not have attended if it was a face-to-face conference. Compared with the previous face-to-face conference the costs were marginal at around £2,500, plus staff commitment from a considerably smaller team, compared with costs of around £30,000 and a larger team in previous years.

The conference generated a significant amount of network publicity, with 3,251 views of the main cloudscape page, 168 comments, 14 separate bloggers and 141 different twitterers using the conference hashtag over 766 tweets.

There are other factors which are difficult to measure but which we gained some insight into through the survey. For instance, most participants reported that they combined participating in the conference with doing some work. Combined with the time saved in not travelling, this ability to engage in some work simultaneously may indicate a more efficient use of time. However, some respondents also suggested that this was a negative effect, in that they value the time away from work which attending a physical conference affords, as this provides them with valuable thinking time.

In terms of socialisation and interaction, most participants thought that the conference allowed a community to form and thought that the open nature of the conference worked well. Opinion was divided as to whether the interaction was less than with a face-to-face conference.

While the responses overall were positive there were also some issues around online conferencing which emerged, which speak to the context within which the academic conference operates and many of the assumptions we hold implicitly about how it operates. Online conferences are probably in a similar position to distance learning 40 years ago or elearning 10 years ago. They have a legitimacy deficit to some and thus have to work hard to overcome this. Some of the practice issues surrounding online conferences include the following:

- Online conferencing doesn't separate from daily tasks sufficiently – this is also one of its strengths, of course, in that people can attend, which a three- or four-day travelling commitment may prevent. But some people commented that either they weren't allowed to prioritise virtual attendance over other work or that if they were in the office, then people assume they are interruptible. If you attend a face-to-face conference the physical separation immediately performs this function.

- Online doesn't command as much attention – although attendance was comparable with the physical event held the previous year, one might have expected it to be higher. When you have a physical conference on campus there are a set of physical cues – signs, catering, attendees. A virtual conference, despite all the communications deployed, loses some of these cues.

- Commitment to online is lower – when you are travelling to a physical conference there is a need to make some preparations: accommodation, transport, child care cover and so on. An advantage of an online conference is that it doesn't require this level of organisation (and thus people attend who couldn't normally). This also means the conference doesn't foreground in an attendee's attention in the same way. Some people experienced connection problems, which were easily fixed, but because it happened on the day of the conference, it was too late and they gave up. Despite issuing instructions detailing how to check connections prior to the conference, it may be that a virtual conference doesn't register in the same way as making physical arrangements.

- The Camelot comparison – when being compared against an existing practice, there is a tendency sometimes to accentuate the positive elements of the entrenched practice. Not every face-to-face conference is a success. Not every speaker is engaging. Not every location wonderful. But the new version is often compared against the idealised version of this.

- Unrealistic burdens – with new formats unrealistic demands are sometimes placed upon them, which are never asked of the existing practice.
  An open, online conference may well bring in different audiences who would not attend physical conferences, and these participants will have different expectations. The traditional conference format doesn't appeal to some people, but their voices are not heard because they don't go to conferences.

Online conferences are different entities to face-to-face conferences. They have different advantages, disadvantages, modes of operation and interactions. Just as with elearning it is a mistake to only compare them with the existing practice because it's what they do *differently* that's intriguing.

Conclusion

This chapter has explored the concept of network weather as a metaphor for the impact of open, digital networked approaches on scholarly practice. The network weather argument suggests that changes in your environment are occurring because of other people's use of these technologies and the behaviour they facilitate, even if as an individual you are not engaged with them.

The example of the academic conference was used to map this onto scholarship as it is a practice common across all disciplines. There are a number of ways in which the interactions, structure and record of a physical conference are being altered by the use of these technologies. This occurs both through the informal adoption of technologies by attendees and the formal deployment of them by conference organisers in order to amplify their event.

This may seem confined to conferences with a technology focus presently, but it is likely to follow the familiar Rogers (1962) diffusion of innovation S-shaped curve. Whenever new technologies are adopted in education, the first examples are where the technology itself is a focus. For example, initial elearning courses were often about the Internet, so the use of the technology was part of the learning experience. As practice becomes standardised and more robust, it spreads and the use of the technology becomes less of a barrier. Now elearning courses are commonplace in all disciplines, from Shakespeare to statistics. The same will occur with changes in conferences. It may start with a handful of attendees blogging an event, and some others sharing photographs from their iPhones on Flickr, while some of the research students connect via Twitter. The following year the conference organisers propose a common hashtag and the conference is on its way to becoming an amplified event, and network weather is gathering.

It is not just in conferences that we see the network weather effect. In teaching, for example, a lecturer may find that a student at the back of the class is asking challenging questions because they are watching a Stanford University professor talk about this subject on iTunes U, or a lecture-based course may find itself in competition with an open, online course on the same topic, or students may be sharing up-to-date resources via Facebook. In most of this book I have been arguing for the positive impact of new technologies, but there is also a more harsh realism stance, which states that it is not whether new behaviours are an improvement but that they are occurring anyway. As with the industries examined in Chapter 3, attempts to prevent this through technical or legislative prohibitions are rarely successful, so the onus is on higher education to adapt and find benefits that are inherent in an open, digital networked approach.

11 Reward and Tenure

Whenever the subject of digital scholarship is raised, it almost inevitably results in the discussion of reward and tenure. This is understandable, not just because individuals wish to progress in their career, but because it exposes what is really valued in academia. If it isn't valued, goes the argument, then it isn't recognised when it comes to getting promotion.

What I want to explore in this chapter are the barriers (perceived and actual) to the recognition of digital scholarship and the ways in which some institutions are attempting to address these.

The tenure process

Promotion and tenure are usually judged on a combination of three factors: research, teaching and service or management. Some universities expand on these to include factors such as contribution to society and academic esteem, but these three represent the main categories. These are supposedly weighted equally, often with candidates required to demonstrate outstanding achievement in at least two of the three. It is often rumoured that there is an unspoken rule that research is regarded as more significant. As Harley *et al.* (2010) summarise it, 'advancement in research universities is often described as a "three-legged stool," with a "research" leg that is far more important'.

In putting together a case for promotion, academics then need to provide evidence to support their case in these three areas (although not all three may be represented equally). For teaching this is usually straightforward – a list of courses that have been taught (perhaps with student ratings). Service can equate to work on committees, or management responsibility, but can also be a little more nebulous, for example, making the case for external work such as work with a professional body. Research is the most difficult to accurately represent, particularly to committee members who are unlikely to be experts in the subject area of the individual and thus will require explanation and clarification on the nature of that individual's contribution to the field.

One can appreciate the complexity of this task across a university with many different niche subject areas, which people in the same discipline may be unfamiliar with, to say nothing of a general university panel. Whereas teaching will usually be to an understood and agreed curriculum and service is predominantly represented by university committees, which are broadly understood and appreciated, research is precisely the area of a scholar's activity that is most specialised. It is the area that is thus most difficult for a general committee to assess. There is thus something of a conundrum around research in the promotion process – it is the most highly regarded of the three strands and yet the most difficult to judge. It is this complexity in quantifying research combined with its significance that sits at the heart of many of the issues relating to digital scholarship and tenure.

Recognising and rewarding digital scholarship is significant for two reasons. The first is the message it sends to individuals within the university. Because they operate in an open, digital, networked manner, digital scholars are often well known in their institution (e.g. many of their colleagues will read their blogs). If a well-known digital scholar struggles to get their work recognised, then it sends a message to the rest of the university that this is not the type of activity that is likely to be rewarded, with a subsequent decline in its uptake. The reverse happens if that digital scholar is rewarded; it sends the positive message that academics should engage in this type of activity.

The second reason to recognise digital scholarship is to encourage institutional innovation. For example, universities are beginning to explore the use of Facebook to support students, or the use of blogs to disseminate research findings to the public, or new models of course development based on third-party content and crowdsourcing. There are very real benefits to the institution from these approaches, for instance reaching new audiences, increasing the university's profile without advertising, increasing student retention through improved peer support, lowering the costs of course production, developing new research methodology and so on. But it is difficult to realise any of these institutional approaches to new media if there is not a solid base of digital scholarship experience to draw upon.

The digital scholarship barriers

Before examining some of the approaches institutions have taken to recognising and rewarding digital scholarship, it is worth considering the barriers and obstacles that many perceive in its recognition. We have already touched upon some of these in Chapter 5, where we saw that a reluctance to engage with new technology or new methods of dissemination was often rooted in fears that this work was not recognised. This is reinforced by advice from senior academics to new researchers to concentrate on traditional, recognised publishing routes as these were the recognised paths to reward. It is worth noting that there is nothing in this argument about the actual benefits or efficacy of traditional publishing over other methods; it is based purely on a pragmatic approach to 'playing the promotion game'.

In a comprehensive study on scholarly communication, Harley *et al.* (2010) found that the strong lock-in with the published journal article and monograph was the overriding factor in consideration for promotion, commenting that

> enthusiasm for the development and adoption of technology should not be conflated with the hard reality of tenure and promotion requirements in highly competitive and complex professional environments. Experiments in new genres of scholarship and dissemination are occurring in every field, but they are taking place within the context of relatively conservative value and reward systems that have the practice of peer review at their core.

Chapter 12 will look at academic publishing in more detail, as it is a practice that runs through scholarship and exerts an enormous influence. It is probably the single most significant influencing factor in recognising digital scholarship.

The first, and fundamental, barrier is the recognition of digital scholarship as an activity that is worthy of appreciation. This is distinct from concerns about how best to represent and measure it. There is, undoubtedly, an element of snobbery in this. Like most bloggers, I have experienced (and still experience) sniggers at the suggestion that blogging is a serious academic practice (to say nothing of the use of social networks). This is based partly on a perception, often perpetuated by traditional media, that the use of such tools is frivolous, egotistical and unprofessional. For instance, when the BBC political broadcaster Andrew Marr dismissed bloggers as 'socially inadequate, pimpled, single, slightly seedy, bald, cauliflower-nosed young men sitting in their mother's basements and ranting. They are very angry people' (Plunkett 2010), there was a degree of sage nodding amongst many academics. Such responses are predictable when a new form of communication presents itself, particularly from entrenched industries, who have the most to lose. We saw similar reactions to radio, television, computers and mobile phones. Cheverie, Boettcher and Buschman (2009) argue that there is a strong bias towards print, or traditional, publication: 'While this community talks about 'publication', the language used implies that digital scholarship is of significantly lesser value, and word of mouth to younger colleagues discourages digital scholarship in the hiring, tenure and promotion process.'

More significantly though the resistance to recognising digital scholarship reflects a more intractable problem – one has to experience the use of these technologies over a prolonged period to appreciate their value and the nature of interactions. In short, you have to do social media to get social media. Given that many senior managers and professors in universities are not people who are disposed towards using these tools, there is a lack of understanding about them at the level which is required to implement significant change in the institution. The membership of promotion committees is most likely to be drawn from senior academics, who have largely been successful with the traditional model of scholarship. Although these academics will have a wealth of experience, they come from a background that may have a limited understanding of the new forms of scholarly practice that utilise different media and technologies.

But there does seem to be a move in many universities to recognise digital scholarship to some extent. This starts with the reasonably uncontroversial recognition that online journals have a similar standing to print ones, particularly when many major publishers are converting many existing titles to online only. Scholfeld and Housewright (2010) reports that there is a general move to online journals with most academics now content to see this shift happen, away from print.

In the arts there has been a tradition of recognising a portfolio of work when considering promotion, and this has inevitably led to inclusion of digital artefacts. In the sciences other components have been recognised prior to more recent developments, including software and data. In an instance of Bellow's Law we now have conditions under which there is sufficient loosening of the strictures on what constitutes evidence to permit a wider range to be considered.

A willingness to recognise new types of output and activity brings into focus the next significant barrier, which is how to measure or recognise quality in these widely varied formats. The problem highlighted above of dealing with complexity in research has essentially been outsourced by universities to publishers. The peer-review process that leads to publication combined with a journal's impact factor act as a quality filter, thus removing the necessity for promotion committees to assess the quality of the outputs themselves. Journals have quality rankings, and therefore publication in any journal of sufficient standing is an indication of quality. As Waters (2000) puts it, 'to a considerable degree people in departments stopped assessing for themselves the value of a candidate as a scholar and started waiting for the presses to decide'.

Peer review is at the core of this practice and is seen as fundamental. Harley et al. (2010) stress that '[t]he degree to which peer review, despite its perceived shortcomings, is considered to be an important filter of academic quality, cannot be overstated.' This highlights the problem with recognising new types of output and activity. The power of many of the new forms of communication lies in their democratisation of the publishing process. They have removed the filter which the tenure process has come to rely on so heavily. Without this filter in place promotion committees are back in the position of having to find a means of assessing the quality of research activity of an individual in a field they know little about. This is now confounded as it may be in a format they know little about too.

Assessing quality in a reliable and transparent manner is a significant problem in the recognition of digital scholarship, and its intangibility and complexity are enough to make many give up and fall back on the practices they know and trust. However, for the reasons I suggested above, it is a problem worth grappling with, and in the next section we will look at some of the ways in which this is being attempted.

Recognising digital scholarship

The response to recognition of digital scholarship can take a variety of forms, some more radical than others. The approaches can be summarised as follows:

- recreating the existing model

- finding digital equivalents

- generating guidelines that include digital scholarship

- using metrics

- peer review

- micro-credit

- developing alternative methods

Recreating the existing model

If we take these in order, recreating existing models is a reasonable first step. Methods of recreating the existing model in digital scholarship terms include adding in a layer of peer review to blog-like practices or making conventional journals more open. For instance, a number of journals now operate a model where the author (or more likely, the author's institution) pays to have an article made open access. Publishers charge between $500 and $3,000 for this model, and as Waltham (2009) reports take-up has been limited with 73 per cent of publishers reporting 5 per cent or less adoption of this model. This is hardly surprising and highlights one of the problems with attempting to recreate current practice. We will look at the economics of the academic publishing industry in more detail later, but given that scholars have provided the writing, editing, and reviewing time free of charge, it seems somewhat unlikely that they will then pay to have the article published online, when it can be done freely by their own means. An attempt then to graft the open, digital, networked approach onto existing practice and then continue as normal fails to address many of the more fundamental issues and also the possibilities afforded by the new technologies.

Digital equivalents

An improvement on this is to seek digital equivalents for the types of evidence currently accepted in promotion cases. In making a case for excellence in one of the three main promotion criteria, the scholar is required to provide evidence. We have become so accustomed to many of these forms of evidence that we have ceased to view them as evidence but rather as an endpoint in themselves. For example, a good track record in peer-review publication should not be the ultimate goal, but rather it is indicative of other more significant contributions including effective research as judged by your peers, impact upon your subject area and scholarly communication. Thus if we examine what each of the accepted pieces of evidence are seen to represent, and assuming these are scholarly values we wish to perpetuate, then it may be possible to find equivalents in an open, digital, networked context which demonstrate the same qualities. For example, the keynote talk at a conference is often cited as one valid piece of evidence of esteem for an individual seeking promotion. The reasons are twofold: Reputation – it demonstrates that they have gained significant standing in their field to be asked regularly to give a keynote talk at a conference; impact – if they are giving the keynote then everyone at the conference hears it, and they can therefore claim a significant impact in their subject.

The important element then is not the keynote itself but what it *signifies*. What might a digital equivalent of this be which meets the two criteria above? For example, if someone gives a talk and converts this to a slidecast of that presentation, a certain number of views might equate to impact (how many people would hear a live presentation?). If the presentation is retweeted, linked to, embedded, then this might give an indication of reputation.

It would be overly simplistic to provide straightforward translations along the lines of 500 views + 5 embeds = 1 keynote, but by focusing on the existing criteria and considering what it is they are meant to demonstrate, it is then possible to consider online equivalents.

The New Media Department at the University of Maine has taken a similar approach in suggesting a number of 'alternative recognition measures' (Blais, Ippolito and Smith 2007):

- Invited/edited publications – if an individual is invited to publish in an online journal that is an indication of reputation.

- Live conferences – they suggest raising the profile of the conference (both face to face and virtual) to a par with peer-review publication, particularly in fast-moving subjects.

- Citations – they suggest using Google and databases to find a better measure of citations and impact.

- Download/visitor counts – downloads of articles or visits to an academic site can be seen as equivalent to citations.

- Impact in online discussions – forums, discussion lists and blogs are 'the proving grounds of new media discourse' with significant impact and a high degree of scrutiny and peer evaluation.

- Impact in the real world – this might be in the form of newspaper references but they also argue that Google search returns can be a measure of real-world impact.

- Net-native recognition metrics – online communities can have their own measures of value, and these represent a more appropriate measure than one imposed upon the contributor from outside.

- Reference letters – they suggest reference letters which may counteract some of the difficulty with traditional recognition systems.

The faculty of the Humanities at the University of Nebraska-Lincoln have similarly developed a set of specific equivalents for recognition, including links to the scholar's research, peer review of digital research sites and technical innovation (http://cdrh.unl.edu/articles/promotion_and_tenure.php).

Digital scholarship guidelines

The recommendations above specify a number of approaches to recognising digital scholarship activity. A more common approach is to produce more general guidelines which set out broader criteria for assessing the quality of scholarly activity. These can include a catch-all term to accommodate new forms of outputs, for example, the Open University promotion guidelines state that 'other appropriate outputs from scholarship can be taken into account including a demonstrable influence upon academic communication mediated through online and related web mediated technologies that influences the discipline'.

The Committee on Information Technology of the Modern Languages Association (MLA) has developed its own guidelines for promotion committees to consider when dealing with digital media in the modern languages (http://www.mla.org/guidelines_evaluation_digital):

- Delineate and communicate responsibilities. When candidates wish to have work with digital media considered, the expectations and responsibilities connected with such work and the recognition given to it should be clearly delineated and communicated to them at the point of employment.

- Engage qualified reviewers. Faculty members who work with digital media should have their work evaluated by persons knowledgeable about the use of these media in the candidate's field. At times this may be possible only by engaging qualified reviewers from other institutions.

- Review work in the medium in which it was produced. Since scholarly work is sometimes designed for presentation in a specific medium, evaluative bodies should review faculty members' work in the medium in which it was produced. For example, web-based projects should be viewed online, not in printed form.

- Seek interdisciplinary advice. If faculty members have used technology to collaborate with colleagues from other disciplines on the same campus or on different campuses, departments and institutions should seek the assistance of experts in those other disciplines to assess and evaluate such interdisciplinary work.

- Stay informed about accessibility issues. Search, reappointment, promotion and tenure committees have a responsibility to comply with federal regulations and to become and remain informed of technological innovations that permit persons with disabilities to conduct research and carry out other professional responsibilities effectively.

Some of these will seem like common sense, for example, reviewing work in the medium in which it was produced, but even such a small step may come up against opposition when there is a strictly regulated promotion process which has bee designed to suit the needs of print outputs.

Metrics

One approach to overcoming, or at least easing, the complexity of judging individual cases is the use of metrics or statistical calculations to measure impact or influence. This has been an area of increasing interest even with traditional publications. This measure of impact is often represented by a statistical measure such as the '*h*-index', which is based upon bibliometric calculations of citations using a specific set of publisher databases. This measure seeks to identify references to one publication within another giving 'an estimate of the importance, significance, and broad impact of a scientist's cumulative research contributions' (Hirsch 2005). Promising though this may sound it is a system that can be cheated, or gamed (Falagas and Alexiou 2008), for instance, by authors referencing previous papers or between groups, and so a continual cycle of detecting such behaviours and then eliminating them is entered into, rather akin to the battle fought between computer-virus makers and antivirus software. The Research Excellence Framework (REF) examined the potential of using such measures as a part of the assessment process and found that currently available systems and data were 'not sufficiently robust to be used formulaically or as a primary indicator of quality; but there is considerable scope for it to inform and enhance the process of expert review' (HEFCE 2010).

There are at least three further degrees of separation from this walled garden approach to citations. The first is to use data outside of a proprietary database as a measure of an article's impact. This 'webometrics' approach was identified early on as offering potential to get richer information about the use of an article, by analysing the links to an article, downloads from a server and citations across the web (e.g. Marek and Valauskas 2002). Cronin *et al.* (1998) argue that this data could 'give substance to modes of influence which have historically been backgrounded in narratives of science'.

The next step is to broaden this webometrics approach to include the more social, Web 2.0 tools. This covers references to articles in social networks such as Twitter and blogs, social bookmarking tools such as CiteULike and recommendation tools such as Digg (Patterson 2009). This recognises that a good deal of academic discourse now takes place outside of the formal journal, and there is a wealth of data that can add to the overall representation of an article's influence.

The ease of participation, which is a key characteristic of these tools, also makes them even more subject to potential gaming. As Priem and Hemminger (2010) report, there are services which can attempt to increase the references from services such as Digg to a site (or article) for a fee. But they are reasonably optimistic that gaming can be controlled, proposing that 'one particular virtue of an approach examining multiple social media ecosystems is that data from different sources could be cross-calibrated, exposing suspicious patterns invisible in single source'.

A more radical move away from the citation work that has been conducted so far is to extend metrics to outputs beyond the academic article. A digital scholar is likely to have a distributed online identity, all of which can be seen to represent factors such as reputation, impact, influence and productivity. Establishing a digital scholar footprint across these services is problematic because people will use different tools, so the standard unit of the scholarly article is lacking. Nevertheless one could begin to establish a representation of scholarly activity by analysing data from a number of sites, such as the individual's blog, Twitter, Slideshare and YouTube accounts, and then also using the webometrics approach to analyse the references to these outputs from elsewhere. A number of existing tools seek to perform this function for blogs; for example, PostRank tracks the conversation around blog posts, including comments, Twitter links and delicious bookmarks. These metrics are not without their problems and achieving a robust measure is still some way off, but there is a wealth of data now available which can add to the overall case an individual makes.

Peer review

The issue of gaming is even more prevalent with metrics, and this is confounded by the mix of personal and professional outputs which are evident in many of these tools. This brings us onto the next approach in recognising digital scholarship, which is the use of peer-assessment. When the filter of peer-review publication is removed, or lowered in significance, then arguably the significance of peer review in the tenure process increases. It will be necessary to determine that the output and activity are indeed scholarly (after all, one could have a popular blog on bee-keeping which had no relevance to your position as professor of English Literature). It is also a response to the increased complexity of judging digital scholarship cases. The MLA guidelines above recommend using external experts to perform this peer review for tenure committees who may be unfamiliar with both the subject matter and the format.

Others have taken this approach further, soliciting commendations from their wider online network (e.g. Becker 2009). There is obviously an issue around objectivity with this approach, but as promotion committees seek to deal with a wider range of activity and outputs, judging their impact will need to involve feedback from the community itself.

Micro-credit

In Chapter 5 on research, I suggested that new methods of communication have allowed a finer granularity of research, that in effect the dissemination route had an influence on what could be deemed research. This finer granularity, or shift to process away from outputs, is another difficulty for recognising digital scholarship. One approach may be to shift to awarding 'micro-credit' for activity – so, for example, a blog post which attracts a number of comments and links can be recognised but to a lesser degree than a fully peer-reviewed article. Finer granularity in the types of evidence produced would allow recognition of not just outputs but also the type of network behaviour which is crucial to effective digital scholarship. Smith Rumsey (2010) suggests that 'perhaps there should be different units of micro-credit depending on the type of contribution, from curating content to sustaining the social network to editing and managing the entire communication enterprise of a collaborative scholarly blogging operation'.

Alternative methods

The last of the approaches to recognising digital scholarship is really a call to encourage new practices which seek to reimagine scholarship. The seven approaches suggested above can be viewed as a continuum of departure from the conventional model. Much of the attempts to gain recognition for digital scholarship seem to be focused around making it behave like traditional scholarship; for example, permitting webometric data for journal article analysis is interesting, but it still foregrounds the peer-reviewed article as the main form of evidence.

Bending new technology to fit existing practice is a common reaction, partly because we are unaware of its potential. Stephen Heppell (2001) declares that 'we continually make the error of subjugating technology to our present practice rather than allowing it to free us from the tyranny of past mistakes'. There is something of this in the approach to recognising digital scholarship – it is often a case of trying to make everything fit into the pre-existing shaped containers, rather than exploring new possibilities.

Promotion committees can play a significant role in this not only by recognising new forms of scholarship but also by positively encouraging them, either through guidelines or through specific projects. For example, a committee might seek to develop the sort of Web 2.0 metrics mentioned above or to encourage alternatives to the peer-review model. In analysing the peer-review process Fitzpatrick (2009) makes a strong case that we need to move beyond merely seeking equivalence measures:

> What I am absolutely *not* arguing is that we need to ensure that peer-reviewed journals online are considered of equivalent value to peer-reviewed journals in print; in fact, I believe that such an equation is instead part of the problem I am addressing. Imposing traditional methods of peer review on digital publishing might help a transition to digital publishing in the short term, enabling more traditionally minded scholars to see electronic and print scholarship as equivalent in value; but it will hobble us in the long term, as we employ outdated methods in a public space that operates under radically different systems of authorization.

Conclusion

The already difficult task of assessing research and scholarly activity in highly specialised fields is only going to be made more difficult by introducing digital scholarship. Previously there has been an agreed set of evidence which could be seen as acting as a proxy for excellence in research. Not only does this list need to be expanded to include digital scholarship outputs but it may also be that no such definitive list can be provided any more.

In recognising digital scholarship activity in the tenure process, the initial barrier to overcome is that it constitutes valid scholarly activity and is not merely an adjunct to the traditional approaches. If this obstacle is overcome in an institution, then the next issue is in finding ways of accurately representing it which don't immediately remove the benefits of these approaches or place inappropriate constrictions. For instance, judging a blog on the same criteria as one might review a journal article fails to recognise the type of discourse which is effective in the blogging community. Many of the characteristics which would be frowned upon in scholarly articles, such as subjectivity, humour, and personal opinion, are vital elements in developing a dialogue in blogs.

There are a number of ways in which promotion committees can begin to address digital scholarship. What they may be leading to is a more portfolio-based approach, perhaps more akin to that found in the arts. Anderson (2009) suggests that the sciences have an advantage in recognising digital scholarship because they are more ready to adopt new technology, but it may be that the arts with its more individual assessment models is well disposed towards incorporating different forms of output. Such a portfolio-based approach is likely to draw on a range of tools and pieces of evidence. These may include a range of digital outputs, metrics demonstrating impact, commendations from the community and recognised experts and an overarching narrative making the case for the work as a whole.

Although the thrust of this chapter has been the ways in which the tenure process inhibits digital scholarship, and the approaches it is beginning to take in recognising it, the tenure process is not solely to blame for the reluctance of many scholars to engage with the open, digital networked approach. About a third of faculty thought that the tenure practice unnecessarily constrained publishing choice, and in assessing the importance of the various functions of a scholarly society it was the publication of peer-reviewed journals that was deemed most significant (Scholfeld and Housewright 2010). It would be inaccurate then to portray the situation as one of a reservoir of digital scholarship activity being held back by the dam of the tenure process. Peer review in particular is a process held dear by the faculty themselves and not an outside imposition by the tenure process. This is for good reason as it is the method by which researchers gain their authority. But we should consider peer review as a method of achieving other goals such as reliability and authority, not an end in itself, and there may be other means of achieving this which the new technologies allow. Peer review in itself should not be the sole determinant of authority or an obstacle to experimentation. Fitzpatrick (2009) rather colourfully suggests that 'peer review threatens to become the axle around which the whole issue of electronic scholarly publishing gets wrapped, like Isadora Duncan's scarf, choking the life out of many innovative systems before they are fully able to establish themselves'.

Even if much of the resistance comes from faculty themselves, the role of the tenure process is still highly significant. If a third of faculty see it as a constraint, that still represents a sufficiently large group that would be encouraged to engage in digital scholarship more if the tenure process were more sympathetic. In addition, there is the message it sends and the positive reinforcement it provides. If digital scholarship activity is a route to tenure, then those seeking it will engage in the types of activity that are recognised.

What is perhaps most interesting in examining the tenure and reward process is that it is yet another example of the unintended consequences of technology adoption. This is what is really fascinating about the open, digital networked technologies – not the technologies themselves but rather what occurs as a consequence of their uptake by individuals. As existing practices are unpicked, it forces us to ask fundamental questions about these practices, which have hitherto been assumed. For example, it may seem a small step to start recognising some of the webometric measures of a journal article's influence, but this leads to questions about what constitutes impact and why is a blog with a higher readership regarded as less influential than a journal article? This in turn leads to an examination of what promotion committees recognise and, more fundamentally, what these are deemed to represent. From a fairly modest and uncontroversial starting position, institutions and individuals can soon find themselves examining some very deep issues about the nature of scholarship and universities themselves. This is another instance of Bellow's law, and it perhaps suggests why many institutions are reluctant to begin the process of recognising digital scholarship – it quickly unravels established practice and raises difficult questions.

Answering difficult questions is the essence of scholarship, and one of the most difficult of all in this area is what is the relationship between scholarship and publishing? This is what Chapter 12 will seek to address.

It is worth emphasising that monetary reward and promotion are not the sole, or even main, driver for most scholarly activity. The reasons why scholars engage in research, disseminate their findings and teach on courses are varied, but they are primarily driven by intellectual curiosity. It is not, therefore, the suggestion of this chapter that digital scholars should pursue any of the digital, networked and open approaches *because* they can lead to tenure. Rather, my purpose is to argue that if these approaches are achieving scholarly functions via different means, that they should be recognised as such and the tenure process acts as something of a proxy for this recognition. To ignore the context within which scholars operate within their institutions would be to disadvantage new practices compared with established ones.

12 Publishing

Chapter 11 examined the tenure and reward process and how closely allied it is to publishing. The printed word has played such a central role in the development of scholarship that at times academia can seem little more than an adjunct to the publishing business; we do after all refer to the academic *paper*. The central role of publishing has a long history in academia, with *The Philosophical Transactions of the Royal Society* being published in 1665. The nature of the academic article and the associated peer-review model developed until it became the accepted practice across most disciplines (it is a model not well suited to the arts, which focuses more on portfolios of work). This chapter will look at how the academic publishing business operates, some of the issues it now faces, the alternatives that are being developed as a result of technologies and where it might be heading. If any practice is central to the nature of scholarship it is that of the academic publication (be it book or article), and no focus better illustrates the tensions between existing practice and the possibilities offered by a digital, networked, open approach.

The academic publishing business

A research student of mine was thinking about submitting his first paper to an academic journal. He casually asked how much he would be paid for his contribution, acknowledging it probably wouldn't be much. I explained that not only would he not be paid but that for some journals the authors were themselves expected to pay for the article to be published. He was shocked by this revelation, 'but, they sell the journals don't they?' In return, my student's reaction caused me to take a backward step and reappraise the model we have come to accept in scholarship. And when you do so, the inevitable conclusion is that academic publishing is a strange business.

The conventional academic publishing model is comprised of the following steps:

1 Research – academics will engage in research, either funded by a research body or as part of their institutional contract.

2 Authoring – either in collaboration or as sole author, academics write articles.

3 Submission and review – the article is submitted to a journal, where the editor will often perform an initial quick review to ascertain whether it is

broadly suitable and then put out to review by recognised scholars in the field. Some journals have paid editors and reviewers, but the majority are volunteers who provide their labour for free.

4   Rejection/modification – following review the paper can be accepted, require revision or be rejected. If rejected the process may begin again with a different journal.

5   Publication – the article is published in a journal after a process of copyediting, adding data and formatting.

6   Dissemination – the journals are sold to libraries and other institutions often on a subscription model, or the article can be purchased via a one-off payment.

When authors agree to publication with a journal, they are usually required to sign a copyright form, assigning the rights of that specific paper, but not all of the intellectual property therein, to the publishers. There are thus three main parties in the process: the academic authors, the publishers and the libraries and purchasers. In most cases the academic authors are employed by universities and institutions, which also house the libraries that purchase the content, with the publishers acting as an intermediary. Other participants include research funders who provide the money for the initial research and the readers of the finished article. Given that the authors provide their services for free, and the same institutions that employ these then purchase the outcome of their labour, it does seem an unusual business model when viewed objectively.

So why do the first and last of our three main parties in the process, scholars and institutions, participate in the process? Here are probably five main elements to the answer:

1   Accepted practice – this is how respected peers in their field operate, and through the process of research studentship it is the practice they have been enculturated into.

2   Academic respectability – journals operate as a quality filter, using the peer-review method to ensure that (usually) journals are of an appropriate standard and have used a sound methodology. Being published in journals then is the accepted method by which research is perceived as credible and respectable.

3   Reward and tenure – as we saw in Chapter 11, the process of tenure is often linked to a strong publication profile.

4 Dissemination – publishers have well-established dissemination routes, so an article in a respectable journal will be made available via libraries, online databases, search engines and so on.

5 Curation – there is a durability and process for preserving articles for future access, through relationships with libraries and their own archiving practice.

This model has operated well for many years, and certainly when there was a reliance on printed journals there seemed little alternative. But as we see an increasing shift to online journals, inevitable questions about the sustainability and desirability of a print-based model have been raised. This is a fine example of Bellow's law in action yet again – once the journal has been liberated from the printed format, a number of related assumptions begin to unravel and lead to more fundamental questions. Before we look at these, however, it is worth examining the publishing business in more detail.

For each of our three players we can look at some recent market analysis. In terms of the authors, the Joint Information Systems Committee (JISC) review by Houghton *et al.* (2009) estimate that in the United Kingdom alone, in 2007, writing peer-reviewed articles costs around £1.6 billion (in terms of academic time), with an additional £200 million for peer review and a further £70 million for editorial costs. For the publishers, Bousfield and Fooladi (2009) size the science, technical and medical 'information marketplace' (which is largely publishing and related products) at $23.1 billion in 2009. There are three big publishing firms, Reed-Elsevier, Springer and Wiley, who account for 42 per cent of all journal articles published. Of these, Elsevier, the academic publishing branch of Reed-Elsevier which focuses on science and medical publication, reported profits of $693 million in 2009, with Reed-Elsevier reporting operating profits of $1.5 billion (Reed-Elsevier 2009). There are about 22,000 peer-reviewed journals in publication, from some 9,900 publishers (Waltham 2009). McGuigan and Russell (2008) report that for the last of the key participants, the libraries, the economic situation has become increasingly tough, with costs for journals increasing 302 per cent from 1986 to 2005, while the number of items purchased has only increased 1.9 per cent per year, and on average journals have increased in price by 7.6 per cent per annum.

What this brief summary indicates is that academic publishing is a significant global business and that in times of financial crisis there is a squeeze on the middle of our participants, the publishers. This pressure is coming from the individual scholars (and more significantly, the research funding bodies) in terms of open access and from libraries with regards to the deals they are making with publishers. We will look at open access in more detail later, but for the libraries the situation is becoming critical. Many libraries have signed what are termed 'big deal' contracts, whereby publishers sell a subscription to their online catalogue, with annual increments. However, if a library wishes to cancel one or two journals then the cost of the others increases. When libraries are facing cuts in their annual budgets, the Big Deal packages become expensive to maintain. A number of universities (e.g. Cornell) have withdrawn from the Big Deal, and many others are seeking to renegotiate. I would contend that it is not these contracts with publishers that are of interest to digital scholarship but rather that the financial pressures and the possibilities offered by new technologies create an environment wherein scholars, libraries, universities and research funders are asking fundamental questions about the scholarly communication process, and often the current model does not stand up to scrutiny.

David Wiley presents a parable, that of the inventor, who having struggled for years finally has an invention she wants to take to market:

> [T]he inventor began contacting shipping companies. But she could not believe what she heard. The truckers would deliver her goods, but only subject to the most unbelievable conditions:
>
> - The inventor had to sign all the intellectual-property rights to her product over to the truckers.
>
> - The truckers would keep all the profits from sales of the inventor's product.
>
> - The shipping deal had to be both exclusive and perpetual, never subject to review or cancellation.
>
> Every shipping company she contacted gave the same response. Dejected, but unwilling to see the fruits of all her labor go to waste, she eventually relented and signed a contract with one of the companies. (Wiley 2009b)

Prior to the advent of new technologies, academics had little choice but to go along with the trucker's deal in Wiley's parable. And, as Edwards and Shulenburger Shulenburger (2003) suggest, it operated successfully when it was seen as a fair exchange, a 'gift economy', but they claim, 'beginning in the late 1960s and early '70s, this gift exchange began to break down. A few commercial publishers recognized that research generated at public expense and given freely for publication by the authors represented a commercially exploitable commodity'. To return to a theme of this book, what we now have are alternatives to a previously rigid system, and these alternatives are driven by new technologies.

Open access publishing

Before addressing alternatives to the current publishing model, it is important to appreciate the functions it provides, to evaluate whether they are necessary and, if so, how they can be realised in any new model. Clarke (2007) suggests the following functions beyond the dissemination of content:

- quality assurance:
    - for relevance to the particular journal;
    - for content (semantics) – which would be perceived by many people as the journal's central function;
    - for expression (syntactics);
    - for presentation (formatting and visual style), including 'branding';
    - for discoverability (in particular, keywords and citation format);
- promotion, marketing and selling;
- logistics (i.e. distribution or access, depending on whether a push or pull model is used);
- revenue collection;
- responsibility for contingent liabilities, including copyright infringement, breach of confidence, defamation, negligence, negligent misstatement, misleading or deceptive conduct, contempt of court and breach of laws relating to censorship, discrimination, racial vilification, harassment and privacy; and
- governance.

Geyer-Schulz *et al.* (2003) meanwhile suggest six 'core processes of value-adding activities': content direction, content packaging, market making, transport, delivery support and services, and interface and systems.

Open access (OA) publishing often seeks to effectively replicate these functions of the publishing model but to make the outputs of that process openly available to all. What constitutes 'open access' is a source of much debate, but the ostensible aim is to remove (not just reduce) barriers to access. The Budapest Open Access Initiative (http://www.soros.org/openaccess) proposes that by open access literature they mean it's free availability on the public internet, permitting any users to read, download, copy, distribute, print, search, or link to the full texts of these articles, crawl them for indexing, pass them as data to software, or use them for any other lawful purpose, without financial, legal, or technical barriers other than those inseparable from gaining access to the internet itself'. A simple definition is 'digital, online, free of charge, and free of most copyright and licensing restrictions' (Suber 2004).

Inevitably there are variations on 'pure open access' and debates as to whether a particular approach is open or not. For example, many journals which still operate a proprietary, closed approach will permit 'self-archiving' of a pre-print by the author, so they can upload this to their blog or a repository. This route can be very successful; for example, the physics pre-print repository arXiv.org has become the *de facto* reference site for physicists. Some publishers will demand an embargo and exclusivity of a set period (typically 6–18 months) before permitting archiving, which most open access advocates would argue contravenes the spirit of open access, and what length embargo is deemed acceptable? With the advent of good search tools self-archiving means a version of the article can often be found for free, although it doesn't guarantee this, and it relies on individual authors to be willing and competent to self-archive. In addition, if reputation and tenure are linked to citations and downloads from a central database it is not in the author's interest to 'dilute' their statistics from the official ones measured in the publisher's database.

Self-archiving is often termed Green OA, while open access journals are labelled 'Gold OA'. The two are not mutually exclusive; the Budapest Open Access Initiative in 2001 was the first attempt to formalise and mobilise the open access movement, and it proposes that 'open access to peer-reviewed journal literature is the goal. Self-archiving and a new generation of open access journals are the ways to attain this goal' (Budapest Open Access Initiative 2002). Peter Suber (2009) agrees, arguing that 'OA archiving and OA journals are complementary and need to proceed simultaneously, much as an organism develops its nervous system and digestive system simultaneously and cannot do one first and the other second'. Stephen Harnad disagrees, suggesting that Green OA is 'faster' and 'surer' (Harnad *et al.* 2004).

Within the 'Gold OA' approach there are a number of alternatives. A model currently favoured by many publishers is that of 'author pays', wherein the cost of open access to the publisher is shifted to the author. Fees range between $1,000 and $3,000 per article although even these fees may not be sufficient to cover current publishing models (Waltham 2009). Having invested heavily in proprietary software systems and infrastructure to maintain a competitive advantage, the cost to existing publishers for open access e-journal articles is calculated at $3,400 per article. Non-profit organisations, such as professional societies, have tended to choose cheaper software options, such as the open source journal management system Open Journal Systems (OJS), and see a significantly reduced cost per article of $730 (Clarke 2007).

Although open access publishing is primarily concerned with the problem of access to journal articles, there is a related issue of the underlying affordability of the publishing model. Author-pays models of open access may not be viable to sustain the current model of publishing, but Clarke's cost-analysis work suggests that this may be a result of excessive costs within the for-profit organisations. As he puts it, 'For-profit publishers have higher cost-profiles than not-for-profit associations, because of the additional functions that they perform, in particular their much greater investment in branding, customer relationship management and content protection.' Few of these additional functions are related to scholarly activity or knowledge dissemination. This raises questions about the additional value that publishers bring to the process. In their paper on the business of scholarly publishing McGuigan and Russell (2008) cite a report from the Deutsche bank, analysing the cost margins of academic publishers and concluding as follows:

> We believe the publisher adds relatively little value to the publishing process. We are not attempting to dismiss what 7,000 people at the publishers do for a living. We are simply observing that if the process really were as complex, costly and value-added as the publishers protest that it is, 40% margins wouldn't be available.

Some of the possibilities of publishers adding value will be explored later, but perhaps the key point here is that once alternatives have become available, it exposes the costs that are used for non-scholarly functions.

A strong driver in the open access movement has been the increasing use of open access mandates by research funding bodies. The US National Institutes of Health (NIH) revealed its Public Access Policy in 2008 (http://publicaccess.nih.gov/) which required all journal articles that arose from NIH funding to be placed in the open access PubMed archive. Many other research bodies have followed suit across the world. Similarly a number of institutions have set out mandates relating to open access; for example, Harvard's Faculty of Science and Arts adopted a self-archiving policy in 2008. The ROARMAP (Registry of Open Access Repository Material Archiving Policy) site lists all such policies, and at the time of writing 249 institutional, departmental, funder and thesis policies had been recorded (http://www.eprints.org/openaccess/policysignup/).

The advantages of open access

In the previous section we saw how cuts in library funding created one form of pressure on the current publishing model. The open access mandates of funders create another challenge. But what of the content producers, the authors themselves; what is their motivation to pursue open access or other models of publishing?

Harnad (2005) suggests six advantages for open access publishing:

1 Early advantage – you can publish earlier in the research cycle.

2 Arxiv advantage – a central repository (or repositories linked by a common data standard) provides one main place for all publications.

3 Quality bias – a self-selecting bias in that higher articles are more likely to be self-archived in the early days, but this effect would disappear as self-archiving approaches 100 per cent.

4 Quality advantage – articles are judged on quality and not on access differences.

5 Competitive advantage – self-archived papers have a competitive advantage over non-self-archived ones, in early days, although this effect would also reduce as the practice increases.

6 Usage advantage – open access articles are read more widely than non-open-access ones.

I would suggest four major motivations for individual scholars to engage with open access, two of which overlap with Harnad's list: citation advantage, the time lag to publication, copyright and alternative publishing methods.

The first is what Harnad terms the 'usage advantage'. There is strong evidence that open access journals have higher citation measures, downloads and views than those in toll-access databases (e.g. Lawrence 2001; Antelman 2004; Harnad and Brody 2004), although Davis (2010) suggests it leads only to increased readership and not citation. In publishing an academic article the author is surely seeking for it to have the greatest impact and widest dissemination (without compromising its quality or findings), and thus given a choice between the two options, the route with the higher potential for reach would seem to be the obvious choice. However, such considerations may be influenced by the range of journals in a particular field and also the reputation of specific journals. These citation improvements usually take into account the green route to open access, self-archiving, so in itself the increased citation effect is probably not sufficient to cause a substantial change beyond the requirement to self-archive.

A second motivation for individual scholars to move beyond their current approaches is an increasing frustration with the time delay between submission and final publication of an article. The process can take up to two or even three years from submission to final publication. Much of this is taken up by the peer-review process, but many journals will still be restricted by the length of each issue and frequency of publication, with many journals only releasing one or two issues per year. The delay in publication reveals a print mentality still in operation in many cases, and for a fast-moving field it renders the journals almost redundant as the main source of scholarly exchange. The advent of e-journals has seen some loosening of this approach, with accepted papers sometimes published online in advance of the actual journal issue.

A related reason for engaging with open access is the copyright agreement required by most publishers. This traditionally signs over the rights of the paper to the publisher (while authors bear all the potential risk of legal action) and places restrictions on the authors' use of their own content. This is an area that has seen considerable change in recent years, when in 2003, 83 per cent of publishers required copyright transfer, falling to 53 per cent in 2008 (Waltham 2009). The standard contract is often the default one provided, with many authors unaware that a less stringent one exists if requested. Many open access journals by contrast operate a Creative Commons licence, whereby the author retains ownership of the article.

The last factor is perhaps the most significant for the publishing model. The preceding three can all be accommodated within the existing model, with a few adjustments. The main reason that academics are beginning to question the publishing model is that they are finding alternative methods for communication, publishing and debate which are more rewarding and have none of these restrictions in place. For most authors academic writing is a creative process, and that personal satisfaction gained from engaging in a creative pursuit is something that can be found elsewhere now. I charted my own publication output before and since becoming a blogger, and found that my annual output of papers halved since becoming a blogger. This wasn't due to the time commitment usurping article-writing time but rather that the desire to write for formal publications waned. Blogging scratched the itch of creative writing and offered more immediate feedback, an opportunity to use a writing style I preferred and more impact in terms of readership. Other academics will have found similar preferences for video, or podcasts or other media. Given the benefits one finds in using a new medium, and that these speak directly to scholarly practice, the traditional journal article begins to seem remote and dry in comparison. Open access approaches seem the best route to acknowledging and utilising these other methods because the article itself is open and can be linked to and merged with other media. How one publisher is attempting to do this is the focus of the next section.

Reimagining publishing

Open access publishing can be seen as a first step in utilising the possibilities of the digital, networked and open approach to scholarly communication. But it is still close to the original model. If publishers merely switched to an author-pays model of open access, then there would be a considerable increase in terms of access, and the funding crisis would shift from libraries to research funders who would bear the brunt of these fees as they are calculated into project costs, but the model would largely remain the same, and some of the opportunities the new technologies permit would be lost.

We can explore what these opportunities might be by looking at some current examples. The first is that of PLoS, the Public Library of Science (http://www.plos. org/). PLoS was founded in 2000 as an advocacy organisation, trying to promote open access in science publishing. Although their campaigning gained support, the kind of change they wanted to happen failed to materialise, so in 2003 they set themselves up as a non-profit, open access publisher. Articles are published under a Creative Commons attribution licence, which means others are free to take them and use them, even for commercial benefit, provided they acknowledge the original author. They operate a Gold OA policy, with the author paying for publication, and have been experimenting with the appropriate price. As well as making their journals free for anyone to read, and employing the Creative Commons licence, PLoS also sought to re-engineer the publication model.

They have a range of journals which represent a continuum of experimentation with the peer-review model. PLoS Biology and PLoS Medicine are reasonably traditional, with the exceptions noted above. These are prestige journals, with paid editors and high impact factors. PLoS One is a journal for all areas of science and medicine and represents a more significant break with the traditional model. Its intention was to address the issue of the time delay in the publication process. Instead of the extensive process of peer review, PLoS One operates a more lightweight model which assesses whether the article is generally suitable, that is, whether the work is done to high scientific and ethical standards, is appropriately described and that the data support the conclusions, but makes no assessment of importance. The PLoS One site then provides tools that allow a degree of post-publication assessment, including reader ranking, comments and metrics. Operating this model they have reduced the peer review to about 100 days, compared with the usual one year. In 2010 they published 6,500 articles, and the journal has a high impact factor.

A further departure from the traditional model is provided by PLoS Currents. These aim to significantly reduce the publication time even further and are focused around particular subjects where breaking developments are essential, for example, Influenza. Using the Google Knol web-based authoring tool, authors write directly into the system. This is then reviewed rapidly by a set of experts who the editor gathers around the particular domain. These experts check for obvious methodological errors and suitability, and the work is then published. This model is free to authors.

As well as exploring variations in the peer-review process, PLoS journals have also widened the types of webometrics used to measure an article's impact. Significantly, they focus at the article level, whereas the current measure of impact is at the journal level. They have expanded impact measures beyond just the standard citation measure to include web links, social bookmarking, blog comments and so on.

Another innovation is the development of PLoS Hubs, which act as information sources for specific subjects, such as Biodiversity. These take advantage of open access by aggregating content from elsewhere and connecting the data. So, for example, if a species is named in an article then photographs from Flickr can be aggregated along with population maps, the Wikipedia definition, museum references and so on. The journal article can be seen as sitting at the heart of a network of data, which add to its richness.

What the PLoS example illustrates is that open publishing allows new forms of representation and communication. Being able to remix data and pull together journal articles and other forms of data means new layers of interpretation can be added to them, and crucially this can be done by anyone because of open licences. The result is that journal articles and their associated data will be subject to the unpredictable, generative features of the Internet, whereas their use has previously been tightly controlled.

Willinsky and Mendis (2007) offer a different take on the possibilities of new publishing models. Using the OJS software they report how a small scholarly association with only 220 members was able to establish, and maintain, a new journal at 'zero cost'. The OJS system was used to manage the review process and with the usual volunteer support for editing and reviewing, combined with online publishing using university systems, this example illustrates that the assumptions in the author-pays model of Gold OA can be challenged and that small associations can take control over their own field of publication.

More ambitious models of reforming the publication process are exploring the role of peer review. It may be that authors bypass publishers altogether; for instance, the referencing tool Mendeley allows users to upload articles, create collections, rate articles and so on. It is not difficult to imagine a scenario where authors simply upload directly to this and let the community decide on the value of an article. As highlighted in previous chapters, this could be another example of Weinberger's (2007) shift from 'filtering on the way in' to 'filtering on the way out', whereby metrics, comments, rankings and search are used to determine what information is filtered.

The issue with post-review models is not whether they are feasible (they obviously are) but whether they are desirable. Academics hold the peer-review process in high regard, and it seems to be one of those practices they are keen to retain. Ware (2008) reports on a large-scale survey of reviewers, where the vast majority felt that peer review greatly helps scientific communication and believed that without it there would be no control. There was a suspicion of open review (over anonymous, blind review), and indeed half of the respondents stated that open review would positively discourage them from reviewing. This would suggest that more radical departures from the peer-review model are unlikely, but as the PLoS example indicates it is not immune to experimentation while still retaining the essential academic function of quality and robustness.

Conclusion

This chapter has explored some elements of the academic publishing business. A number of factors are conspiring to create pressure on the standard model, with a resulting interest in open access publishing. There are strong arguments for open access, most powerfully that the publications are usually the result of tax-payer funding in terms of research or staff time. There is also a strong financial case, with Houghton *et al.* (2009) demonstrating that research funding could probably divert sufficient funds to pay for the Gold OA method to be successful and that the increased savings from both Gold and Green OA would significantly outweigh the costs.

Even without the public good or financial arguments, the case for openness in publication can be made on the basis of what it allows. If we return to Zittrain's (2008) argument that innovation occurs when you have a generative system, then storing journal publications in proprietary database acts as a restriction. The case of PLoS hubs is one example of this, with open data being aggregated around journals. But this is only a start; the key to the generative system is that it is unpredictable. One can easily imagine collections of articles being gathered together, open courses being created around open reading lists, data analysis across articles to explore connections between concepts, visual representations of arguments that link to articles and so on. In terms of scholarship it is this additional layer of interpretation and use that is perhaps of the greatest interest.

The economic and access argument against open access is difficult to sustain, so the question remains why is it that toll access is still the norm and that only a minority of authors self-archive? The answer is that we may well be in a transition state, and the picture will look different in a decade or so. But we should also explore some of the barriers to open access. The greatest of these is the current strong bonds with metrics such as the journal impact factor and the link with reward and tenure explored in Chapter 14. The opportunity to any individual for open access publishing is also a major factor. For example, if a scholar operates in a highly specialised domain, there may only be two or three reputable journals suitable for their work. If none of these operate an open access policy it is a difficult decision to eschew publication in any of them. This is where, as Harnad would argue, the Green OA route is most effective, and if authors begin to ask for this then more publishers will grant it.

I would go further and argue that given the contribution scholars make for free to the business (producing, editing and reviewing the content), we should not undervalue our work. I have committed to a personal policy of publishing solely in open access journals and also only reviewing for such journals. It is noticeable that when I reply to a request for a review by politely stating my policy it is often the first time the editor has considered the open access model. I would suggest a similar bottom-up approach from scholars in all disciplines would soon effect change.

The primary reasons reviewers gave for engaging in the peer-review process (Ware 2008) were as follows:

- to play your part as a member of the academic community,

- to enjoy being able to improve the paper,

- to enjoy seeing new work ahead of publication, and

- to reciprocate the benefit when others review your papers.

None of these motivations is undermined by an individual open access policy, and this represents the type of action whereby scholars can gain ownership over the key practices in their discipline.

A further avenue of action is to explore further the peer-review model, and how this can be modified, when it is appropriate and what other forms of evaluation are useful. No lesser a figure than the Astronomer Royal Sir Martin Rees (2010) prophesises that 'arXiv.org archive transformed the literature of physics, establishing a new model for communication over the whole of science. Far fewer people today read traditional journals. These have so far survived as guarantors of quality. But even this role may soon be trumped by a more informal system of quality control, signaled by the approbation of discerning readers'.

An approach that combines this kind of experimentation with the recognition and evaluation of other forms of digital scholarship as detailed in Chapter 11 has the potential to significantly alter both the communication and practice of research. To merely continue with the current model in a slightly modified format would overlook many of the opportunities made possible by a digital, networked, open approach. Christine Borgman (2007) warns that '[u]niversities and higher education agencies risk undermining their efforts to reform scholarly communication if they merely reinforce the norms that serve print publication and that preserve the disciplinary boundaries of the past'.

13 The Medals of Our Defeats

My argument thus far in this book has been to set out how a digital, networked, open approach *can* change scholarship. I have attempted to demonstrate that it offers alternatives to a previously limited set of options which were often created to meet the needs of physical requirements, be it the pedagogy we use to teach, the way in which we meet to share knowledge at conferences or the form of knowledge dissemination we adopt in publishing. I may not have portrayed the adoption of technology as an unalloyed force for good in scholarship, but it has largely been an argument based on the potential positive impacts. In this chapter then I want to counter this and explore some of the potential negative effects of technology because as we adopt new practices we may well find others being abandoned, and we should be aware what the cost of this is to our practice overall. I would contend that the benefits will outweigh the negatives, but just as we can't know what those benefits are if we don't engage with technology, so will we be unaware of what we lose if we do not apply our critical faculties to technology adoption.

Avoiding extremism

The use of technology seems to divide people into strong pro- and anti-camps or perhaps utopian and dystopian perspectives. Lessig (2007) points out that such an extremist divide is occurring with regard to intellectual property, on both sides, as the law intersects with the digital remix culture. On one side there are the copyright owners who will prosecute any misuse or, as with YouTube, enforce a takedown of any copyrighted material regardless of fair use. This is the type of response I categorised as a 'scarcity response' in Chapter 8. But, as harmful, Lessig suggests, are the other extremists, who reject all notions of copyright and intellectual ownership. Similar extremism can be seen with the use of technology, in society in general and in education in particular. The pro-camp will make some of the more outlandish claims we saw in Chapter 2, about the imminent revolution, the irrelevancy of higher education and the radically different net generation. The anti-technology camp will decry that it destroys social values, undermines proper scholarly practice, is always superficial and is even damaging our brains. Lessig seeks a balance between the intellectual property extremes, and a similar balance can be sought between the pro- and anti-technology camps. The remainder of this chapter will examine some of the anti-technology charges in more detail, some of which have more substance than others.

Superficiality

Nicholas Carr's (2008) article 'Is Google Making Us Stupid?' struck a chord with many people. Carr's (2010) argument, which he fleshes out in his book *The Shallows*, is that our continual use of the net induces a superficiality to our behaviour. He says this is felt particularly when trying to read a complex piece:

> Immersing myself in a book or a lengthy article used to be easy. My mind would get caught up in the narrative or the turns of the argument, and I'd spend hours strolling through long stretches of prose. That's rarely the case anymore. Now my concentration often starts to drift after two or three pages. I get fidgety, lose the thread, begin looking for something else to do.

Carr cites the British Library's Google Generation study (Rowlands *et al.* 2008) as evidence that people are losing the ability to read deeply, and when they are online they tend to skim, jumping from one site to another. The pervasiveness of the Internet means that this behaviour is then carried over into other, offline activity.

The reason Carr's article resonated with people was that many have intuitively begun to suspect this of themselves. On a less significant level than deep reading, I know that, for instance, I cease trying to remember small pieces of information: people's telephone numbers being a good example. As a child it was a point of honour to be able to recite the numbers of most friends and family from memory. Now I'm lucky if I can remember my own number. This is partly a result of changing practice; one doesn't type the number in any more but dials from a contact list, and so the learning by rote that occurred previously has diminished, but it is also a form of cognitive economy – I don't *need* to remember those numbers because I always have them in a list somewhere. Similarly, I don't need to remember an exact article or book reference because as long as I have enough salient pieces of information, Google will find it for me. I am effectively outsourcing some of that mundane memory to Google.

The real question is 'does this matter?' Is remembering small, precise pieces of information a kind of intellectual morning stretching routine? It isn't difficult and won't make you super-fit, but it has long-term benefits. Or are we just being practical, not wasting time remembering the rote information, which frees us up to engage in more creative pursuits? When Clay Shirky (2010) talks of cognitive surplus he is referring to it at a societal level, but maybe it operates at an individual level also; now that we don't have to waste mental capacity remembering what film a certain actor was in (because we have instant access to imdb.com) we are free to think how the narrative might have been better conveyed in that scene.

The answer is that we don't know which of these two is correct, and I suspect neither of them is, as they both suggest a rather simplistic mental model.

Carr's charge that superficiality bleeds over into other activities such as deep reading and analysis is a serious one for scholarship, which is almost entirely constituted of such activity. In this view engagement with technology is not just a distraction, or another pressure on an overloaded academic, but is positively dangerous. It becomes something akin to a virus, infecting the key critical engagement skills required for scholarship to function.

There may be some evidence that this occurs online. Wijekumar *et al.* (2006) reported that this skittish 'bouncing' behaviour was exhibited by students with more computer experience, resulting in poorer performance when they needed to engage in an academic task. They concluded that the students were transferring negative affordances from their prior experience, when they may have been playing a game, while indulging in instant chat and reading email:

> [T]he students who had used computers for a long time tended to have multiple windows open on their desktop and then believed they were not affected by the multi-tasking. The results of their recall showed that their synthesis of the chat room was actually disjointed and quite incomplete. (Wijekumar *et al.* 2006)

What we don't know is the extent to which this is transferred offline. Carr makes a strong correlation between deep reading and deep thinking. One might suppose that if the type of behaviour he indicates was strongly manifested in society then we would see a decline in book sales because people would not find them useful or they didn't suit their new found behaviour. The opposite is true, however, with book sales increasing from $24 billion to $37 billion over 2000–2008 and internet sales being a main driver of this (Brynjolfsson, Hu and Smith 2010). Of course, we don't know that people are reading, or indeed engaging in 'deep reading' of these books, but the figures do at least suggest that reading is not an activity in decline.

What is also not clear is if people are engaging in new types of activity that replace the function of deep reading. For instance, if someone is writing a blog post they may be gathering several articles together to construct an argument. Similarly, is a student who creates a video mashup from images, video, text and music to make an argument learning less than one who writes an essay? The answer is that at the moment it is probably too early to know, but we should note Carr's caution about superficiality for now.

Quality

Much of the success of Web 2.0 has been driven by its simplicity. This has seen a mass democratisation of expression, as anyone can now create a blog, or share a video or a photo. This has led to innovation and inventiveness which would not have arisen through conventional broadcast channels. However, it has also given rise to an unprecedented amount of what we might charitably label 'ephemera'. This shift in filtering from pre- to post-dissemination raises a key issue for scholars: How do they maintain and judge quality in a world where everyone is a broadcaster or publisher?

Some of these issues were addressed in Chapter 12 on publishing. One response is to resist any such shift and to retain the peer-review model, which has served scholars very well. This is a viable approach, but even then, as PLoS have demonstrated, there are different models that may be explored.

The issue of quality is perhaps more keenly felt when we consider teaching. I raised the idea of pedagogy of abundance in Chapter 8, and in such a pedagogy the content will vary greatly in terms of quality. In *The Cult of the Amateur*, Andrew Keen (2007) argues that such abundance does not produce high-quality, merely an outpouring of low-quality, content: 'instead of creating masterpieces, these millions and millions of exuberant monkeys – many with no more talent than our primate cousins – are creating an endless digital forest of mediocrity.' If you compare any random piece of Web 2.0 content with that produced by a professional, this is likely to be true. But the question is not whether some people produce poor quality content, obviously they do and the majority in fact, but whether *as a whole* this system can produce high-quality content.

Keen argues that it does not, and it may be that we are making false comparisons. It is not whether a YouTube clip is as good as a professional television show or movie but rather whether it is a good YouTube clip that is important. These often trade off high production quality for inventiveness. A blog post may not be the equivalent of the inside story of investigative journalism, but because it is free from constraints of readership, word length or deadlines, the blog post may provide more thoughtful and detailed analysis of the subject than is found in the mainstream media.

From a scholarly perspective then, quality will depend on the purpose. As I proposed in Chapter 9 when looking at open educational resources (OERs), there is an implicit message within different types of content. High-quality content, such as professionally produced teaching or research material, suggests authority. Students will have one set of behaviours associated with this, for example, reading, dissecting and summarising. Low-quality, individual items, however, because of their obvious ease of production, can be seen as an invitation to participate. Therefore if the intention is to encourage engagement then low-quality routes may be more fruitful than seeking to produce professional broadcast material. Around a research project then one might imagine a range of different types of output, all realising different functions.

Keen's fear is that the cult of the amateur drives out the professional, that there is no room for newspapers if everyone reads blogs and that society will be the poorer. This is beyond the scope of this book, but in terms of education, the range of content can be beneficial, since 'amateurs' often create content which addresses subjects that academics may not and also in a manner which differs from traditional teaching.

For learners the issue becomes one of assessing the quality and appropriateness of resources. The role of education here seems vital, in both providing the critical framework for evaluating and assessing content and also in demonstrating how such content can be used to develop deep understanding of a topic.

Brain damage

Carr makes reference to the Internet changing our cognitive capacity, that it is rewiring our brains. In one sense, this is a facile truism; any time you learn anything your brain is 'rewired' at a synaptic level. If you remember anything from this book, it will have rewired your brain, but you probably won't need to worry about it. There is a trend, however, to promote this rewiring to a grander scale, to suggest it is some kind of evolutionary change. Susan Greenfield is fond of making pronouncements of this nature, for example, that "these technologies are infantilising the brain into the state of small children who are attracted by buzzing noises and bright lights, who have a small attention span and who live for the moment" and even 'we do not know whether the current increase in autism is due more to increased awareness and diagnosis of autism, or whether it can – if there is a true increase – be in any way linked to an increased prevalence among people of spending time in screen relationships' (Derbyshire 2009).

These arguments seem both vague and ill-founded. The suggestion is that because the brain rewires itself (what is termed 'brain plasticity') it can therefore be influenced by the amount of time spent playing games, being online and so on (although the activities are rarely differentiated and often grouped together as 'screen time'). This is as true of playing a computer game as it is of riding a bicycle or writing a book. It is the subsequent conclusion that it is necessarily harmful that lacks evidence and, as with the quotes above, is based on supposition and anecdote. Brain plasticity is also, surely, an antidote to these concerns, since if an individual's brain has been rewired by one set of behaviour, it can be rewired again. The intention of referring to brain circuitry seems to be to instigate fear. As neuroscientist Joshua Greene puts it, 'the Internet hasn't changed the way we think anymore than the microwave oven has changed the way we digest food. The Internet has provided us with unprecedented access to information, but it hasn't changed what we do with it once it's made it into our heads' (Gerschenfeld 2010).

Whether there are social and behavioural impacts of operating online is a serious question, however. Just as the television had serious social impacts, we must accept that computers and Internet will also have consequences. These will undoubtedly be a mixture of positive and negative, but I would argue that using pseudo-scientific explanations to back up prejudices will not help us address these issues.

Forgetting and identity

One such serious issue relates to online identity, particularly for young people. There have been numerous stories about people losing their jobs because they have posted injudicious content online. Sometimes this seems justified, and at other times, an overreaction. For instance, most of us would sympathise with teacher Ashley Payne who was dismissed from her job when she posted photographs of herself on her vacation holding a glass of wine to her private Facebook account and was reported to her principal. But maybe it is less clear in other cases, for example, the Labour MP Stewart MacLennan who was sacked after referring to David Cameron and Nick Clegg in rather unsavoury terms on Twitter.

What such cases demonstrate is that the boundary between personal and professional life is increasingly blurred, and what may seem like a joke between friends has the potential to be taken out of context and, with a global distribution, suddenly transmitted everywhere. When 22-year-old student Connor Riley was offered an internship at Cisco, she tweeted 'Cisco just offered me a job! Now I have to weigh the utility of a fatty paycheck against the daily commute to San Jose and hating the work'. A Cisco employee picked it up, and something of a witch-hunt ensued as the message was shared as an example of how to lose a job (she had in fact already declined the internship). A more recent, and sinister, case is that of Paul Chambers, who, because of airport closures, was unable to fly to see his girlfriend. He tweeted 'Crap! Robin Hood airport is closed. You've got a week and a bit to get your shit together otherwise I'm blowing the airport sky high!!' This message saw him prosecuted and fined using an obscure telephony law, which resulted in him losing his job twice.

Both of these cases demonstrate the strained boundary between public communication systems and social chat. For young people who now grow up using such media, the possibility of leaving a trace of some indiscretion increases due to the time they spend in such environments and because so much of their social life is conducted there. If it is not to have a damaging effect on their lives, they need to learn techniques of handling their online identities early on and, equally, society at large needs to learn to view these in the proper light.

In his book *Delete: The Virtue of Forgetting in the Digital Age* Mayer-Schonberger (2009) argues that forgetting is an important psychological process. It allows us to construct new versions of our identity, which are suited to different contexts and different ages. With a digital, networked and open online memory, however, this is becoming increasingly difficult. As well as leading to the types of problems of misinterpretation and heavy-handed responses listed above, it may also affect our own personal development. We cannot shake off the memory of the inconsiderate adolescent we once were so easily because its record is always there. He proposes that internet communications have a shelf life, that they should be allowed to expire unless the individual takes specific action to preserve them.

For educators there are two main issues; the first is the extent to which they help students manage their online identity, and the second is how they manage their own boundary between personal and professional life. There are a range of options available from complete withdrawal from online life to using pseudonyms to speak openly. Knowledge of the type of information that can be gathered about you and how that might be used is important, but if it comes at the cost of a sterile online exchange where people become scared to say anything beyond a form of corporate message, then that would be a price too high for many. So developing an appropriate online persona and voice is an important skill as our digital footprint expands. As is developing a good relationship with your employer one suspects.

It is not just young people who may have behaved foolish, who need to forget or at least remould their past. Scholars make judgements, suggestions and proposals all the time. An open approach inevitably results in more such pronouncements, as scholarly output is not restricted to just conference papers and journal articles. An increase in both quantity and type of outputs (which may include casual conversations, jokes, half-thought-out ideas etc.) must increase the possibility of being wrong. Most scholars will revise their positions based on new evidence or changing circumstances. Scholarship is closely bound with authority; the opinions of scholars count because they are deemed as being an authority in this area. Will a digital audit trail reveal contradictions, which undermine current authority?

I know that I have shifted position with regard to technology over the years. In 2004 I was an advocate of LMSs, but subsequently I have become a critic of the manner in which they stifle innovation. In 2008 I wrote a (not entirely serious) blog post suggesting that you 'Google up your life' (Weller 2008). I am certainly more wary of some of the issues around cloud computing now and would be unlikely to write such a post today (although I still find the Google suite of tools superior to those offered in-house by my university).

Do such modifications to opinion undermine the authority of this book? Or are they part of a natural progression as someone develops an argument in response to changing contexts? If so, is this a subtlety that everyone can appreciate? Does the process of ongoing engagement and openness create a different type of authority?

I will leave you to determine your own responses to these questions, but I would suggest that perfect digital memory is not just an issue for teenagers with hangovers.

Next-big-thingism

If failing to engage with technology is one problem, then over-eager adoption of every new technology is another. One of the effects of a digital, open, networked culture is that it amplifies success. The network effect sees some very big winners, as a piece of content goes 'viral'. Suddenly a YouTube clip of a child on the way back from the dentist has 75 million views (http://www.youtube.com/watch?v=txqiwrbYGrs). As argued in Chapter 7, these big successes are a distraction, however; they are outliers, freaks – they are not the norm. The norm is a hundred hits or so. Similarly some projects achieve great success, and the obvious approach is to emulate them. Wikipedia is such an oft-quoted example of how crowdsourcing can be successful that it is a cliché. That Wikipedia works *is* amazing, but that doesn't mean the same approach will work for every project. Similarly, Twitter may be an excellent means of expanding a professional network, but forcing students to use it may be seen as irrelevant.

As we saw in Chapter 2, it is something of a myth that a digital generation of students is clamouring for these new technologies in their education. Cann and Badge (2010) created a course on developing a personal learning environment using a variety of tools. The module was not popular with students and seen as a distraction, for example, one student commenting, 'I didn't feel this course was necessary in my degree course; it took up a lot of my time. Time which I feel would have been better spent doing work more related to my degree, such as practical reports and essays'. However, the next iteration of their course which focused on using Friendfeed to act as a form of social eportfolio met with more success, indicating that the choice of tools and the perceived relevance to the main area of study are crucial elements.

The over-adoption of tools can lead to what has been termed 'creepy tree house' syndrome (Stein 2008) when authority is seen to try and invade a young person's social space. There is strong resistance from students to universities and lecturers making formal use of social networks as this is seen as an invasion of their social space (e.g. Madge *et al.* 2009). When parents and professors start inhabiting these spaces it creates a role conflict (Selwyn 2009) for students, as they struggle to know which face to present and find their communication stifled. These tools may have significant potential for learning, but students don't want them to become the next LMS: organisationally controlled, bland and singular in focus (i.e. teaching). For the teaching function of scholarship then the question is 'How can educators utilise the potential of these tools without destroying what makes them valuable to students?'

The answer is one that doesn't always sit well with educators and students, particularly when students face rising costs for their education, which in turn alters the educator–student relationship to a more supplier–customer oriented one. But, nevertheless, the answer is: *by making mistakes.* Undoubtedly wikis will be unedited, community forums silent, crowdsourced database projects empty, but each iteration will generate improvement and insight as to what works effectively.

Fortunately the investment is not high with many technologies, both in terms of finance and time taken to use them, so this iteration can occur rapidly. It may seem unprofessional to 'experiment' with a student's education, but as long as there is a sound basis for exploring the new approaches, and flexibility on the part of the educator, then the damage is limited. Erik Duval (2010) argues that we should be less cautious and that we can afford to disrupt education, largely because the existing systems are far from perfect anyway. An argument can also be made that exposure to new approaches and critical analysis of these are of benefit across all disciplines of study, and it is more harmful to create a sterile, artificial environment for students which will not be replicated as they continue to learn throughout their lives.

It is also the case that experience is required to appreciate what tools and approaches are suitable. Crowdsourcing, for example, works well for particular problems, often when there is a simple contribution to make, which can be aggregated to produce an overall answer. It is not good at producing singular works of creativity or genius, where individuals fare better. It also requires a reasonable mass of contributions to work, a motivation for those contributions and an easy means to contribute. So crowdsourcing an essay probably won't be successful, but getting students to create a set of links to useful resources via social bookmarking might be, particularly over several presentations of a course. And the latter might work better if it builds on a tool that students are already using rather than requiring them to adopt a different one. Knowing which approach to try, and then which tool to use to implement it, is something that workshops, training courses and examples can help with, but it arises much more from experience and experimentation.

In his essay on Churchill, Christopher Hitchens (2002) complains that 'Churchill was allowed by events to flaunt the medals of his defeats'. Churchill's defeats had costly consequences; however, our experiments with technology do not, but defeats will be inevitable.

Property and ownership

Like many people I am somewhat conflicted over cloud computing. On the one hand, being able to share and store content in the ubiquitous cloud has been a great benefit, and many of the tools that allow me to do this possess a vibrancy and ease of use that is sadly lacking in bespoke academic tools. But, at the same time, I am conscious of surrendering more of my ideas, content and identity to companies who make use of my data for their own ends. We can view this anxiety from an individual and broader perspective.

For the individual an oft-voiced concern is that of intellectual property and ownership when adopting an open approach. Creative Commons licences go some way to addressing these, but a bigger concern may be that scholars feel under pressure to release data, ideas or results because of a culture of openness, which are then taken by others and exploited. I suspect the fear of this is disproportionate to the reality for most areas of study; it is only in the highly commercial fields that it is likely to be the case, such as medicine (and even then, there is a strong argument for adopting an open source model of drug development). Indeed openness can be its own defence, since content stolen and unattributed is more likely to be recognised (particularly if the 'thief' places their content online).

But undoubtedly an open approach makes these issues more likely, and the boundaries of fair use become blurred. Like many bloggers I have found my content appearing in unusual places, sometimes unattributed. For example, I recently found a feed of my blog being used as the 'Blog' link on a commercial software site. The post linked back to my site, but there was no explicit attribution, or context provided, nor was permission requested. This would seem to stretch the Creative Commons licence I use on my blog – does a link count as attribution? Does this constitute commercial use? I emailed the company involved, but didn't receive a response. This mild misuse didn't cost me anything, but one could argue that it could be damaging to reputation if you were interpreted as endorsing a product. Obviously this situation could not have arisen if I didn't keep a blog, or kept it private, or maybe even if I used a very traditional copyright notice. The question I had to answer then was whether keeping a public blog with an open licence brings me more benefit overall than the potential damage which might arise. So far, my experience has come down strongly in favour of the benefits, but balancing this equation will vary for individuals.

Perhaps more significant is the potential cost of adopting cloud-based solutions not for individuals but to scholars as a whole. At the time of writing, the Wikileaks release of US diplomatic cables is causing considerable controversy. What this has revealed is the extent to which many cloud services have embedded themselves within the fabric of our society. For example, Wikileaks was hosted by Amazon, who removed this service, seemingly under pressure from a US senator. MacKinnon (2010) points out that 'a substantial if not critical amount of our political discourse has moved into the digital realm. This realm is largely made up of virtual spaces that are created, owned and operated by the private sector'.

Scholars have a long tradition of holding governments to account and questioning policy, so could a shift to cloud computing put this in jeopardy? Even if it is not political, the Wikileaks episode has highlighted the dangers of relying on the cloud to host all scholarly discourse. As John Naughton (2010) puts it, 'For years people have extolled cloud computing as the way of the future. The lesson of the last week is simple: be careful what you wish for.'

Sustainability

For Web 2.0 critics like Keen (2007) the issue is not just that the democratisation of publishing creates low-quality content but that it undermines the business practice of established industries, as I examined in Chapter 2. This may be the case; the changes we are seeing in content industries are still relatively new. Lanier (2010) similarly suggests that the open content movement will ultimately harm creativity. He reports that he failed to find any significant number of musicians who were making a living using the 'new economy' models. When people download pirated content he argues that '[t]he problem in each case is not that you stole from a specific person but that you undermined the artificial scarcities that allow the economy to function. In the same way, creative expression on the internet will benefit from a social contract that imposes a modest degree of artificial scarcity on information' (Lanier 2010).

The argument from sustainability then can be summarised as 'who pays?' The focus of this book is scholarship, and despite the analogies that can be drawn with other sectors such as newspapers, music and film, there are also significant differences. What will work in those sectors may not work in academia, and conversely, what is disastrous for them may not be for scholars. Piracy, for instance, is less of an issue when it comes to scholarship, for two very significant reasons: revenue does not flow directly from this content, and content forms only a part of the overall offering. In terms of research, money comes from research councils, industry, professional bodies, government agencies, charities and the scholar's own institution. This is not to suggest that these funding sources are not facing pressure, but piracy, or free open dissemination, is not a factor that undermines this model. Indeed the opposite would seem to be the case, in that most funders will want the findings of the research disseminated, shared, downloaded, reused and copied as many times as possible (provided it is acknowledged and isn't commercially sensitive).

The situation is a little more complex with teaching. If a university releases all of its teaching content as OERs, will that result in fewer students? From the OER projects that have been initiated so far the answer seems to be no, and it may even attract students. What is unclear is if this is a temporary effect – if *every* university and college released *all* of their teaching content, would we witness a decline in student numbers? What OERs highlight is that education is, of course, about more than content, as I explored in Chapter 3. Accreditation, support, structure and expertise are all valuable elements which are difficult (but maybe not impossible) to disaggregate.

Sustainability is an issue for the OER movement, but as argued in Chapter 7, much of what scholars currently do can be realised as open, digital outputs with relatively little cost. We are also blind to many of the costs that operate in our current system because we have not had alternatives to realising them previously.

So while the open content movement may well have profound implications for the survivability of other sectors, this is not the case with scholarship. Most revenue relating to scholarship does not arise directly from selling content. Scholars are thus in a better position to explore the possibilities of an open approach because they are protected to a degree from the financial implications, and in fact their relevance and value to learners, society and research funders can be increased by such an approach. These differences with other sectors, and the implications for experimenting in higher education, are explored in more detail in Chapter 14.

Conclusion

Of the objections, or reservations, covered in this chapter, I would suggest the following as the most challenging for digital scholarship:

- Moving beyond the superficial – many successful Web 2.0 services essentially allow a very simple function, for example, sharing a photograph. Can we use the same techniques for deeper, more difficult tasks?

- Understanding quality – this is not just about maintaining current quality, as this may not be appropriate in many forms, but appreciating when different levels of quality can be used.

- Managing online identity – there is a tension for scholars and their students in gaining the benefits of a social network, which thrives on personal interactions, while not compromising professional identity.

- Ownership of scholarly functions – there is also a dilemma regarding how much of scholarly discourse and activity we give over to cloud computing services and whether the benefits in terms of widespread use and (often) superior tools outweigh the potential risks.

These issues will be explored in more detail in Chapter 14, as they represent some of the recurring themes of this book.

A theme of this chapter has been the need to engage with new approaches, to have the space to explore these, and to get things wrong. Gartner (2008), an IT research company, proposes a hype cycle for technologies with five phases: technology trigger, peak of inflated expectations, trough of disillusionment, slope to enlightenment, and finally a plateau of productivity. It is a useful model, although one that should not be interpreted too seriously (Aranda [2006] provides a good overview of the problems with it). What it reminds us is that our attitude to technology goes through phases. This is particularly pertinent when one finds oneself in the peak of inflated expectations, when it seems the technology can do no wrong, is great fun and will probably overthrow dictatorships along the way. It isn't long ago that we were praising email as a means of flattening hierarchies in organisations, but now it is often regarded as a nuisance, partly because it has become such a standard tool that we fail to see the benefits it still provides.

Bearing in mind something akin to the Gartner Hype cycle is useful for both technology advocates and critics. For the advocates they should appreciate that after initial enthusiasm may come a period of rejection, before the tool settles into a pattern in their working life. For critics being able to differentiate between hype and the sustained long-term uses is a challenge as they dismiss the tool on the basis of the inflated claims. Social networks are a useful recent example of this; both Facebook and then Twitter were met by an initial burst of enthusiasm. People felt compelled to update their status continually, sometimes even at the expense of their real relationships. First with Facebook, and more recently with Twitter, previous advocates and users have started to reject these tools and delete accounts. Sometimes these people come back but with a more low-key use, as the tool, and the online network, accommodates itself into their broader life at an appropriate level.

I know I've done this, and what's more I'll do it again. Just as with the initial dot-com bubble, the fact that there is hype doesn't mean that the overall direction isn't correct. A technology may not completely change the world in the next 18 months, but it may significantly change practice in the next decade. It is difficult to pick out these salient features when you are immersed in a change. For example, Clifford Stoll in 1995 dismissed online shopping:

> Then there's cyberbusiness. We're promised instant catalog shopping – just point and click for great deals. We'll order airline tickets over the network, make restaurant reservations and negotiate sales contracts. So how come my local mall does more business in an afternoon than the entire Internet handles in a month?

Few would doubt we do all of those things online now and much more. So even if the e-commerce enthusiasts were wrong about the speed and extent of change back then, they were more right than Stoll was in dismissing it. Roy Amara is credited with summing this up: We tend to overestimate the effect of a technology in the short run and underestimate the effect in the long run.

And that's the case with many of the technologies and approaches that constitute a digital, networked, open form of scholarship: social networking, Web 2.0, user-generated content, open content, blogs and so on. Even if their use in scholarship doesn't lead to some of the changes I have proposed, there is one key point – *it will never go back to how it was*. After Wikipedia, Flickr, YouTube, iTunes and so on the idea that anyone will go back to the previous model is more fanciful than any hype. Whatever comes after the current trends will build on top of them – just as Web 2.0 built on what had happened in the first wave of Web development. And the people who instigated this wave of development weren't people who had dismissed the Web initially and insisted it would go away. They were people who engaged with it and could see how to take it forward. So whatever comes after Web 2.0 (and I don't mean Web 3.0), the people best placed to understand it and adapt to it will be those who have immersed themselves in the current technological climate.

For scholars, then, the challenge is to engage with the technology, while avoiding some of the hype, and being mindful of the challenges described in this chapter. A willingness to experiment with new approaches and to explore the tensions between new possibilities and established practice is essential in addressing this chapter. In Chapter 5 I referenced Saul Bellow's novel *The Adventures of Augie March*, and the closing lines of that book seem relevant to this attitude: 'I may be a flop at this line of endeavour. Columbus too thought he was a flop, probably, when they sent him back in chains. Which didn't prove there was no America.'

14 Digital Resilience

The concluding chapter of this book aims to draw out some of the themes that have recurred and to address the context within which the impact of a digital, networked, open approach will exist. One such theme is the reluctance of scholars to adopt some of the new practices now afforded to them, and particularly some of the anxieties surrounding these are examined first of all. It is proposed that this has previously led to a failure of ownership over some key scholarly practices which have been grounded in technology. The solution to this is not resistance but engagement with technology and reflection on changing scholarly practice. Different types of engagement are then delineated, and resilience is proposed as a means of considering the core scholarly practices. Such engagement is both necessary and possible, I contend, because higher education has within it the ability to disrupt some of its own practice without undermining its own economic basis.

Techno-angst

There is often some anxiety, resistance or scepticism around the adoption of new technology and related approaches. As mentioned in Chapter 13 there is a danger of extremism in these attitudes, which are either dismissed as people 'who don't get it' or, conversely, as technology fetishism lacking in critical reflection. I am in agreement with Lanier (2010) when he argues that 'technology criticism shouldn't be left to luddites', but the reverse is also valid, in that technology engagement shouldn't be left to the evangelists.

One theme of this book has been the relative reluctance of academia to engage with new technologies or to change established practice, for example, the lack of uptake by researchers covered in Chapter 5. I have suggested some reasons for this, including the impact of the reward and tenure process, the nature of research practice and the established communication channels. But a more general psychology may also be at work, which is worth considering.

For the title of one of his novels Martin Amis (2010) borrowed from this Alexander Herzen quote:

> The death of contemporary forms of social order ought to gladden rather than trouble the soul. Yet what is frightening is that the departing world leaves behind it not an heir, but a pregnant widow. Between the death of the one

and the birth of the other, much water will flow by, a long night of chaos and desolation will pass.

In his novel, Amis is writing about the sexual revolution of the 1970s, but I suggest the same can be applied to the digital revolution. This is what causes so much angst in the popular media and amongst society in general. We can see what is passing, but what is forming is still unclear. Clay Shirky (2009) talking about newspapers puts it thus:

> So who covers all that news if some significant fraction of the currently employed newspaper people lose their jobs?

> I don't know. Nobody knows. We're collectively living through 1500, when it's easier to see what's broken than what will replace it. The internet turns 40 this fall. Access by the general public is less than half that age. Web use, as a normal part of life for a majority of the developed world, is less than half *that* age. We just got here. Even the revolutionaries can't predict what will happen.

We can think about some general directions of travel, we can make some guesses, and most of all, we can experiment. The focus of this book is what the changes mean for scholarly practice, how will academics perform research, what will education look like twenty years from now, how can we best be engaged in public debates? We have a very well-established set of methods for all of these currently, but it is unlikely that any of them will remain untouched by the impact of a digital, networked, open approach. And as with other industries we saw in Chapter 3, trying to find ways to preserve them as they are, or with a digital veneer, won't be sufficient when others find innovative ways to achieve the same ends using new tools.

As Amis puts it in his novel, 'it was a revolution. And we all know what happens in a revolution. You see what goes, you see what stays, you see what comes.'

What goes, what stays and what comes – each element of this trio is significant. Often we concentrate on 'what comes', but it's just as interesting to consider what stays. This reveals what is important to us (will journalism stay? will universities stay?) or at least what is so ingrained culturally or commercially as to be immovable. The QWERTY keyboard has stayed thus far in the digital age, despite being an analogue solution, not through any sense of value but because it was too entrenched to overthrow.

What goes is equally revealing because it demonstrates that practices and values that we may have seen as unassailable are suddenly vulnerable because the assumptions they are based upon are no longer valid. The scarce, rivalrous nature and distribution model of many goods and content is one such example. When they became abundant, non-rivalrous and freely distributed, whole industries began to look weak. The 'what goes' element may also reveal to us what was important and not so important after all.

We generally assume that after a peaceful social revolution the resulting practice is an improvement for the majority of people; otherwise it wouldn't occur. Unless the revolution is imposed upon the people, the general direction will be towards a utilitarian improvement. But this doesn't mean the post-revolutionary world will be better for everyone. There are those whose profession and identity will be strongly allied to the existing practices. There will be practices and values that are lost that we find we did in fact hold dear but which were too closely attached to the older methods to survive. In short, there will be winner and losers. A revolution may be bloodless but is rarely painless for all.

This is why we see scare stories about games damaging children's health, social networks ruining the nature of friendship, piracy killing artistic endeavour or the fabric of society being damaged irrevocably by a general addiction to computers. We are learning what role these new tools play in our lives, and there will inevitably be mistakes, misapplication, overuse and correction.

If we have the triumvirate of what comes, goes and stays, this may also explain some of the reluctance to change existing practice. Kahneman and Tversky's prospect theory (1979) sets out the different evaluations we have of loss and gain. The two are not weighted equally by individuals, with loss-aversion being more psychologically important than possible gain. While we are in this period of transition, it is not entirely clear what it is that will be gained, and even if cogent arguments are made for benefits, these gains may still not be sufficient to outweigh the psychological risk-aversion to the possible losses. The gain of new methods of communicating and working are not perceived as sufficient to overcome the potential pain of losses. We tend to exaggerate the feeling of loss, so changing scholarly practice highlights the potential of losing authority, for example, by undermining the peer-review process, weakening the higher education system by offering the components separately or losing some ownership by releasing content under an open licence. The possible (if not probable) losses are more palpable. This emphasises the significance of framing, of placing both the benefits and losses in an appropriate perspective, which I will return to in the section on disruption.

The impact of technology on society in general is something we are only beginning to appreciate. The world my daughter will inhabit is likely to differ from the one I know more significantly than the one I grew up in compared to my parents. Who can predict how these changes will affect her professional and social life? In Chapter 2 I suggested that the prophecies about the impending irrelevance of universities were overblown, but we can recast these prophecies in terms of how scholars can change their own practice. Without addressing some of the issues set out in this book, scholars may find themselves excluded from discussions in the wider social network, their work hidden away in obscure repositories and their research ignorant of social issues. This would be the real tragedy of scholars, even if they continued to be successful in terms of employment and research funding.

When Wikipedia founder Jimmy Wales gave a talk for the Open University conference I said that as a father of an inquisitive eight-year-old, not a week went by when I didn't give thanks for the existence of Wikipedia. He responded that it was a double-edged sword; when he was young his father could give him an answer and he'd accept it, but he found now that his kids were back-checking his answers on Wikipedia. There was no getting away with fabricating answers anymore. This small example seems to encapsulate much of the challenge facing scholarship – some things are coming and some are going, and we don't yet know how significant these will be, but key to the successful implementation of changes, or appropriate continuation of current practice, is a sense of ownership over them, which is the subject of the next section.

A failure of ownership

Academics should not be passive recipients of this change. If we, as scholars, truly believe that some elements of a digital, networked, open approach will harm some core functions of scholarship, then the correct response is not to decry the new approach and retreat, it is to engage and determine for ourselves how these functions might be preserved. For example, if peer review is deemed essential then scholars can construct methods of achieving this which utilise the technology to the improvement of the process. An insistence on maintaining the current model, with the current journals, and denigrating the new models runs the risk that research is out of date and hidden away. Or worse, it allows others to control the process because scholars deem it too complex or not their domain. The solution provided then will not be suited to their needs but to those of external agents.

I would argue that this has happened to a significant extent in academia already, particularly where technology has played a key role. Inevitably this has meant academia have outsourced functions to for-profit companies. There is nothing intrinsically wrong about the involvement of for-profit companies with scholarship; it is often a mutually beneficial relationship. But for complex activities that go to the heart of scholarship, once they were outsourced then academia became reliant on them and effectively lost control. Here are three examples of this in action:

1 LMSs/VLEs – the central role that elearning would come to play in teaching was underestimated by many academics, and so simple solutions were

sought. The commercial VLEs offered this, but this has seen increasingly costly contracts, an attempt by the company Blackboard to patent many of the core concepts in elearning, and in general a reliance on commercial providers to lead development. Once a VLE becomes embedded in practice with all the requisite staff development programmes, policy guidelines and links to university systems, then it becomes difficult to dislodge.

2 Tenure, assessment and publications – as discussed in Chapter 11, one view of the promotion system is that the complexity of measuring excellence in different fields was effectively outsourced to the peer-review process. This placed publishers in a central position in academia, since they controlled the routes to career progression. Related to this was the manner in which scholars ceded control to various initiatives which sought to quantify the quality of research. This reinforced the publishers' position since their journals were linked directly to institutional funding.

3 Publication – as addressed in Chapter 12, many professional societies and university presses handed over their publications to for-profit publishing firms, effectively outsourcing the process, the proceeds of which they would then have to buy back.

George Siemens (2010) has argued that academia should take ownership of the open education debate before it is hijacked, and given the above history, I would agree.

The loss of ownership of some of these core academic functions occurred not because of the technology but rather because the scholarly community failed to engage with it. Large-scale open source projects could have solved many of these problems (and in cases such as OJS and Moodle have been successful), and the overall cost to universities would have been much less than being in an unequal relationship with commercial companies for whom scholarship is not their primary interest.

Commercial partnerships in education can be very fruitful, and academia is not always best placed to develop or innovate in technology. Many of the popular free services are undoubtedly better, or exist at all, because they were developed by commercial operations (imagine an academic Flickr or YouTube), but we should be aware of what it is we are handing over. As we face the question of 'what do we do about Web 2.0/cloud computing/social media?' a full understanding of what it can do is essential, and simply handing over the problem to someone else will not serve us well.

A potential nightmare scenario for many involved in scholarship is what we might term the 'Googling of higher education'. In this scenario, libraries, and in particular the human expertise of librarians, are replaced by digital copies of all content, with efficient data and search mechanisms. Teaching is replaced by automatically generated 'playlists' of open content. Accreditation of learning is performed by metrics and scores which are too complex to cheat or game. The only research that gets funded is that which offers commercial incentives, and its merit is judged by the number of hits the results generate.

This is maybe a bit far-fetched, and there are a number of external factors which would mitigate against it. But it, or a flavour of it, is not beyond the realms of possibility.

One response to this might be to resist, adopting the exact opposite of many of the approaches proposed in this book. There is a strong logic to this – if scholars don't make research and teaching content available, then Google can't sweep it up. The danger of such an approach is that if this content is made available by other means (maybe by academics in different countries who sign a deal with Google or by non-academics) then scholars lack any position of power and, worse, sufficient knowledge of how to compete.

Back in 1998, when elearning was new, critics such as David Noble (1998) argued that it was part of a process of commercialisation and commoditisation of higher education. While there was more than a touch of anti-technology sentiment about Noble's argument, some of what he predicted has come to pass. He argued 'universities are not simply undergoing a technological transformation. Beneath that change, and camouflaged by it, lies another: the commercialization of higher education. For here as elsewhere technology is but a vehicle and a disarming disguise'.

Quite rightly he suggested that this should be resisted. In this sense resistance meant not engaging, withdrawing cooperation, refusing to put course notes online and engage with technology. One could argue that the result was that the commercialisation of education did indeed occur, but not because academics went along with it unwittingly but because insufficient numbers engaged with the technology itself.

Levels of engagement

So what does engagement with technology mean? First, I would suggest, it acknowledges that the changes afforded by new technology are not peripheral but fundamental to all aspects of scholarship. Then there is engagement at a number of levels to be considered. This is not intended as a manifesto or a manual, but the following suggestions demonstrate the type of responses scholars might undertake once the first principle is accepted, which would address the ownership and engagement issues. Such strategies can be considered at four levels:

1 governmental and funding body

2 institutional

3 disciplinary

4 individual

Governmental and funding body level

For those at the most strategic level of governments, funding bodies, national policy and so on the scope for influence is considerable. Most research funding flows from such bodies, and so legitimisation of other forms of impact beyond conference papers and journal articles is one way of encouraging engagement with new communication tools. But the strategy could go much further than simply making the use of new tools a desired element in any bid, and a more radical rethinking of both the bidding process and the type of research that is funded which fully utilises a digital, networked, open approach is possible. One of the themes of this book has been how new technologies offer alternatives to existing methods, but the onus is on practitioners to examine current practice and explore how these alternatives may be realised.

For example, most research is structured around medium- to large-scale projects operating over a two- to three-year time scale. Such projects are constructed around milestones, work packages and deliverables. There is a great deal of effort and time involved by all parties at every stage of this process: creating the initial call, preparing and costing a bid, evaluating proposals, allocation of funds, managing a successful project, reporting, monitoring and independent evaluation of the project once it has completed. Such large-scale projects are indeed necessary for much of the in-depth research in scholarship. But the process is also a product of the tools we had available. A research funding approach which had digital, networked and open as its main characteristics may look different. For example, if the granularity of research becomes smaller (or at least more variable), as suggested in Chapter 5, then such a top-heavy approach will struggle to accommodate this. An alternative might be a shift in emphasis to more fellowship-based approaches, rather than project-based ones, where an individual with a digital, networked identity is given funds to explore a particular theme. One of the benefits of an open approach is that a significant quantity of data is already available, as are a wide range of tools, so for some research subjects, the cost of equipment and data gathering are not great, and exploratory research performed by an individual is a more fruitful approach. More radically, research funding could be realised through micropayments, based on *post hoc* recognition of shared outcomes, that is, a research group or individual gets small payments after they have published a small piece of research. Funders might also look to create research outcomes as the aggregations of a network of individuals and not just the outputs of large formal groupings.

Undoubtedly there is research that will always require the large funding model as we currently know it to exist (this may be particularly true in the sciences), and I do not suggest that any of the alternatives sketched above are superior. What they demonstrate hopefully though is that there are different models of how research can be funded, recognised and disseminated, which national and international bodies could explore.

Institutional level

At the institutional level the first task is to recognise the issues set out in Chapter 11 regarding the recognition of digital scholarship. While reward and promotion are not the sole motivation for academics, failure by institutions to recognise them and to promote established practices sends a clear message which does not help to create an innovative environment.

In conjunction with recognition is facilitation. Each institution will need to determine what, if any, the benefits will be if academic staff become active digital scholars. For example, it may be seen as a route to public and community engagement, as a means of rejuvenating the curriculum or of raising the profile in particular research disciplines. It is not, however, a shift in practice that will occur overnight, and so if there are perceived institutional benefits then investment in developing the appropriate skills will be required some time before these benefits can be realised. This does not necessarily mean a range of training courses (although some may opt for this), but for instance, it could be realised through an allocation of time to explore new technologies, similar to Google's 20 per cent time, where staff are allowed that allocation to work on projects outside of their normal remit, but which might be of interest (to them and Google). This removal of emphasis on deliverables and reporting creates an environment where people are perhaps less fearful of failure, and as anyone who has experimented with using new technologies can testify, failure is a certainty at some stage. Other options might be to reward and publicise the most innovative use of technology in teaching or to regularly share informal outputs such as blog posts and videos in an internal forum. The methods are varied, but the aim is similar – to turn technology engagement into a virtue.

Discipline level

At the level of a particular subject discipline or community, a combination of the previous two approaches might apply, with recognition and encouragement of new forms of output as well as supportive research funding. In addition it is at the disciplinary level that much of the knowledge exchange occurs, so there is an opportunity to nurture new forms of this, particularly, for example, in the case of conferences. As proposed in Chapter 10, the bottom-up adoption of technology by participants is beginning to alter the nature of conferences, but in their format many are unchanged. In terms of disseminating knowledge the one-to-many lecture was a viable solution prior to the Internet, but it now seems like a misuse of the face-to-face medium. If you can easily broadcast the content online (e.g. through video, slidecast, blog posts, articles), then to spend much of the conference time replicating this function doesn't utilise the face-to-face interaction to its fullest potential. As covered in that chapter, a number of alternatives to the traditional conference have been attempted. The barcamp and unconference models have experimented with this, but this more fluid, practical or discussion-based approach has not been adopted widely in academic circles. At the discipline level then societies and conference organisers might be more experimental about the format of conferences. Some possibilities include the following:

- disseminating presentations online prior to the event as videos or slidecasts and then using the face-to-face segment for discussion;

- an open peer-review model where proposals or papers are debated and voted on for further discussion at the conference;

- practical sessions with the aim of producing a tangible output, such as a site, a learning resource, some code, a set of guidelines and so on;

- open presentation formats, for example, having to speak on a random subject for two minutes; and

- group formation about possible research topics, with the aim of developing a research proposal, to be shared back to the wider conference later.

As with the possible experiments with research models suggested previously, these need not completely replace all existing conferences or presentations, and many might be unsuccessful, but few disciplines are exploring the possibilities that are now available.

Individual level

Finally, at the level of the individual scholar, the actual approaches and technologies used will vary depending on preference, role, purpose and ability, but I would suggest that taking the role technology can play in transforming practice seriously is important. This will require engagement with technology and, perhaps more significantly, reflection on practice. The technologies that underpin the digital, networked, open approach are too prevalent and significant to be dismissed as stuff for techies – what I have tried to demonstrate in this book is that they can impact upon all aspects of scholarship. So just as a scholar is willing to commit time to aspects of scholarship for which there may be no direct outcome, such as reviewing articles, preparing research bids, attending seminars, so allocating some time to exploring a particular technology with the aim of integrating it into scholarly practice can be seen as a legitimate and necessary task. Creating the space for this is undoubtedly difficult, and it is why technology is often seen as yet another burden piled onto the academic. One way to make this space is to use formal recording mechanisms to raise its profile, for example, in an annual workplan to specifically allocate a number of days to a technology-related activity (e.g. 'starting a blog') or in research returns to record other outputs as measure of impact (e.g. '3,000 views of this presentation'). These may well be ignored, but by formally recording them individuals can raise the significance of digital scholarship in their practice and also create a discussion with the institution regarding its attitude and support.

The emphasis at all four levels should not be on the technology itself but on the approaches the technology now facilitates and how these can improve scholarly practice. I would contend that engagement at all levels is necessary to create the environment within which scholarship continues to perform the functions we value. Any of the suggestions here, and many more besides, should be viewed as a means by which scholars can retain (and even regain) ownership of their own practice. This requires a strategy of resilience, which I will explore next.

Resilience

In his 1973 paper on the stability of ecological systems, Holling defined resilience as 'a measure of the persistence of systems and of their ability to absorb change and disturbance and still maintain the same relationships between populations or state variables'. It is a perspective that has been evolved beyond the ecosystems Holling applied it to and has found particular relevance to sustainable development and climate change. Hall and Winn (2010) have applied the concept of resilience to education and open education in particular. Walker *et al.* (2004) propose four aspects of resilience:

1 latitude: the maximum amount a system can be changed before losing its ability to recover;

2 resistance: the ease or difficulty of changing the system; how 'resistant' it is to being changed;

3 precariousness: how close the current state of the system is to a limit or 'threshold'; and

4 panarchy: the influences of external forces at scales above and below. For example, external oppressive politics, invasions, market shifts or global climate change can trigger local surprises and regime shifts.

This is a useful means of considering the response of academia to the potential impact of new technologies. This applies across all four of the levels given above, providing a 'digital scholarship resilience matrix' as shown in Table 14.1. Completing this is an exercise you might like to attempt for your own discipline and institution and relevant research council or agency. For each entry, attempt to match the level against the resilience factor, to provide an overall picture of resilience.

How you complete each entry will vary considerably depending on discipline (medical research, for instance, is arguably less precarious than historical research), geographical location (venture capital funding for technology research will be easier to come by in San Francisco), institution (Cambridge University is likely to be more resistant to change than a modern one) and recent events (universities in Ireland and Greece, for example, will be subject to the panarchic influence of recent years).

Building on Holling's work, resilience is now often defined as 'the capacity of a system to absorb disturbance and reorganise while undergoing change, so as to retain essentially the same function, structure, identity and feedbacks' (e.g. Hopkins 2009).

It is this capacity to retain function and identity that is particularly relevant to scholarship. To return to my contention in the section on ownership, this does not equate to resistance. Indeed, a high resistance is not necessarily a benefit to an ecosystem, as Holling observed how some insect populations fluctuate wildly depending on environmental factors but overall they are resilient.

In terms of scholarship resilience is about utilising technology to change practices where this is desirable but to retain the underlying function and identity which the existing practices represent. It is a mistake to think of the practices *themselves* as being core scholarship, rather that they are the methods through which we realise them, and these methods can change. Peer review, for example, is a method of ensuring quality, objectivity and reliability. But it may not be the only way of realising this, or at least its current incarnation may be subject to change. A resilience

Table 14.1 Digital scholarship resilience matrix

	National agency	Discipline	Institution	Individual
Latitude				
Resistance				
Precariousness				
Panarchy				

perspective would seek to ensure these core functions were protected and not just resist at the level of the method.

As an example of resilience, I will take a rather prosaic example but one which reflects some of the anxieties and issues for an individual. One of the popular web 2.0 services amongst academics has been the social bookmarking tool Delicious. This allows users to easily tag and share bookmarks, so very quickly large resource collections can be built, which are open to all. In December 2010 Yahoo, who own Delicious, announced they were seeking to find a buyer for it. This caused much consternation amongst users, who began asking whether it would mean the end of Delicious, what would happen to their collections, what alternative tools were available and so on.

More significantly users began to wonder whether it signalled the death knell for cloud computing. If cloud services could not be relied upon should academics abandon the cloud altogether and rely on internally hosted solutions?

If one views this from a resilience perspective, the following responses seem appropriate:

- Use cloud solutions when they are best suited to the task. If the aim is to share content, to have it easily embedded, to be part of a wider community of participants, then cloud solutions are often ideal. It is possible for individuals to be open and digital by placing their presentations in their own database, but this lacks the network element, and services such as Slideshare offer a better option where more people will find them. If connections, views and ease of use are paramount, then the commercial cloud is a sensible option.

- Store locally, share globally. Placing content online doesn't entail surrendering it completely. Perhaps a reasonable assumption is that these services will disappear at some point, so a local store acts as backup.

- Find alternatives. One advantage of the cloud-based approach is that there are numerous services that perform the same function. When the news about Delicious broke many people looked for alternatives, for example, Diigo, and exported their bookmarks. The cloud itself offers a degree of resilience.

- Develop academic solutions. Academic projects don't always have a good track record in keeping things simple, but there are services that it may be useful to share between universities, such as storing research data in a specialised cloud. The Flexible Services for the Support of Research (FleSSR) project, for example, is exploring a hybrid of private and public cloud solutions between universities "for the on-demand provision of computational and data resources in support of research" (http://www.jisc. ac.uk/whatwedo/programmes/flexibleservicedelivery/flessr.aspx). There could be benefits in terms of efficiency, shared data and agreed standards for similar projects focused on very specific academic needs, which general cloud solutions do not meet.

- Accept that such services are temporary. Even if Delicious did close down (which doesn't seem to be the case), it has lasted seven years, giving users a service they wouldn't have had if they'd waited for an institutionally hosted version to materialise.

- Develop service-level agreements. This model accepts that some cloud-based solutions are viable, and the institution either pays for these or guarantees a number of users in return for a service-level agreement. This doesn't guarantee the durability of the providing company or that the services won't be removed, but it does provide a level of reassurance.

- Self-hosting. A range of open source and low-cost software options are available, which mean that individuals can host their own versions. For example, the blogging software Wordpress can be installed on individuals' server, which means they are not reliant on external services.

I would argue that an appropriate approach is not to retrench to solely internally developed systems, not to simply resist, but to engage in a resilient manner.

Room for disruption

In Chapter 3 some of the impacts of new technology in other industries were examined. While the lessons these sectors offer are instructive, it also provides a basis for considering in what ways higher education differs and thus may not be subject to the same influences. The major difference is that higher education is not purely a content industry. As I argued in Chapter 7, it *produces* a considerable amount of content, which could be distributed and shared digitally, but its revenue is not predicated on selling this content, unlike music or newspapers.

It is undoubtedly the case that the vast amount of online content means that people now conduct a lot of their learning informally, using free resources. Combined with financial pressures, this creates a pressure or an alternative competition for learning that is new to higher education. Anya Kamenetz (2010) details the convergence of these two factors in her book *DIY U*, arguing that 'Do-It-Yourself University means the expansion of education beyond classroom walls: free, open-source, vocational, experiential, and self-directed learning'. This certainly represents a challenge to the monopoly on learning that universities and colleges have held for centuries and one they should take seriously (through engagement with technology and approaches).

However, even in times of financial crisis higher education has a certain resilience for two reasons: the social value of formal education is often increased in times of financial hardship and learning is not a zero-sum game. It is this latter reason that I think is of real significance to higher education. Even if people are learning much of what they require via open, online resources mediated through their social network, that in itself can generate the desire for further learning and can generate interest in formal education. Competition with informal learning is true to an extent, but it presupposes a set amount of learning by an individual, as if they have a limited number of cognitive learning tokens to be used up in a lifetime. But it is more often the case that learning begets learning. In this respect open, informal education is complementary to formal education, indeed something of a gift, rather than a threat. In a world that generates vast amounts of niche content which people are increasingly engaged with, either through generating their own, sharing or discussing, the outcome is a larger population of active learners. A population of active learners are more likely to engage in formal study than a population of passive consumers.

The challenge for universities is to remain relevant to these learners. This means developing an appropriate curriculum, having flexible course options, using technology effectively and generating interest. An example of this symbiotic relationship would be between a photo-sharing service such as Flickr and university courses on digital photography. A great deal of informal learning occurs through the communities on Flickr, which can focus on themes or techniques, or the Daily Shoot site, which gives photographers a daily task to perform (http://dailyshoot.com/). At some stage though many photographers want to further their understanding or have a more structured approach and sign up for a course on digital photography. The Open University's short course in this area has been one of its most popular, which since 2007 has two presentations a year with between 1,000 and 1,500 students per cohort.

More radically, Jim Groom set up an open course on digital storytelling (http://ds106.us/), which combines learners from a global community with those based on his own campus of University of Mary Washington. Participants are required to create digital artefacts and to share these on their own blogs and sites, which are aggregated together on this course blog. The course is fluid, with participants suggesting assignments, and distributed across many sites, using the hashtag #ds106 to group content. It combined 32 campus-based students who are studying for credit, with more than 250 learners from a global community studying for their own interest, and even had its own radio station.

These two examples demonstrate how the open, informal learning which many people partake in online is not necessarily a threat to the existence of higher education and, given some adjustments by universities, can be a benefit.

There are two messages that higher education can take from this: the first is that it needs to engage in the sort of experimentation Jim Groom's course represents if it is to turn the digital, networked and open approaches of learners to its advantage; the second is that it has the capacity to do so.

It is this second message that marks another difference with the sectors reviewed in Chapter 3. Many of those industries did not have the revenue streams which come from accreditation and research funding to counter any loss of revenue from consumers finding alternative content freely available online. Higher education is in a position where not only does it need to disrupt its own practice but it can *afford* to. It has sufficient resilience to do so because unlike content industries, that disruption does not completely undermine its current model. In Chapter 7 I argued that higher education can be viewed as a long tail content production system, and with little effort much of what it produces could be shared as open, digital resources. Higher education can afford to do this because their 'customers' (if we use that term by way of analogy with other sectors) are not purchasing that content directly – they are instead students who are paying for a learning experience which comprises that content along with the other elements outlined in Chapter 3, most notably support, guidance and accreditation. Other customers include research councils, commercial partners, media, charities and governmental agencies. Again these customers are not directly paying for content, and with the exception of cases of commercial sensitivity and privacy issues, they often have much to gain from openness and wide dissemination.

Some of the concerns relating to the impact of new technologies in other sectors then do not apply in scholarship, or their impact is reduced. The concerns regarding how artistic endeavour is to be rewarded in a world where all content can be easily distributed for free are very real if you are a musician, for example. These concerns are not the same for academics, however, who are usually employed and so are not deriving their income from content in the same manner. This is not to underestimate the impact and challenges that face higher education, but to highlight that disruption by new technologically driven approaches is not as threatening to core practice as it has been in other sectors. This may account for why the innovation and adoption of such approaches have been less prevalent in higher education, since the urgency to respond is not as great.

Conclusion

In Chapter 2 I argued that some of the rhetoric about revolution in higher education was ill-founded. But that is not to say that considerable changes to practice are not occurring and that education itself is operating within a broader social and economical upheaval driven by digital technologies. If a complete revolution in higher education is not necessarily imminent, this does not equate to a life of immutable practice either.

It is necessary to acknowledge then that the adoption of a digital, networked, open approach is not without its problems, and what is more we are at a stage when there is still considerable uncertainty as to how such approaches will affect scholarship. Higher education is facing challenges beyond technological ones as funding models and the role of education in society come under scrutiny. Technology should not be seen as a panacea for all of these issues, but also we should not romanticise some scholarly Camelot of yesteryear either.

If there is some room for disruption within higher education, then the kind of changes that are witnessed in broader society as a result of a global, digital network represent an opportunity for higher education. The first wave of user-generated content has largely focused on easy-to-share artefacts: photos, videos, audio. Having begun sharing, people are now constructing meaning around these, for example, the groups that form on Flickr. It is this next step, in using these artefacts to construct deeper knowledge, that higher education has a role to play. This can be in constructing an appropriate curriculum, developing tools and structure for facilitating this, generating outputs that can be used and researching how this type of knowledge construction occurs. Scholarship which met these challenges would be one that is not only of increased relevance to society but also a resilient practice.

This argument can be furthered by an example. Lanier (2010) argues against what he perceives as the prevailing wisdom around cloud computing in *You Are Not a Gadget*. The resultant disaggregation of our self is depersonalising, he suggests, and superficial (to echo an earlier objection). This is partly a result of the way the software is designed; for example, he argues that the sort of anonymous, consequence-free commenting on YouTube leads to the sort of negative 'Trolling' behaviours one often observes there. It is also partly a result of people lowering the behaviour to meet that of the software, for example, allowing the simple classifications of Facebook. This may not be true; a rich picture of someone emerges from their Facebook updates regardless of the simplistic classifications they start their profile with, but the perceived superficiality of much online discourse is often raised.

Lanier does not propose withdrawing from online environments as a solution but rather suggests some simple approaches to overcoming this depersonalisation:

1   Don't post anonymously unless you really might be in danger.

2   If you put effort into Wikipedia articles, put even more effort into using your personal voice and expression outside of the wiki to help attract people who don't yet realise that they are interested in the topics you contributed to.

3 Create a website that expresses something about who you are that won't fit into the template available to you on a social networking site.

4 Post a video once in a while that took you one hundred times more time to create than it takes to view.

Whether you accept Lanier's view, the suggestions above represent an example of how, having mastered sharing, there is a desire to utilise the possibilities for structured, thoughtful pieces, and higher education should surely be able to play a role in this.

In this book I have attempted to set out three themes: the changing practice that is occurring; the potential of digital, networked, open approaches to enhance scholarship; and the context within which this is taking place. This is a period of transition for scholarship, as significant as any other in its history, from the founding of universities to the establishment of peer review and the scientific method. It is also a period that holds tension and even some paradoxes: it is both business as usual and yet a time of considerable change; individual scholars are being highly innovative and yet the overall picture is one of reluctance; technology is creating new opportunities while simultaneously generating new concerns and problems. One should therefore be wary of any simplistic solutions and rhetoric which proclaims a technological utopia or equally dismisses technology as secondary.

In this period of transition the onus is on us as scholars to understand the possibilities that the intersection of digital, network and open approaches allow. If Boyer's four main scholarly functions were research, application, integration and teaching, then I would propose that those of the digital scholar are engagement, experimentation, reflection and sharing. It is the adoption of these functions that will generate the resilient scholarship of the next generation. For scholars it should not be a case of you see what goes, you see what stays, you see what comes, but rather you *determine* what goes, what stays and what comes.

References

Aemeur, E., Brassard, G. & Paquet, S. (2005), 'Personal Knowledge Publishing: Fostering Interdisciplinary Communication', *IEEE Intelligent Systems*, 20(2): 46–53.

Amis, M. (2010), *The Pregnant Widow*, London: Jonathan Cape.

Andersen, D.L. (2008), *Digital Scholarship in the Tenure, Promotion, and Review Process*, New York: M.E. Sharpe.

Anderson, C. (2006), *The Long Tail: Why the Future of Business Is Selling Less of More*, New York: Hyperion.

Anderson, C. (2008), 'Freemium Math: What's the Right Conversion Percentage?' Available at http://www.longtail.com/the_long_tail/2008/11/freemium-math-w.html [accessed 11 February 2011].

Anderson, C. (2010), 'How Web Video Powers Global Innovation'. Available at http://www.ted.com/talks/chris_anderson_how_web_video_powers_global_innovation.html [accessed 11 February 2011].

Anderson, P. (2007), 'What Is Web 2.0? Ideas, Technologies and Implications for Education', JISC. Available at http://www.jisc.ac.uk/media/documents/techwatch/tsw0701b.pdf [accessed 11 February 2011].

Anderson, T. (2009), 'ALT-C Keynote'. Available at http://www.slideshare.net/terrya/terry-anderson-alt-c-final [accessed 11 February 2011].

Antelman, K. (2004), 'Do Open-Access Articles Have a Greater Research Impact?' *College and Research Libraries*, 65(5): 372–82.

Aranda, J. (2006), 'Cheap Shots at the Gartner Hype Curve'. Available at http://catenary.wordpress.com/2006/10/22/cheap-shots-at-the-gartner-hype-curve/ [accessed 11 February 2011].

Bacon, S. & Dillon, T. (2006), 'The Potential of Open Source Approaches for Education'. Futurelab, TeLearn Online. Available at http://telearn.noe-kaleidoscope.org/warehouse/bacon-2006-OpenSource.pdf [accessed 11 February 2011].

Barrows, H. & Tamblyn, R. (1980), *Problem-Based Learning: An Approach to Medical Education*, New York: Springer.

Bauer, H. (1990), 'Barriers Against Interdisciplinarity: Implications for Studies of Science, Technology and Society (STS)',Science, Technology & Human Values, 15(1): 105–19.

Becker, J. (2009), 'What I've Learned from/with Dr Alec Couros'. Available at http://edinsanity.com/2009/11/25/what-ive-learned-fromwith-dr-alec-couros-a-k-a-courosa-alec/ [accessed 11 February 2011].

Bellow, S. (1953), *The Adventures of Augie March*, New York: Viking Press.

Bennett, S., Maton, K. & Kervin, L. (2008), 'The "Digital Natives" Debate: A Critical Review of the Evidence', *British Journal of Educational Technology*, 39(5): 775–86.

Birney, E., Hudson, T., Green, E., Gunter, C., Eddy, S., Rogers, J., Harris J. & Dusko, S. (2009), 'Prepublication Data Sharing', *Nature*, 461: 168–70.

Blais, J., Ippolito, J. & Smith, O. (2007), 'New Criteria for New Media', *Leonardo*, 42(1): 71–5.

Borgman, C. (2007), *Scholarship in the Digital Age: Information, Infrastructure, and the Internet*, Cambridge, MA: MIT Press.

Bousfield, D. & Fooladi, P. (2009), 'Scientific, Technical and Medical Information: 2009 Final Market Size and Share Report',Outsell. Available at http://www.outsellinc.com/store/products/938-scientific-technical-medical-information-2009-final-market-size-and-share-report [accessed 11 February 2011].

Boyd, D. (2009), 'Spectacle at Web2.0 Expo... from My Perspective'. Available at http://www.zephoria.org/thoughts/archives/2009/11/24/spectacle_at_we.html [accessed 11 February 2011].

Boyd, D., Golder, S. & Lotan, G. (2010), *Tweet, Tweet, Retweet: Conversational Aspects of Retweeting on Twitter*, HICSS-43, IEEE: Kauai, HI, January 6. Available at http://www.danah.org/papers/TweetTweetRetweet.pdf [accessed 11 February 2011].

Boyer, E. (1990), *Scholarship Reconsidered: Priorities of the Professoriate*, San Francisco: Jossey-Bass.

Brown, M. (2009), 'The NetGens 2.0: Clouds on the Horizon', *EDUCAUSE Review*, 44(1): 66–7.

Brynjolfsson, E., Hu, Y.J. & Simester, D. (2007), 'Goodbye Pareto Principle, Hello Long Tail: The Effect of Search Costs on the Concentration of Product Sales', *Social Science Research Network.* Available at http://ssrn.com/abstract=953587 [accessed 11 February 2011].

Brynjolfsson, E., Hu, Y.J. & Smith, M.D. (2010), 'The Longer Tail: The Changing Shape of Amazon's Sales Distribution Curve', SSRN. Available at http://ssrn.com/abstract=1679991 [accessed 11 February 2011].

Budapest Open Access Initiative (2002), Available at http://www.soros.org/openaccess/read.shtml [accessed 11 February 2011].

Burton, G. (2009), 'The Open Scholar'. Available at http://www.academicevolution.com/2009/08/the-open-scholar.html [accessed 11 February 2011].

Callender, C. & Jackson, J. (2008), 'Does the Fear of Debt Constrain Choice of University and Subject of Study?' *Studies in Higher Education*, 33(4):405–29.

Cann, A. & Badge, J. (2010), 'Reflective Social Portfolios for Feedback and Peer Mentoring'. Forthcoming.

Capps, R. (2009), 'The Good Enough Revolution: When Cheap and Simple Is Just Fine', *Wired Magazine: 17.09*. Available at http://www.wired.com/gadgets/miscellaneous/magazine/17-09/ff_goodenough?currentPage=1 [accessed 9 February 2011].

Carpenter, J., Wetheridge, L. & Smith, N. (2010), 'Researchers of Tomorrow: Annual Report 2009–2010', British Library/JISC. Available at http://explorationforchange.net/attachments/056_RoT%20Year%201%20report%20final%2020100622.pdf [accessed 11 February 2011].

Carr, N. (2007), 'The Long Player'. Available at http://www.roughtype.com/archives/2007/05/long_player.php [accessed 9 February 2011].

Carr, N. (2008), 'Is Google Making Us Stupid?' *Atlantic*. Available at http://www.theatlantic.com/magazine/archive/2008/07/is-google-making-us-stupid/6868/ [accessed 11 February 2011].

Carr, N. (2010), *The Shallows*. London: W. W. Norton & Company.

Carson, S. (2005), 'MIT OpenCourseWare 2005 Program Evaluation Findings Report'. Available at http://ocw.mit.edu/ans7870/global/05_Prog_Eval_Report_Final.pdf [accessed 11 February 2011].

Cheverie, J.F., Boettcher, J. & Buschman, J. (2009), 'Digital Scholarship in the University Tenure and Promotion Process: A Report on the Sixth Scholarly Communication Symposium at Georgetown University Library', *Journal of Scholarly Publishing*, 40(3): 219–30. Available at http://muse.jhu.edu/citation/journals/journal_of_scholarly_publishing/v040/40.3.cheverie.html [accessed 9 March 2011].

Clarke, R. (2007), 'The Cost Profiles of Alternative Approaches to Journal Publishing', *First Monday*, 12(12). Available at http://www.uic.edu/htbin/cgiwrap/bin/ojs/index.php/fm/article/viewArticle/2048/1906 [accessed 11 February 2011].

Clayton, N. (2002), 'SCOT: Does It Answer?' *Technology and Culture*, 43(2): 351–60.

Clow, D. (2009), '@stephenfry 20 Times Better than BBC News'. Available at http://dougclow.wordpress.com/2009/03/31/new-media-better-for-new-media/ [accessed 11 February 2011].

Comscore (2010), 'comScore Reports Global Search Market Growth of 46 Percent in 2009'. Available at http://www.comscore.com/Press_Events/Press_Releases/2010/1/Global_Search_Market_Grows_46_Percent_in_2009 [accessed 11 February 2011].

Conole, G. (2008), 'New Schemas for Mapping Pedagogies and Technologies', *Ariadne*, 56. Available at http://www.ariadne.ac.uk/issue56/conole/ [accessed 11 February 2011].

Conole, G., Scanlon, E., Mundin, P. & Farrow, R. (2010), 'Interdisciplinary Research: Findings from the Technology Enhanced Learning Research Programme', ESRC. Available at http://www.tlrp.org/docs/TELInterdisciplinarity.pdf [accessed 11 February 2011].

Cope, B. & Kalantzis, M. (2009), 'Signs of Epistemic Disruption: Transformations in the Knowledge System of the Academic Journal', *First Monday*, 14(4).

Coughlan, S. (2010), 'Majority of Young Women in University', BBC News. Available at http://news.bbc.co.uk/1/hi/education/8596504.stm [accessed 11 February 2011].

Cronin, B., Snyder, H.W., Rosenbaum, H., Martinson, A. & Callahan, E. (1998), 'Invoked on the Web', *Journal of the American Society for Information Science*, 49(14): 1319–28.

Crowston, K. & Howison, J. (2005), 'The Social Structure of Free and Open Source Software Development', *First Monday*, 10(2). Available at http://firstmonday.org/issues/issue10_2/crowston/index.html [accessed 11 February 2011].

Curtis, P. (2008), 'Record Number of Pupils Suspended', *The Guardian*, 25 October. Available at http://www.guardian.co.uk/politics/2008/oct/25/truancy-school-suspensions [accessed 12 February 2011].

Czerniewicz, L. & Brown, C. (2008), 'A Virtual Wheel of Fortune? Enablers and Constraints of ICTs in Higher Education in South Africa', in S. Marshall, W. Kinuthia & W. Taylor (eds), *Bridging the Knowledge Divide: Educational Technology for Development*, Colorado, CO: Information Age Publishing, pp. 57–76.

Davis, P.M. (2010), 'Does Open Access Lead to Increased Readership and Citations? A Randomized Controlled Trial of Articles Published in APS Journals', *The Physiologist*, 53(6). Available at http://www.the-aps.org/publications/tphys/2010html/December/open_access.htm [accessed 11 February 2011].

Dempsey, L. (2007), 'The Amplified Conference'. Available at http://orweblog.oclc.org/archives/001404.html [accessed 11 February 2011].

Derbyshire, D. (2009), 'Social Websites Harm Children's Brains: Chilling Warning to Parents from Top Neuroscientist', *Daily Mail*, 24 February. Available at http://www.dailymail.co.uk/news/article-1153583/Social-websites-harm-childrens-brains-Chilling-warning-parents-neuroscientist.html#ixzz1DSPdY7Pu [accessed 11 February 2011].

Drewes, T. & Michael, C. (2006), 'How Do Students Choose a University?: An Analysis of Applications to Universities in Ontario, Canada', *Research in Higher Education*, 47(7): 781–800.

Dunbar, R. (1992), 'Neocortex Size as a Constraint on Group Size in Primates', *Journal of Human Evolution*, 22(6): 469–93.

Duval, E. (2010), 'Removing Friction in Open Education'. Available at http://erikduval.wordpress.com/2010/11/08/removing-friction-in-open-education/ [accessed 11 February 2011].

Edwards, R. & Shulenburger, D. (2003), 'The High Cost of Scholarly Journals (and What to Do About It)', *Change*, 35(6): 10.

Ehrlich, P.R. & Levin, S.A. (2005), 'The Evolution of Norms', *PLoS Biol*, 3(6): e194.

Falagas, M. & Alexiou, V. (2008), 'The Top Ten in Journal Impact Factor Manipulation', *Archivum Immunologiae et Therapie Experimentalis*, 56(4): 223–26.

Ferguson, D. (2009), 'The Keynote and the Harshtag'. Available at http://www.daveswhiteboard.com/archives/2874 [accessed 11 February 2011].

Fitzpatrick, K. (2009), 'Peer-to-Peer Review and the Future of Scholarly Authority', *Cinema Journal*, 48(2): 124–9.

Foster, I. (2006), 'A Two-Way Street to Science's Future', *Nature*, 440: 419.

Fry, J. (2004), 'The Cultural Shaping of ICTs within Academic Fields: Corpus-Based Linguistics as a Case Study', *Literary and Linguistic Computing*, 19(3): 303–19.

Galison, P. & Hevley, G. (1992), *Big Science: The Growth of Large-Scale Research*, Stanford, CA: Stanford University Press.

Gannes, L. (2010), 'The Short and Illustrious History of Twitter #Hashtags'. Available at http://gigaom.com/2010/04/30/the-short-and-illustrious-history-of-twitter-hashtags/ [accessed 11 February 2011].

Gartner (2008), 'Gartner Hype Cycle'. Available at http://www.gartner.com/it/products/research/methodologies/research_hype.jsp [accessed 11 February 2011].

Gerschenfeld, A. (2010), 'Is the Internet Changing the Way We Think?' *The Edge*. Available at http://www.edge.org/documents/press/publico2010.html [accessed 11 February 2011].

Geyer-Schulz, A., Neumann, A., Heitmann A. & Stroborn, K. (2003), 'Strategic Positioning Options for Scientific Libraries in Markets of Scientific and Technical Information: The Economic Impact of Digitization', *Journal of Digital Information*, 4(2). Available at http://journals.tdl.org/jodi/article/viewArticle/101/100 [accessed 21 April 2011].

Ghosh, R. & Glott, R. (2005), 'FLOSSPOLS: Skills Survey Interim Report'. Available at http://flosspols.org/deliverables/D10HTML/FLOSSPOLS-D10-skills%20survey_interim_report-revision-FINAL.html [accessed 11 February 2011].

Ghosh, R.A., Glott, R., Krieger, B. & Robles, G. (2002), *Free/Libre and Open Source Software: Survey and Study. Part IV: Survey of Developers*, Maastricht: International Institute of Infonomics/Merit.

Ginsberg, J., Mohebbi, M., Patel, R., Brammer, L., Smolinski, M. & Brilliant, L. (2009), 'Detecting Influenza Epidemics Using Search Engine Query Data', *Nature*, 457,

19 February. Available at http://dx.doi.org/10.1038/nature07634 [accessed 11 February 2011].

Glott, R., Meiszner, A. & Sowe, S. (2007), 'Report on the Learning Environment of FLOSS Communities', FLOSScom project. Available at http://openedworld. flossproject.org/index.php/flosscom-project-2006-to-2008 [accessed 21 April 2011].

Graham, J. (2006), 'Flickr of Idea on a Gaming Project Led to Photo Website', *USA Today*, February 27. Available at http://www.usatoday.com/tech/products/2006-02-27-flickr_x.htm [accessed 12 February 2011].

Green, T. (2009), 'We Need Publishing Standards for Datasets and Data Tables', *OECD Publishing White Paper*, OECD Publishing. Available at http://www.oecd.org/docu ment/25/0,3746,en_21571361_33915056_42600857_1_1_1_1,00.html [accessed 11 February 2011].

Greenfield, A. (2010), 'Don't Get Me Wrong'. Available at http://speedbird.wordpress. com/2010/05/04/dont-get-me-wrong/ [accessed 11 February 2011].

Griffiths, M. (2008), 'Changing Media Environments Are Providing an Alternative Space for Young People to Meet Up', Creating Second Lives Conference, 24/25 October 2008, Bangor, Wales.

Grunwald, P. (2003), 'Key Technology Trends: Excerpts from New Survey Research Findings', *Exploring the Digital Generation*, Educational Technology, U.S. Department of Education, Washington, DC, 23–4 September.

Hajjem, C., Harnard, S. & Gingras, Y. (2005), 'Ten-Year Cross-Disciplinary Comparison of the Growth of Open Access and How It Increases Research Citation Impact', *IEEE Data Engineering Bulletin*, 28(4): 39–47. Available at http://eprints.ecs.soton. ac.uk/12906/ [accessed 11 February 2011].

Hall, R. & Winn, J. (2010), 'The Relationships between Technology and Open Education in the Development of a Resilient Higher Education', Open Education Conference, Barcelona, 12 August. Available at http://www.learnex.dmu.ac.uk/ wp-content/uploads/2010/09/hall_winn_OpenEd_resilience.12.09.10.pdf [accessed 11 February 2011].

Hanson, T. (2008), 'A Vision of Students Today – Some Additional Thoughts from Michael Wesch'. Available at http://www.openeducation.net/2008/10/28/ a-vision-of-students-today-some-additional-thoughts-from-michael-wesch/ [accessed 12 February 2011].

Harley, D., Acord, S., Earl-Novell, S., Lawrence, S. & King, C. (2010), 'Assessing the Future Landscape of Scholarly Communication: An Exploration of Faculty Values and Needs in Seven Disciplines', Berkeley, CA: Center for Studies in Higher Education, UC Berkeley. Available at http://escholarship.org/uc/cshe_fsc [accessed 11 February 2011].

Harnad, S. (2005), 'OA Impact Advantage = EA + (AA) + (QB) + QA + (CA) + UA'. Available at http://eprints.ecs.soton.ac.uk/12085/ [accessed 11 February 2011].

Harnad, S. & Brody, T. (2004), 'Comparing the Impact of Open Access (OA) vs. Non-OA Articles in the Same Journals', *D-Lib Magazine*, 10(6). Available at http:// www.dlib.org/dlib/june04/harnad/06harnad.html [accessed 11 February 2011].

Harnad, S., Brody, T., Vallieres, F., Carr, L., Hitchcock, S., Gingras, Y., Oppenheim, C., Stamerjohanns, H., & Hilf, E. (2004), 'The Access/Impact Problem and the Green and Gold Roads to Open Access', *Serials Review*, 30(4). Available at http://dx.doi. org/10.1016/j.serrev.2004.09.013 [accessed 11 February 2011].

Hart, A., Northmore, S. & Gerhardt, C. (2009), *Auditing, Benchmarking and Evaluating Public Engagement*, National Coordinating Centre for Public Engagement. Available at https://www.publicengagement.ac.uk/sites/default/files/EvaluatingPublicEngagement.pdf [accessed 11 February 2011].

Hartman, J., Moskal, P. & Dziuban, C. (2005), 'Preparing the Academy of Today for the Learner of Tomorrow', in D. Oblinger & J. Oblinger (eds), *Educating the Net Generation*, Washington, DC: Educause, pp. 6.1–6.15.

HEFCE (2007), 'Bridging the Gap between Higher Education and the Public', HEFCE News. Available at www.hefce.ac.uk/news/hefce/2007/beacons.asp [accessed 11 February 2011].

HEFCE (2010), 'REF 2014: Bibliometrics'. Available at http://www.hefce.ac.uk/research/ref/biblio/ [accessed 11 February 2011].

Hendler, J., Shadbolt, N., Hall, W., Berners-Lee, T. & Weitzner, D. (2008), 'Web Science: An Interdisciplinary Approach to Understanding the Web', *Communications of the ACM*, 51(7): 60–9.

Heppell, S. (2001), 'Preface' in V. Ellis & A. Loveless (eds), *ICT, Pedagogy and the Curriculum: Subject to Change*, London: Routledge, p. xv. Available at http://books.google.co.uk/books?id=i8a0qAOsBiMC [accessed 11 February 2011].

Hevner, A.R. & March, S.T. (2003), 'The Information Systems Research Cycle', *Computer*, 36(11): 111–13.

Hiatt, B. & Serpick, E. (2007), 'The Record Industry's Decline', *Rolling Stone*, June 19.

Hirsch, J.E. (2005), 'An Index to Quantify an Individual's Scientific Research Output'. Available at http://arxiv:physics/0508025 [accessed 15 April 2011].

Hirst, T. (2009), 'Comment on Digital Britain at WriteToReply.org'. Available at http://blog.ouseful.info/2009/02/04/comment-on-digital-britain-at-writetoreplyorg/ [accessed 11 February 2011].

Hirst, T. (2010), 'Structural Differences in Hashtag Communities: Highly Interconnected or Not?' Available at http://blog.ouseful.info/2010/09/13/structural-differences-in-hashtag-communities-highly-interconnected-or-not/ [accessed 11 February 2011].

Hitchens, C. (2002), 'The Medals of His Defeats', *Atlantic Monthly*, April. Available at http://www.theatlantic.com/past/docs/issues/2002/04/hitchens.htm [accessed 12 February 2011].

Holling, C.S. (1973), 'Resilience and Stability of Ecological Systems', *Annual Review Ecology Systems*, 4: 1–23.

Hopkins, R. (2009), 'Resilience Thinking', *Resurgence*, 257: 12–15.

Horrigan, S. (2009), 'Twitter Mysteries and Twettiquette'. Available at http://kindalearning.blogspot.com/2009/04/twitter-mysteries-and-twetiquette.html [accessed 11 February 2011].

Houghton, J., Rasmussen, B., Sheehan, P., Oppenheim, C., Morris, A., Creaser, C., Greenwood, H., Summers, M. & Gourlay, A. (2009), 'Economic Implications of Alternative Scholarly Publishing Models: Exploring the Costs and Benefits', JISC. Available at http://www.jisc.ac.uk/publications/reports/2009/economicpublishingmodelsfinalreport.aspx [accessed 11 February 2011].

Hoyle, M. (2009), 'OER and a Pedagogy of Abundance'. Available at http://einiverse.eingang.org/2009/11/18/oer-and-a-pedagogy-of-abundance/#more-181 [accessed 11 February 2011].

Huberman, B., Romero, D. & Wu, F. (2009), 'Social Networks that Matter: Twitter under the Microscope', *First Monday*, 14(1). Available at http://firstmonday.org/htbin/cgiwrap/bin/ojs/index.php/fm/rt/printerFriendly/2317/2063 [accessed 11 February 2011].

IFPI (2009), 'Digital Music Report'. Available at http://www.ifpi.org/content/library/DMR2009.pdf [accessed 11 February 2011].

James, L., Norman, J., De Baets, A., Burchell-Hughes, I., Burchmore, H., Philips, A., Sheppard, D., Wilks, L. & Wolffe, J. (2009), 'The Lives and Technologies of Early Career Researchers', JISC. Available at http://www.jisc.ac.uk/publications/reports/2009/earlycareerresearchersstudy.aspx [accessed 11 February 2011].

Jonassen, D. (1991), 'Objectivism vs Constructivism: Do We Need a New Philosophical Paradigm?' *Educational Technology, Research and Development*, 39(3): 5–13.

Kahneman, D. & Tversky, A. (1979), 'Prospect Theory: An Analysis of Decision under Risk', *Econometrica*, 47(2): 263–91.

Kamenetz, A. (2010), *DIY U: Edupunks, Edupreneurs, and the Coming Transformation of Higher Education*, White River Junction, VT: Chelsea Green Publishing.

Keen, A. (2007), *The Cult of the Amateur: How Today's Internet Is Killing Our Culture.* London: Crown Business.

Keen, A. (2009), 'Free Market Maoism'. Available at http://andrewkeen.typepad.com/the_great_seduction/2009/03/where-are-we-now-1500-or-1848.html [accessed 9 February 2011].

Kelly, B. (2008), 'Defining an Amplified Conference'. Available at http://ukwebfocus.wordpress.com/2008/08/28/defining-an-amplified-conference/ [accessed 10 February 2011].

Kerr, B. (2007), 'Which Radical Discontinuity?' Available at http://billkerr2.blogspot.com/2007/02/which-radical-discontinuity.html [accessed 11 February 2011].

Kirschner, P.A., Sweller, J. & Clark, R.E. (2006), 'Why Minimal Guidance During Instruction Does Not Work: An Analysis of the Failure of Constructivist, Discovery, Problem-Based, Experiential, and Inquiry-Based Teaching', *Educational Psychologist*, 41(2): 75–86.

Klein, J.T. (1991), *Interdisciplinarity: History, Theory, and Practice*, Newcastle upon Tyne: Bloodaxe Books.

Kling, R., McKim, G. & King, A. (2003), 'A Bit More to IT: Scholarly Communication Forums as Socio-Technical Interaction Networks', *Journal of the American Society for Information Science and Technology*, 54(1): 46–67.

Kockelmans, J. (1979), *Interdisciplinarity and Higher Education*, University Park, PA: Pennsylvania State University Press.

Kroll, S. & Forsman, R. (2010), 'A Slice of Research Life: Information Support for Research in the United States' OCLC Online Computer Library Center, Inc., Available at http://www.oclc.org/research/publications/library/2010/2010-15.pdf [accessed 11 February 2011].

Lamb, B. (2010), 'Open Contempt'. Available at http://wiki.ubc.ca/Open_Contempt [accessed 11 February 2011].

Lanier, J. (2010), *You Are Not a Gadget: A Manifesto*, New York: Knopf.

Lave, J. & Wenger, E. (1991), *Situated Learning: Legitimate Peripheral Participation*, Cambridge, UK: Cambridge University Press.

Lawrence, S. (2001), 'Free Online Availability Substantially Increases a Paper's Impact', *Nature*, 31 May. Available at http://www.nature.com/nature/debates/e-access/Articles/lawrence.html [accessed 11 February 2011].

Le Meur, L. (2005), 'Is There a Blog Culture?' Available at http://loiclemeur.com/english/2005/05/is_there_a_blog.html [accessed 21 April 2011].

Lenhart, A., Arafeh, S., Smith, A. & MacGill A. (2008), 'Writing, Technology and Teens', *Pew Internet and American Life Project*. Available at http://www.pewinternet.org/Reports/2008/Writing-Technology-and-Teens.aspx [accessed 21 April 2011].

Leslie, S. (2008), 'Planning to Share Versus Just Sharing'. Available at http://www.edtechpost.ca/wordpress/2008/11/08/just-share-already/ [accessed 11 February 2011].

Lessig, L. (2007), 'Larry Lessig on Laws that Choke Creativity'. Available at http://www.ted.com/talks/larry_lessig_says_the_law_is_strangling_creativity.html [accessed 11 February 2011].

Levine, A. (2009), 'Amazing Stories of Openness'. Available at http://cogdogblog.com/stuff/opened09/ [accessed 11 February 2011].

Lipsett, A. (2008), 'Truancy Rate Rises to 63,000 Pupils a Day', *The Guardian*, 27 February. Available at http://www.guardian.co.uk/education/2008/feb/27/schools.uk1 [accessed 12 February 2011].

Livingstone, S. & Bober, M. (2005), 'UK Children Go Online: Final Report', LSE. Available at http://www.lse.ac.uk/collections/children-go-online/ [accessed 12 February 2011].

Lyon, L. (2007), 'Dealing with Data: Roles, Rights, Responsibilities and Relationships',UKOLN. Available at http://www.ukoln.ac.uk/ukoln/staff/e.j.lyon/reports/dealing_with_data_report-final.pdf [accessed 11 February 2011].

MacFadgen, L. (2008), 'Mature Students in the Persistent Puzzle: An Exploration of the Factors that Contribute to Mature Students' Health, Learning and Retention in Post-Secondary Education', Canadian Council on Learning. Available at http://www.ccl-cca.ca/NR/rdonlyres/D17D6EC1-6894-4E65-A08F-1921E039DD32/0/MacFadgenFinalExecSummEAL2006.pdf [accessed 15 April 2011].

MacKinnon, R. (2010), 'WikiLeaks, Amazon and the New Threat to Internet Speech', CNN. Available at http://edition.cnn.com/2010/OPINION/12/02/mackinnon.wikileaks.amazon/ [accessed 11 February 2011].

MacMillan, R. (2008), '*New York Times* Ad Revenue Falls 20 Percent', *Reuters*. Available at http://uk.reuters.com/article/2008/12/24/businesspro-us-newyorktimes-idUKTRE4BN39Q20081224 [accessed 12 February 2011].

Madge, C., Meek, J., Wellens, J. & Hooley, T. (2009), 'Facebook, Social Integration and Informal Learning at University: "It Is More for Socialising and Talking to Friends About Work than for Actually Doing Work', *Learning, Media and Technology*, 34(2): 141–55.

Marek, K. & Valauskas, E.J. (2002), 'Web Logs as Indices of Electronic Journal Use: Tools for Identifying a "Classic" Article', *Libri*, 52(4): 220–30.

Mayer, R. (2004), 'Should There Be a Three-Strikes Rule against Pure Discovery Learning? The Case for Guided Methods of Instruction', *American Psychologist*, 59(1): 14–19.

Mayer-Schonberger, V. (2009), *Delete: The Virtue of Forgetting in the Digital Age*, New Jersey: Princeton University Press.

McAndrew, P., Santos, A., Lane, A., Godwin, S., Okada, A., Wilson, T., Connolly, T., Ferreira, G., Buckingham Shum, S., Bretts, J. & Webb, R. (2009), *OpenLearn Research Report 2006–2008*. Milton Keynes, UK: The Open University. Available at http://oro.open.ac.uk/17513/ [accessed 11 February 2011].

McAndrew, P., Scanlon, E. & Clow, D. (2010), 'An Open Future for Higher Education', *Educause Quarterly*, 33(1). Available at http://www.educause.edu/EDUCAUSE+Quarterly/EDUCAUSEQuarterlyMagazineVolum/AnOpenFutureforHigherEducation/199388 [accessed 11 February 2011].

McAuley, A., Stewart, B., Siemens, G. & Cormier, D. (2010), 'The MOOC Model for Digital Practice'. Available at http://davecormier.com/edblog/wp-content/uploads/MOOC_Final.pdf [accessed 11 February 2011].

McGuigan, G. & Russell, R. (2008), 'The Business of Academic Publishing: A Strategic Analysis of the Academic Journal Publishing Industry and Its Impact on the Future of Scholarly Publishing', *E-JASL: The Electronic Journal of Academic and Special Librarianship*, 9(3), ICAAP. Available at http://southernlibrarianship.icaap.org/content/v09n03/mcguigan_g01.html [accessed 9 March 2011].

McKenzie, J. (1996), 'We Weave the Web', *Educational Leadership*, 54(3): 30–2.

Meiszner, A. (2010), 'The Emergence of Free/Open Courses – Lessons from the Open Source Movement', PhD Thesis, Milton Keynes, UK: The Open University. Available at http://www.scribd.com/doc/33852509/The-Emergence-of-Free-Open-Courses-Lessons-from-the-Open-Source-Movement [accessed 12 February 2011].

Morris, E. (1997), Fast, Cheap and Out of Control. Producer: Errol Morris.

Morrison, J. (2003), 'U.S. Higher Education in Transition', *On the Horizon*, 11(1): 6–10.

Moti, N. (1995), 'Fruits, Salads, and Smoothies: A Working Definition of Interdisciplinarity', *Journal of Educational Thought*, 29: 119–26.

Naughton, J. (2009), 'The Future of Newspapers (and Lots More Besides)'. Available at http://memex.naughtons.org/archives/2009/03/17/6998 [accessed 9 February 2011].

Naughton, J. (2010), 'WikiLeaks Row: Why Amazon's Desertion Has Ominous Implications for Democracy', *Guardian*, 11 December. Available at http://www.guardian.co.uk/technology/2010/dec/11/wikileaks-amazon-denial-democracy-lieberman [accessed 12 February 2011].

NEA (2007), 'To Read or Not to Read'. Available at http://www.nea.gov/research/ToRead.pdf [accessed 12 February 2011].

The New York Times (1908), 'Truancy Rates Increasing in City Schools', *The New York Times*, 8 May 1909. Available at http://query.nytimes.com/gst/abstract.html?res=9502E3D71738E033A2575BC0A9639C946897D6CF [accessed 12 February 2011].

Nielsen (2010), 'Social Networks/Blogs Now Account for One in Every Four and a Half Minutes Online'. Available at http://blog.nielsen.com/nielsenwire/online_mobile/social-media-accounts-for-22-percent-of-time-online/ [accessed 12 February 2011].

Noble, D.F. (1998), 'Digital Diploma Mills: The Automation of Higher Education', *First Monday*, 3(1). Available at http://firstmonday.org/htbin/cgiwrap/bin/ojs/index.php/fm/article/view/569/490 [accessed 11 February 2011].

Nowak, M. & Roch, S. (2007), 'Upstream Reciprocity and the Evolution of Gratitude', *Proceedings of the Royal Society B: Biological Sciences*, 274: 605–10.

Oblinger, D. & Oblinger, J. (2005), 'Is It Age or IT: First Steps Towards Understanding the Net Generation', in D. Oblinger & J. Oblinger (eds), *Educating the Net Generation*, Bolder, CO: Educause. Available at http://net.educause.edu/ir/library/pdf/pub7101b.pdf [accessed 21 April 2011]

OCLC (2007), 'Sharing, Privacy and Trust in Our Networked World'. Available at http://www.oclc.org/reports/sharing/default.htm [accessed 9 February 2011].

OECD (2007), 'Giving Knowledge for Free: The Emergence of Open Educational Resources'. Available at http://www.oecd.org/dataoecd/35/7/38654317.pdf [accessed 10 February 2011].

O'Reilly, T. (2004), 'The Architecture of Participation'. Available at http://oreilly.com/pub/a/oreilly/tim/articles/architecture_of_participation.html [accessed 9 February 2011].

Ortega, F. (2009), *Wikipedia: A Quantitative Analysis*, PhD Thesis, Madrid: Universidad Rey Juan Carlos. Available at http://libresoft.es/Members/jfelipe/thesis-wkp-quantanalysis [accessed 12 December 2010].

Palmer, C., Teffeau, L. & Pirmann, C. (2009), 'Scholarly Information Practices in the Online Environment: Themes from the Literature and Implications for Library Service Development', OCLC Research. Available at www.oclc.org/programs/publications/reports/2009-02.pdf [accessed 11 February 2011].

Patterson, M. (2009), 'Article-Level Metrics at PLoS – Addition of Usage Data', Public Library of Science (PLoS) Blog. Available at http://www.plos.org/cms/node/485 [accessed 11 February 2011].

Pinch, T.J. & Bijker W.E. (1984), 'The Social Construction of Facts and Artefacts: Or How the Sociology of Science and the Sociology of Technology Might Benefit Each Other', *Social Studies of Science*, 14: 399–441.

Plunkett, J. (2010), 'Andrew Marr Says Bloggers Are "Inadequate, Pimpled and Single"', *Guardian*, 11 October. Available at http://www.guardian.co.uk/media/2010/oct/11/andrew-marr-bloggers [accessed 11 February 2011].

Prensky, M. (2001), 'Digital Natives, Digital Immigrants', *On the Horizon*, 9(5): 1–6.

Price, D. (1963), *Little Science, Big Science*, New York: Columbia University Press.

Priem, J. & Hemminger, B. (2010), 'Scientometrics 2.0: Toward New Metrics of Scholarly Impact on the Social Web', *First Monday*, 15(7). Available at http://firstmonday.org/htbin/cgiwrap/bin/ojs/index.php/fm/article/viewArticle/2874/2570 [accessed 10 December 2010].

Procter, R., Williams, R., & Stewart, J. (2010), 'If You Build It, Will They Come? How Researchers Perceive and Use Web 2.0', Research Information Network. Available at www.rin.ac.uk/system/files/attachments/web_2.0_screen.pdf [accessed 21 April 2011].

Raymond, E. S. (1999), *The Cathedral & the Bazaar: Musings on Linux and Open Source by an Accidental Revolutionary.* Sebastopol, CA: O'Reilly Press.

Reed-Elsevier (2009), 'Annual and Financial Reports 2009'. Available at http://reports.reedelsevier.com/ar09/index.html [accessed 12 February 2011].

Rees, M. (2010), 'How Has the Internet Changed the Way You Think?' The Edge. Available at http://www.edge.org/q2010/q10_2.html [accessed 11 February 2011].

Rennie, F. & Weller, M. (eds) (2010), 'Open to All: Designing Digital Courses Using Open Educational Resources'. Available at http://www.blurb.com/bookstore/detail/1267854 [accessed 11 February 2011].

Robbins, L. (1932), *An Essay on the Nature and Significance of Economic Science*, London: Macmillan.

Roberts, G. (2005), 'Technology and Learning Expectations of the Net Generation', in D. Oblinger & J. Oblinger (eds), *Educating the Net Generation*. Bolder, CO: Educause. Available at http://net.educause.edu/ir/library/pdf/pub7101c.pdf [accessed 21 April 2011]

Roco, M. & Bainbridge, W. (2003), *Converging Technologies for Improving Human Performance: Nanotechnology, Biotechnology, Information Technology, and Cognitive Science*, The Netherlands: Springer.

Rogers, E.M. (1962), *Diffusion of Innovations*, Glencoe: Free Press.

Rosenzweig, R. (2007), 'Can History Be Open Source? Wikipedia and the Future of the Past', *Journal of American History*, 93(1): 117–46.

Rowlands, I., Nicholas, D., Williams, P., Huntington, P., Fieldhouse, M., Gunter, B., Withey, R., Jamali, H.R., Dobrowolski, T. & Tenopir, C. (2008), *The Information*

Behaviour of the Researcher of the Future, British Library/JISC. Available at http://www.jisc.ac.uk/media/documents/programmes/reppres/gg_final_ keynote_11012008.pdf [accessed 21 April 2011].

Ryan, S. (2000), *The Virtual University: The Internet and Resource Based Learning*, London: Routledge.

Schonfeld, R.C. & Housewright, R. (2010), 'Faculty Survey 2009: Key Strategic Insights for Libraries, Publishers, and Societies', Ithaka. Available at http://www.ithaka.org/ithaka-s-r/research/faculty-surveys-2000-2009/Faculty%20Study%202009.pdf [accessed 11 February 2011].

Schutz, J. (2007), 'Google Searches per Day'. Available at http://notes.jschutz.net/2007/11/google-searches-per-day/ [accessed 12 February 2011].

Seely-Brown, J. (2006), 'New Learning Environments in the 21st Century: Exploring the Edge', Forum Futures 2006. Available at http://www.educause.edu/ir/library/pdf/ff0604S.pdf [accessed 11 February 2011].

Seely-Brown, J. & Adler, P. (2008), 'Minds on Fire', *EDUCAUSE Review*, 43(1): 16–32. Available at http://www.educause.edu/EDUCAUSE+Review/EDUCAUSEReviewMagazineVolume43/MindsonFireOpenEducationtheLon/162420 [accessed 21 April 2011].

Selwyn, N. (2009), 'Faceworking: Exploring Students' Education-Related Use of Facebook', *Learning, Media and Technology*, 34(2): 157–74.

Shaohui, W. & Lihua, M. (2008), 'The Application of Blog in Modern Education', *Proceedings of CSSE 08*, 4:1083–1085

Shirky, C. (2007), 'New Freedom Destroys Old Culture: A Response to Nick Carr'. Available at http://many.corante.com/archives/2007/08/01/new_freedom_destroys_old_culture_a_response_to_nick_carr.php [accessed 9 February 2011].

Shirky, C. (2008a), 'Gin, Television and Cognitive Surplus'. Available at http://www.edge.org/3rd_culture/shirky08/shirky08_index.html [accessed 11 February 2011].

Shirky, C. (2008b), *Here Comes Everybody: The Power of Organizing without Organizations*, New York: Penguin Press.

Shirky, C. (2009), 'Newspapers and Thinking the Unthinkable'. Available at http://www.shirky.com/weblog/2009/03/newspapers-and-thinking-the-unthinkable/ [accessed 9 February 2011].

Shirky, C. (2010), *Cognitive Surplus: Creativity and Generosity in a Connected Age*, New York: Penguin.

Siegler, M. (2010), 'Eric Schmidt: Every 2 Days We Create As Much Information As We Did Up To 2003', Techchrunch. Available at http://techcrunch.com/2010/08/04/schmidt-data/ [accessed 12 February 2011].

Siemens, G. (2005), 'Connectivism: A Learning Theory for the Digital Age', *International Journal of Instructional Technology*, 2(1). Available at http://www.itdl.org/Journal/Jan_05/article01.htm [accessed 12 February 2011].

Siemens, G. (2008), 'New Structures and Spaces of Learning: The Systemic Impact of Connective Knowledge, Connectivism, and Networked Learning'. Available at http://elearnspace.org/Articles/systemic_impact.htm [accessed 12 February 2011].

Siemens, G. (2010), 'The University Lacks Capacity to Change Education'. Available at http://www.elearnspace.org/blog/2010/10/23/the-university-lacks-capacity-to-change-education/ [accessed 11 February 2011].

Smith Rumsey, A. (2010), 'Scholarly Communication Institute 8: Emerging Genres in Scholarly Communication',University of Virginia Library. Available at http://www.uvasci.org/wp-content/uploads/2010/09/SCI-8-report-final.pdf [accessed 11 February 2011].

Smits, P.B.A., Verbeek, J. & de Buisonjé, C. (2002), 'Learning in Practice: Problem Based Learning in Continuing Medical Education: A Review of Controlled Evaluation Studies', *BMJ*, 324: 153. Available at http://www.bmj.com/content/324/7330/153.full [accessed 21 April 2011].

Snow, C.P. (1960), *The Two Cultures*, Cambridge: Cambridge University Press.

Soutar, G.N. & Turner, J.P. (2002), 'Students' Preferences for University: A Conjoint Analysis', *The International Journal of Educational Management*, 16(1): 40–5.

Stein, J. (2008), 'Defining Creepy Treehouse'. Available at http://flexknowlogy.learningfield.org/2008/04/09/defining-creepy-tree-house/ [accessed 11 February 2011].

Stoll, C. (1995), 'The Internet? Bah!' Newsweek. Available at http://www.newsweek.com/1995/02/26/the-internet-bah.html [accessed 11 February 2011].

Suber, P. (2004), 'Open Access Review'. Available at http://www.earlham.edu/~peters/fos/overview.htm [accessed 11 February 2011].

Suber, P. (2009), 'Will OA Progress Lead to Pyrrhic Victory?' Available at http://www.earlham.edu/~peters/fos/2009/03/will-oa-progress-lead-to-pyrrhic.html [accessed 11 February 2011].

Swan, A. & Brown, S. (2008), 'To Share or Not to Share: Publication and Quality Assurance of Research Data Outputs', Research Information Network. Available at http://www.rin.ac.uk/our-work/data-management-and-curation/share-or-not-share-research-data-outputs [accessed 11 February 2011].

Sweney, M. (2008), 'Trinity Mirror Ad Revenue Slumps by a Fifth since June', *The Guardian*, 13 November. Available at http://www.guardian.co.uk/media/2008/nov/13/trinity-mirror-advertising [accessed 11 February 2011].

Tapscott, D. & Williams, A.D. (2006), *Wikinomics: How Mass Collaboration Changes Everything*, New York: Portfolio.

Unsworth, J. (2000), 'Scholarly Primitives: What Methods Do Humanities Researchers Have in Common, and How Might Our Tools Reflect This?' Symposium on 'Humanities Computing: Formal Methods, Experimental Practice', King's College, London, May 13. Available at http://www3.isrl.illinois.edu/~unsworth/Kings.5-00/primitives.html [accessed 11 February 2011].

Vernon, D. & Blake, R. (1993), 'Does Problem Based Learning Work? A Meta Analysis of Evaluation Research', *Academic Medicine*, 68: 550–63.

Waldrop, M. (2008), 'Science 2.0: Great New Tool, or Great Risk? Wikis, Blogs and Other Collaborative Web Technologies Could Usher in a New Era of Science. Or Not', *Scientific American*, January 9. Available at http://www.scientificamerican.com/article.cfm?id=science-2-point-0-great-new-tool-or-great-risk [accessed 11 February 2011].

Walker, B., Holling, C.S.,Carpenter, S.R. & Kinzig A. (2004), 'Resilience, Adaptability and Transformability in Social–Ecological Systems', *Ecology and Society*, 9(2): 5. Available at http://www.ecologyandsociety.org/vol9/iss2/art5 [accessed 12 February 2011].

Waltham, M. (2009), 'The Future of Scholarly Journals Publishing among Social Science and Humanities Associations', Report on a study funded by a Planning Grant from the Andrew W. Mellon Foundation. Available at http://www.nhalliance.org/bm~doc/hssreport.pdf [accessed 11 February 2011].

Ware, M. (2008), 'Peer Review: Benefits, Perceptions and Alternatives', *Publishing Research Consortium*. Available at http://www.publishingresearch.net/documents/PRCsummary4Warefinal.pdf [accessed 11 February 2011].

Waters, L. (2000), 'A Modest Proposal for Preventing the Books of the Members of the MLA from Being a Burden to Their Authors, Publishers, or Audiences', *PMLA*, 115: 316.

Weinberger, D. (2007), *Everything Is Miscellaneous: The Power of the New Digital Disorder*, New York: Times Books. Weingarten, G. (2007), 'Pearls Before Breakfast', *The Washington Post*, April 8. Available at http://www.washingtonpost.com/wp-dyn/content/article/2007/04/04/AR2007040401721.html [accessed 28 May 2011].

Weller, M. (2009a), 'Using Learning Environments as a Metaphor for Educational Change', *On the Horizon*, 17(3): 181–9. Available at http://nogoodreason.typepad.co.uk/welleronthehorizon.pdf [accessed 12 February 2011].

Weller, M. (2009b), 'Remote Conference Participation Results'. Available at http://nogoodreason.typepad.co.uk/no_good_reason/2009/11/remote-conference-participation-results.html [accessed 11 February 2011].

Weller, M. (2010), 'The Podstars Lessons'. Available at http://nogoodreason.typepad.co.uk/no_good_reason/2010/07/podstars-as-.html [accessed 11 February 2011].

Weller, M. & Dalziel, J. (2009)), 'Bridging the Gap between Web 2.0 and Higher Education' in S. Hatzipanagos & S. Warburton (eds), *Handbook of Research on Social Software and Developing Community Ontologies*, London: IGI Global, pp. 466–78.

Wenger, E. (1998), *Communities of Practice: Learning, Meaning, and Identity*, Cambridge: Cambridge University Press.

Wesch, M. (2007), 'The Machine Is Us/ing Us'. Available at http://www.youtube.com/watch?v=6gmP4nk0EOE [accessed 11 February 2011].

Wesch, M. (2008), 'A Portal on Media Literacy'. Available at http://www.youtube.com/watch?v=J4yApagnr0s [accessed 12 February 2011].

Wijekumar, K.J., Meyer, B.J.F., Wagoner, D. & Ferguson, L. (2006), 'Technology Affordances: The "Real Story" in Research with K-12 and Undergraduate Learners', *British Journal of Educational Technology*, 37(2): 191–209.

Wiley, D. (ed.), (2001), *The Instructional Use of Learning Objects Online Version*, Logan: University of Utah. Available at http://www.reusability.org/read/ [accessed 11 February 2011].

Wiley, D. (2007), 'On the Sustainability of Open Educational Resource Initiatives in Higher Education', OECD. Available at http://www.oecd.org/dataoecd/33/9/38645447.pdf [accessed 11 February 2011].

Wiley, D. (2009a), 'OA and OER Policy Reviews'. Available at http://opencontent.org/blog/archives/1008 [accessed 11 February 2011].

Wiley, D. (2009b), 'The Parable of the Inventor and the Trucker', *Chronicle of Higher Education*. Available at http://chronicle.com/blogs/wiredcampus/david-wiley-the-parable-of-the-inventorthe-trucker/7244 [accessed 11 February 2011].

Willinsky, J. (2006), *The Access Principle: The Case for Open Access to Research and Scholarship*, Cambridge, MA: MIT Press.

Willinsky, J. & Mendis, R. (2007), 'Open Access on a Zero Budget: A Case Study of Postcolonial Text', *Information Research*, 12(3). Available at http://InformationR.net/ir/12-3/paper308.html [accessed 11 February 2011].

Windham, C. (2005), 'The Student's Perspective'. In D. Oblinger & J. Oblinger (eds), *Educating the Net Generation*, Boulder, CO: Educause, pp. 5.1–5.16. Available at http://www.educause.edu/6061&bhcp=1 [accessed 11 February 2011].

Wu, S. & Neylon, C. (2008), 'Open Science: Tools, Approaches, and Implications', Nature Proceedings. Available at http://dx.doi.org/10.1038/npre.2008.1633.1 [accessed 11 February 2011].

Zittrain, J. (2008), *The Future of the Internet – and How to Stop It*, New Haven, CT: Yale University Press.

Index